'C'

'C'

A BIOGRAPHY OF
Sir Maurice Oldfield

RICHARD DEACON

Macdonald

A Macdonald Book

Copyright © Donald McCormick 1984

First published in Great Britain in 1985
by Macdonald & Co (Publishers) Ltd
London & Sydney

British Library Cataloguing in Publication Data

Deacon, Richard, 1911-
    'C': a biography of Sir Maurice Oldfield.
    1. Oldfield, Sir Maurice   2. Spies—
    Great Britain—Biography
    I. Title
    327.1'2'0924   UB271.G7204

ISBN 0-356-10400-1

Photoset in North Wales by
Derek Doyle & Associates, Mold, Clwyd.
Printed and bound in Great Britain by
Biddles Ltd, Guildford and King's Lynn

Contents

List of Illustrations

ACKNOWLEDGEMENTS

Acknowlegements are gratefully made for the following permissions to reproduce and quote:

The BBC for the quotations from their programme, 'The Profession of Intelligence', broadcast on Radio 4 on 30 August 1981.

Transcripts of Crown-copyright records in the Public Record Office from the Controller of H.M. Stationery Office.

The British Library for a quotation from the Charles Babbage Papers in the Department of Manuscripts.

The author is especially appreciative of all those (some of whom must remain anonymous) who have assisted him in compiling this biography.

FOREWORD

THE OFFICE OF 'C'

One of Maurice Oldfield's favourite stories concerned a retired British Secret Service officer who took holy orders and became a prison visitor. The latter was talking with a prisoner who had been convicted of burglary and happened to mention that he had once been given a job which entailed repair work in the offices of the SIS (Secret Intelligence Service) at Century House in South London.

In the course of the conversation the prisoner revealed that he had taken the opportunity to 'case the joint' in these very offices. 'Proper rum place it was,' he continued. 'People didn't talk to one another in the lifts and they left nothing on their desks. All you need to get into Century House is a ladder and a bag of tools. But it would be a waste of time. Nothing worth nicking there, guv'nor!'[1]

Sir Maurice would cap his little anecdote by adding that, if ever he wrote his autobiography, 'Nothing Worth Nicking' would be its title.

Needless to say he did not write his autobiography. But though an absolute model of discretion in or out of his office, nobody was more aware than Oldfield of the need to see the funny side of some of the pomposity and ridiculous extremes of secrecy with which members of the Secret

1

Service, civil servants and politicians tended to surround this esoteric organisation. 'Not so much hush-hush, as what does it all mean?' was how he once succinctly summed up the web of obfuscation which the Establishment threw around the Service of which he became the chief.

In many respects the British Secret Service is still the most passionately secretive in the whole world. This ultra-secrecy is a symptom of the hypocrisy which periodically besots the British race, the pretence that one must not admit the existence of a Secret Service because its activities hardly conform with polite behaviour. One can understand secrecy being essential in all matters of national security, or the protection of agents, but quiet often the dragon of the Official Secret Acts is brought forth to prevent the SIS from being given due credit for successes long since past. The KGB (*Komitet Gosudarstvennoy Bezopasnosti*), the Soviet Secret Service, manages this sort of thing so much better. When the Russians lauched their campaign to glorify Soviet spies in the mid-1960s, Colonel Rudolf Abel was the first to get this treatment while he was still alive.

It is inconceivable that any similar campaign to glorify British secret agents would ever be sanctioned in Whitehall. Yet Israel's *Mossad* has flourished by publicizing its own coups in the field of intelligence and America's Freedom of Information Act has not ruined the CIA. Countless copies of declassified documents concerning the CIA, FBI, State Department and the White House in the archives of the British Library of Political and Economic Science provide ample testimony on this score. On the other hand it could justifiably be argued that occasionally Britain's reputation has been damaged by the excessive secrecy surrounding its Secret Service. Nor is there much sign that censorship regulations are being relaxed even to the extent of permitting historians and biographers to chronicle events of sixty years ago. The activities of the SIS are regarded by the mandarins of the Cabinet Office and others as being so sensitive that papers dating back to 1919 still cannot be released to the Public Record Office. This may in part explain why nobody has previously written a biography of any 'C', or, to give this office its full title Director-General of MI 6, sometimes known as the Secret Intelligence Service.

Even where papers have been released to the Public Record Office, many of the secret reports are unintelligible, as Sir Winston Churchill himself discovered more than once. Often they have not merely been censored, but so unskillfully edited as to give a totally misleading picture. Sometimes this may have resulted from a machiavellian intention to deceive or mislead, but more often it has been downright incompetence and mindless obstruction.

In Victorian times the task of collecting intelligence had become much less professional than it was in the eighteenth century, or even under that great intelligence chief, John Thurloe, in Cromwellian times. A nucleus of the modern Secret Service was started at Queen Anne's Gate in 1871. It was closely linked with Military Intelligence at the War Office, and other premises for organizational work were found in such modest accommodation as an abandoned coach-house and stables near Government offices in Whitehall and then in 1874 at Adair House, Nell Gwynn's old home in Pall Mall.

Nevertheless, it was still somewhat amateurish and inadequate, and there was a tendency to rely rather more on naval than any other form of intelligence. A declassified War Office document of 1907 suggests that in this period Britain was completely without agents in Europe, but most probably many of the agents were not even listed at the War Office, but communicated only with some individual. External evidence shows quite clearly that, while Britain may have had fewer agents overseas than other major powers, throughout the early part of this century the nation was well served by spies in most European countries as well as the Middle East and Far East.

A foreign department of the Secret Service Bureau was created in 1909 during a period of reorganization. This first became known as MI 1 C, and it was not until about 1911 that MI 6 emerged. It should be pointed out that this is an anachronism. Originally there was a close link between the War Office and MI 6, but that, like the War Office itself, has long since passed into oblivion. MI 6 is today totally separate from the Defence Ministry even though some purists insist that it should be known as DI 6, the 'D' being for Defence. Nor has it any connection with the Military Intelligence Corps.

The two main operative bodies for the safety and security of the realm are the SIS and the SS (Security Service), usually known as MI 5. Both are represented on the co-ordinating intelligence body of the British Government, the Defence Intelligence Committee. There has been a mistaken idea that the heads of MI 5 and MI 6 always take the code initial by which they are known from the first letter of their surnames. This was true of Major-General Sir Vernon Kell, who, as Captain Kell, became the first chief of MI 5. On official documents he was invariably referred to as 'K'. It was also true of the very first 'C', Captain Sir Mansfield Cumming. But it was not true of Sir Stewart Menzies, a later head of MI 6, despite the fact that Ian Fleming in his James Bond stories referred to the head of MI 6 as 'M'. MI 6's chief is still known as 'C' regardless of the first letter of the name of the occupant of the post.

'C' became the Secret Service's symbol for its passion for secrecy. Although the name of almost every other Secret Service chief in the world was fairly well known long before World War One, that of the British was carefully, jealously, fanatically and, on the whole, successfully guarded. It was all part of the myth that, officially, the British Secret Service did not exist. From the viewpoint of the British Foreign Office and its ambassadors overseas it was a most convenient myth to perpetuate.

Not only was the identity of 'C' looked upon as a State secret, but the very letter itself became sacrosanct. This was illustrated by a prize example of British legal buffoonery in 1933 when the author Compton (later Sir) Mackenzie was charged under the Official Secrets Act and brought to trial at the Old Bailey, where he was fined £100. The Establishment, and particularly some senior figures in the Foreign Office, had been trying to discredit Mackenzie for some time. He had himself served in Intelligence in Greece and Syria during the First World War. In his book, *Greek Memories*, Mackenzie had told of some British Secret Service activities in Greece and Turkey in that war and actually referred to the head of that service as 'C'.

MI 6 managed to protect its image with the same archaic methods of security for many years after the war. Curiously, the name of the head of MI 5, the Security Service, had nearly always been well-known to outsiders. Yet when MI 6 was suffering from a series of catastrophes in the 1950's and 1960's there was still no letting down of the mask of silence. The disappearance of Burgess and Maclean to Moscow, the treachery which ruined Albanian operations, the unfortunate incident of Commander Crabb's underwater inspection of a Soviet warship in Portsmouth Harbour, and the slow tracking down of 'Kim' Philby did not make the same deadly impact on MI 6 which similar happenings in the USA would undoubtedly have had much sooner on the CIA. It was not until the mid-sixties that there was a still fairly muted call for an overhaul of Britain's Intelligence and Security Services.

However, foreign observers began to take a much closer look at the SIS. In October 1967, extracts were published in the American magazine, *Saturday Evening Post*, from a book entitled *The Espionage Establishment*, by Thomas B. Ross and David Wise. They wrote that No. 21 Queen Anne's Gate, round the corner from Whitehall, was the office of 'Sir Dick Goldsmith White, head of MI 6, one of the most powerful, but least known men in England.'

No action could, of course, be taken against the *Saturday Evening Post*, or the publishers of the book. Some civil servants would have liked to muzzle the British newspapers which referred to these matters. The Ministry of Defence and the head of MI 6 had nothing to say. The secrecy surrounding 'C' had finally been broken and the appointment of every holder of this office from then on has sooner or later appeared not only in the foreign press, but in that of the United Kingdom, too.

In February 1973, it was announced that the then head of MI 6 (Sir Dick White's sucessor), Sir John Rennie, would retire before his sixtieth birthday in the following year. Restrictions on press mention of Sir John's name were lifted after his post as 'C' had been revealed in the foreign press. Until then Sir John's name was covered by a D-notice, which in theory prevents the publication of anything which might, allegedly, harm the country's security. Yet in any real show-down between government and media the powers of the D-Notice Committee are negligible. Only if it can be shown that the Official Secrets Act has been positively breached can there be a case for instant action.

When Maurice Oldfield took over from Sir John Rennie as head of MI 6, his role as an Intelligence officer had long since been made public by 'Kim' Philby in his autobiographical work, *My Silent War*. Thus Richard Eder was able to report from London in the *New York Times* that Oldfield, Sir John Rennie's deputy, was 'a likely candidate to head the organization officially known as the Secret Intelligence Service'. He added the comment: 'Why the British insist that such a commonly availiable bit of information is a secret puzzles foreigners and many Britons. They note that the indentities and policies of the heads of the American CIA and many of its Western European equivalents are widely discussed in the press of each country.'[2]

It was the first 'C', then known as Commander Mansfield Smith-Cumming, who built up MI 6 and created its aura of élite amateurism and esoteric mystery. A fifty-year-old naval officer when appointed as head of the service, he later dropped the name Smith and became simply Mansfield Cumming. He insisted on being known as 'C' both inside and out of office. So effectively did he ensure the anonymity of his organization that many of his greatest successes, especially in war-time, have never been recorded. Of all the 'C's' Mansfield Cumming was perhaps the most improbable, so extraordinary a figure that he would have seemed unreal as a fictional spy-master. In a car accident in France in 1914 his son was killed and he himself lost a leg. Despite the fact that he had been driving the car himself, this tragedy in no way deterred him from continuing to drive cars at a reckless speed, usually (or so he claimed) to test the nerve of any agent he might have as passenger. He revelled in displaying his wooden limb in the most eccentric and ostentatious manner. When interviewing people, he drew attention to his wooden leg by tapping it with a paper-knife, or striking matches on it before lighting his pipe. He also terrified female typists when he worked in the War Office by speeding down the corridors at an alarming speed with his wooden leg placed on a child's scooter, propelling it along with his good leg.

Such conduct would hardly be considered a satisfactory qualification for an Intelligence chief today, but then seventy years ago a modicum of eccentricity was admired as providing a certain *élan*. It is really surprising that Mansfield Cumming's quixotic behaviour did not lead to a breaking down of cover. But there is no doubt that he was a forceful and inspiring leader. Prior to his arrival the Secret Service had been somewhat staid and pompous in outlook and methods. Any philandering or play-boy antics by agents were very much frowned upon. Cumming, a notorious womanizer, changed all that. He rather liked his agents to philander, especially when it 'furthered the cause', as he put it. According to Sir Compton Mackenzie, Cumming frequently compared espionage to a game of cricket, actually describing the notorious Sidney Reilly as 'rather a good googly bowler'. He was fearless and ruthless to the point of having no qualms about ordering an assassination, even if this meant killing one of his own agents, if deemed necessary.[3]

The next 'C' was Admiral Hugh ('Quex') Sinclair, a conscientious man, but one who was never strong enough to withstand the pressures of government economy demands, or to weld the organization into an effective peace-time service. There were drastic cuts in the money made available for Secret Service operations and from the mid-twenties onwards the Secret Service was run on a very small budget until World War Two. In 1921 it had been recommended that the service should be financed from the Foreign Office secret vote. Some records (again misleading, because sometimes intelligence is obtained through the spending of private or non-State funds) suggest that the total cost of the SIS network was far less than £100,000 a year! While some figures given for Secret Service costs certainly cover the actual payment of key personnel, they omit the funding of SIS activities by departments and organizations other than the Treasury. Treasury documents in the past few years suggest that the SIS costs have risen from about £15.7 millions twelve years ago to about £33 millions in the late seventies and up to more than £66 millions in 1983, according to the appropriation accounts on 'overseas aid and other overseas services'.[4]

Under Sinclair salary costs were often reduced or saved by appointing ex-Servicemen who lived chiefly on their pensions. The tragedy was that many of these were either too old, or, if much younger, not much good, as otherwise they would not have been retired from the Services so early.

Between the wars there had been a tendency for MI 6 too become too departmentalized, with each section forming its own policies and plans. The result was that very often one section did not know what another was doing, occasionally with overlapping complications, sometimes with disastrous results. This caused inter-departmental vendettas. There was also some confusion over what had priority in intelligence-gathering and some departments concentrated more on Soviet Russia than the up-and-coming main potential enemy of the day – Nazi-Germany. Consequently Sinclair was never able to provide sufficient factual evidence to back up reports of the extent of German rearmament. When Winston Churchill was campaigning against the National Government on this very subject in the thirties, he relied mainly on his own private intelligence service.

As war approached and a somewhat belated re-organization of the Secret Service was being worked out, Sinclair not only suffered from ill health, but from awkward and sometimes uncooperative heads of departments. Colonel Claude Dansey, an assistant director of MI 6, was constantly feuding with Colonel Valentine Vivian, the deputy head of the Service. Dansey argued, quite realistically, that it was nonsense for the Secret Service to pretend it did not exist and that it was not recognized by Common Law, while every foreign nation in Europe knew perfectly well that its offices were sited in the Passport Control offices of each British Embassy or Consulate. Dansey urged the creation of an alternative secret service as a precautionary measure. Somewhat reluctantly, Sinclair agreed to this and so 'Z' Section was established as a second and reserve string of agents.[5]

Alas, when war came it was decreed that the two services should be merged. The result was that when the Germans swooped down on two British agents, Stevens and Best, at Venlo on the Dutch frontier in October, 1939, they obtained sufficient information to destroy the SIS's entire espionage service in Western Europe in a single afternoon. Yet, despite this, the legend of a supremely powerful and machiavellian secret service lingered on and the Germans were still somewhat overawed by it. Probably they were suspicious of their own luck. But the legend was a factor in deterring them from invading Britain in 1940.

Paradoxically, other nations, especially the Germans and Russians, knew far more about the successes of the SIS in its earlier days than did the British public. To some extent this is still largely true, as all the British people ever seem to learn about the SIS is its failures. At the outset of World War Two MI 6 was understaffed, had many mediocre officers and was totally unprepared for the Nazi onslaught across Western Europe. Sinclair was even more of an amateur than Cumming. He had brought his sister Evelyn into the SIS, and he is said to have shared solely with her the secret of the location of at least some of the various 'dead letter boxes' used for communication with agents. Had brother and sister died together in an accident, some sections of the Secret Service might have been temporarily disrupted.

One other myth about the office of 'C' needs to be destroyed. Many highly intelligent foreigners still believe, as did some of the Nazi leaders, that the head of MI 6 had enormous powers and great influence. It is worth noting that when the American writers, Ross and Wise, revealed the name of Sir Dick Goldsmith White, they referred to him as 'one of the most powerful men in Britain'. This, of course, is a nonsense. The heads of MI 6 may be influential, some more than others, but it would be true to say that most of them have often wished they had greater powers.

To grasp the implications of the Intelligence set-up in 1939, it must be realized that there was no real overlord of intelligence, thus unsatisfactorily dividing responsibility between the Joint Intelligence Committee and the Prime Minister. Once war had been declared, however, the Prime Minister often had to be the sole arbiter in this sphere. To prevent this from putting too much power in one man's hands, or giving him the burden of too much responsibility, there was the theoretical safeguard that the head of MI 5 had direct access to the Home Secretary, and the head of MI 6 to the Foreign Office while those of Military and Naval Intelligence had access to the War Minister and the First Lord of the Admiralty. This system worked well with a strong Prime Minister such as Churchill, but as events in the early 1960's showed, it could be disasterous with a Prime Minister such as Macmillan who gave the impression of being slightly bored with the subject of intelligence.

Colonel (as he then was) Stewart Menzies became 'C' shortly after war broke out, when Sinclair was forced to retire through ill health. Though mild and quiet in manner, he had some of the qualities of a first-class diplomat. He was very much better than Sinclair in setting the right targets for intelligence-gathering and also in establishing his own authority. 'C' needed to be a diplomat in those dark days. From the spring of 1940 onwards his most exacting task was dealing with a Prime Minister in Churchill who was much more inquiring, critical and demanding than any of his predecessors since Lloyd George.

Menzies was the epitome of as Establishment 'C'. A meticulously orthodox background was, however, enhanced with a certain mystique in that he was reputed to be one of King Edward VII's various illegitimate children. Menzies was not only aware of this legend, but he sometimes cleverly exploited it because it was just the kind of information which gave him added status with his various friends inside

Germany. Educated at Eton, he served in the Grenadier Guards in World War One, winning the DSO and the MC. He was a member of White's Club and, more recently, had served in Army Intelligence. At last the Secret Service had broken with tradition of having a naval chief, much to the resentment of Admiral Sir John Godfrey, who had not only set his heart and mind on succeeding Sinclair, but had even started to set up a team to take with him from the Admiralty where he was Director of Naval Intelligence.

Some said that Menzies had an almost infallible intuition. He lacked any intellectual pretensions, but relied on his own judgements in the last resort, while taking pains to avoid premature assessments of his staff, with whom he was generally popular. Yet, despite the infallible intuition theory, one of his staff once told me: 'Menzies understood his opposite number in the German *Abwehr* (Secret Service) better than he did me. He could get inside the minds of Canaris, and even Beria, the head of the NKVD, but he had his blind spots. He never got inside the mind of Kim Philby and he would never believe that his Service could be infiltrated by the Russians.'

It is certainly true to say that if Menzies had followed up his hunches on Canaris, he might have brought off the biggest coup of the war. From the very beginning he had a great respect for and curiosity about Canaris and believed that the SIS made a great mistake in not establishing better contacts in that quarter many years before. Menzies set out to establish links with Canaris through intermediaries, but he had to go very carefully because he received no encouragement from on high and no cooperation from other Intelligence departments. Also Menzies recalled how his predecessor had received an approach shortly before war broke out, suggesting that Reichsmarschall Göring should pay a secret visit to England to meet Chamberlain. Lord Halifax, who was then Foreign Secretary, recorded in his diary of 21 August 1939 that 'C' had told him of this and that 'it was decided to send an affirmative answer to this curious suggestion and arrangements we̅re accordingly set in hand for Göring to come over secretly on Wednesday, the

11

23rd.' Three days later Halifax noted that 'the Göring idea has, temporarily at least, faded out.'[6]

This suggestion was never revived, but by the end of 1942 Menzies was in a position to open direct negotiations with Canaris. 'C' had no illusions about the head of the *Abwehr*: he knew that the Admiral's aim was to preserve German power intact as a price for helping to end the war. But Menzies was sufficiently realistic to know that, with Canaris's help, it might be possible for Hitler to be removed from office, the war shortened and the bringing about of a negotiated peace which would not leave the Russians master of large areas of Eastern Europe. Long afterwards he stated that he was 'thwarted in certain Foreign Office quarters for fear of offending Russia'. He never realized that he was thwarted just as much by Philby's deliberate obstruction of any moves towards Canaris when this egregious mole in the SIS was in charge of the Iberian section of the Service.

Menzies' supreme success in World War Two was unquestionably obtaining the secret of the Enigma encoding device through Polish intermediaries in July 1939, and its subsequent exploitation by the Bletchley Park codebreakers. In acquiring this secret Menzies himself went to Warsaw to supervise the final arrangements. At this time he was Sinclair's deputy.

In 1951 Menzies retired with the rank of major-general and a knighthood. Yet another Sinclair then became 'C', this time Major-General Sir John Alexander Sinclair, who had been Director of Military Intelligence at the War Office from 1944-45. Known as 'Sinbad' Sinclair because he had served as a midshipman in the Royal Navy after being educated at Winchester and the Royal Naval College, Dartmouth, the new 'C' was a relatively recent member of MI 6. He had entered the Royal Academy, Woolwich, in 1918 and was commisioned in the Royal Artillery the following year. In World War Two he was made Deputy Director of Military Operations.

His was what might be called a 'seniority appointment', made in Civil Service manner. Sinclair lacked Menzies' experience and knowlege of agents. However, it is doubtful whether he was to blame for the incident which led to his retirement, or, to put it another way, he probably had the excuse that he was never put fully in the picture.

Commander Crabb, one of the Royal Navy's best underwater sabotage experts and divers, dived into Portsmouth Harbour in April 1956, on a secret mission for MI 6 near the Russian cruiser,*Ordkhonikidze*, which had brought Bulganin and Khrushehev, the Russian leaders, to Britain. He never reported back and the Russians made sure that the incident had full publicity so that his disappearance would create a Parliamentary storm. There were, of course, the usual denials that Crabb was working for British Intelligence and some rather clumsy propaganda to the effect that he might have been employed as a free lance agent for the American CIA.

However, despite the denials, this was a Secret Service operation controlled by an SIS senior officer still living, and clumsily conducted by a middle-aged diver not fully fit for the job. Sir Anthony Eden, the Prime Minister, regarded any incident like this as an implied criticism of his own statesmanship and a blow to his ego. Some thought that the SIS had linked up with the CIA to sabotage the Bulganin-Khrushchev so-called goodwill visit to Britain, and some Opposition members of Parliament said as much. There was no evidence whatsoever of this, but there was an immediate demand from Eden for a shake-up in the SIS and the Foreign Office adviser to MI 6 was the first to go. In retrospect both the Foreign Office and the Prime Minister agreed that a categorical order specifically forbidding any such opperations in espionage should have been issued before the Russians' visit.

Not long after this Sinclair was replaced by Sir Dick Goldsmith White, who had been head of MI 5. This marked a distinct departure in policy in the appointment of 'C', for it was the first time that the post had not gone either to a naval or military officer. Educated at Bishops Stortford College, Christ Church, Oxford, and the universities of Michigan and California, Sir Dick was originally a schoolmaster who joined MI 5 with a view to making a permanent career in intelligence. He succeeded in the sphere of counter-espionage by his capacity for sheer hard work. Under Sir Percy Sillitoe he had been in charge of B Division of MI 5 (counter-espionage section) and in 1953 he became head of that organization. The idea of someone from MI 5 becoming head of MI 6 was anathema to some of the older members of the latter Service who affected to despise those they termed rather patronizingly as 'spy-catchers'.

Although cooperation between MI 5 and MI 6 was usually reasonably close, there had been ill feeling between the two services on occasions. To this extent Sir Dick White was at a disadvantage and he came under criticism from two fronts, firstly from those who, as later revelations showed, were shocked at the extent of infiltration of MI 5 by the Soviet Union, and secondly from the pro-Philby faction who took the view that the new man was appointed to take a closer look at their own activities. Indeed he was, and indeed he did. No doubt he was astounded to find that, despite his official resignation from MI 6, Phiby was still highly regarded by some. At this time, of course, the controversy as to whether or not Philby was a Soviet agent had not been absolutely resolved.

Sir Dick had no easy task, but he was at least able to look objectively at some of MI 6's past performances and to assess his staff from an independent viewpoint. Perhaps he proceeded rather too cautiously in the early years of his term of office, sometimes decisions were delayed, but he could look back on some substantial successes in the end. George Wigg (the late Lord Wigg), who, as Paymaster-General in the earlier Wilson governments, kept a watch on intelligence matters, regarded Sir Dick very highly indeed, even urging the idea of creating an intelligence overlord with powers over MI 5 and MI 6, Sir Dick being his choice for the job.

When Sir John Rennie succeeded Sir Dick White a new trend in the history of MI 6 began. It marked the beginning of a campaign to bring the Service under much tighter control by the Foreign Office. John Ogilvy Rennie was very much a Foreign Office man. Educated at Wellington and Balliol College, Oxford, he had worked with the firm of

Eckhardt, Inc., in New York from 1935-39. Then, from being Vice-Consul in Baltimore in 1940, through British Information Services in New York and various appointments in Warsaw, Washington and Buenos Aires, as well as a spell at the Foreign Office from 1946-49, he eventually became an Under-Secretary of State. He was never an Ambassador, but, as SIS chief he was officially described and listed as the Superintending Under Secretary of the Planning, the Research and the Library Records Departments of the Foreign Office.

The trend towards appointing a Foreign Office man as chief was cut short in 1973 when Maurice Oldfield, who was the deputy to 'C', succeeded Rennie. Oldfield was a professional in the same sense that Sir Dick White was, with a continuous experience in various fields of Intelligence from the early forties. Oldfield held strongly to the view that whatever may have been argued in ringing the changes from one Service to another in selecting any future 'C', the post should always go to a professional intelligence officer. Thus it was that another such experienced officer succeeded him in 1978: Arthur Temple Franks. Sir Arthur, as he now is, was educated at Rugby and Queens College, Oxford. He entered the SIS largely on the strength of his wartime service in the SOE (Special Operations Executive), the British sponsored organization set up to aid and collaborate with Resistance Movements in Nazi-occupied Europe. Joining the Foreign Office in 1952, he went to Teheran as Second Secretary the following year at the time of the Iranian Coup and after another spell in London was appointed MI 6 chief of station in Bonn in 1962. He retired in 1981.

Recommendations for chiefs of MI 5 and MI 6 are now made by a five-man committee which takes its choices from a short list of candidates submitted by the Prime Minister's office. Following confirmation of Soviet infiltration into the ranks of MI 5 and the proven infiltration of MI 6 by such a man as Philby (who might easily have become 'C' himself, but for the defection of Burgess and Maclean to Russia), it was decided some few years ago that the normal succession in both 5 and 6 should be broken from time to time by the appointment of a chief from outside. But it was soon realised that while such a policy was relatively easy in the case of MI 5, it was much more difficult with MI 6. To choose a chief from outside the Service is to risk ruining the vital continuity of MI 6's work. To appoint a man who has only had experience of Intelligence work in Army, Navy or RAF might have worked pre-war, but not today. Similarly, to pick a Foreign Office man, however able, tends to create a feeling of frustration and diplomatic claustrophobia inside the Secret Service.

There have always been members of the Diplomatic Service who not only have a loathing of espionage and the SIS, but who actually go out of their way to frustrate this service. The view of such types of diplomat is that overt intelligence is always better, and certainly safer, than covert intelligence. Sometimes that view prevails to the extent that there is an attempt to 'take over' and muzzle MI 6. In the late 1970's there were some fears that Foreign Office advisers would exercise an almost total control over not only the SIS, but the Security Service as well. Not only was there talk of appointing a one hundred per cent diplomat as the next 'C', but Sir Howard Smith, a former Ambassador in Moscow and Prague, was actually made Director-General of MI 5. In addition Sir Francis Brooks Richards, another diplomat, was charged with Security Co-Ordination in Ulster, and Sir Antony Duff, a Foreign Office man of wide experience, was made security and intelligence co-ordinator in the Cabinet Office.

Sir Antony was, in fact, remarkably successful and soon commended himself to the Prime Minister, Mrs Thatcher. Not only was he successful, but he soon made it clear that he was acting quite independently of the Foreign Office. During Mr Francis Pym's term of office as Foreign Secretary, a determined campaign was waged by some inside the Foreign Office to ensure that Mr Patrick Wright, a senior FO official, should remain chairman of the Joint Intelligence Committee, although moving into the Cabinet Office. The Prime Minister, no doubt mindful of the criticism of the Foreign Office's role in the events leading up to the

Falklands invasion, took the view that the Foreign Office should lose the chairmanship of the JIC, as had been suggested in the Franks Report which stated that the JIC had not given enough weight to indications that Argentina's position on the Falklands was hardening long before the invasion.

So Sir Antony was made chairman of the JIC and in 1982 the Prime Minister showed her confidence in MI 6 by recommending a professional Intelligence officer from inside the Service as the new 'C'. Eventually the appointment was confirmed and Colin Frederick Figures became the new chief of MI 6. He worked originally with the Control Commission in Germany (1953), then went to Amman as first a Third, then Second Secretary, served for a few years in Warsaw and in 1966 was appointed First Secretary and Head of the Visa Section in Vienna. He was given the rank of Counsellor in the Foreign Office in 1975. Sir Colin Figures, who is one of the few 'Cs' not to have found his way into *Who's Who*, is not without a sense of humour. Asked what his recreations were, he replied: 'Watching sport, gardening and beachcombing.'

Doubtless there are many in Whitehall who would like to see the office of 'C' brought much more directly under Foreign Office control, or at least to ensure that he never made any move without clearing his proposals with that ministry. This would not merely stifle the work of the SIS, but rob the government of the day of an independent intelligence service by which it could assess the advice of the diplomats. Another school of thought would like to appoint an intelligence overlord who would have access to and control over both MI 5 and MI 6. Superficially, this plan might seem attractive and, so it has been argued, would enable each service to be kept under tighter control. But it is extremely doubtful whether it would make for greater efficiency.

There is no reason why 'C' should not remain much as he was in the past – a supreme, independently operating chief of the Service, jealously guarding his own prerogatives with the minimum of interference from any quarter, answerable in the last resort to the Prime Minister of the day rather than the Foreign Secretary.

As will be seen from this very brief history of the office of 'C' there has been a gradual change from amateurism to professionalism in holders of the post. In the past thirty years there has been tighter control at the top of MI 6 and far fewer rogue elephant tactics of the type employed by Mansfield Cumming. On the whole British intelligence gathering still rates quite highly compared with that of other major powers and especially in value for money. As far as the latter qualification is concerned, its expertise and skill in getting intelligence 'on the cheap' must put the SIS in the top four Intelligence services in the world. The future depends upon how well that intelligence is analysed and interpreted not only by the JIC, but in the last resort by the politicians.

1

History Has 'Many Cunning Passages'

Sometimes in later life, when asked how he managed to explain his passion for history and apparent zeal for intelligence work, Maurice Oldfield would answer by quoting from T.S. Eliot:

'History has many cunning passages, contrived corridors
And issues: deceives with whispering ambitions,
Guides us by vanities.'

Having made this point with an amused chuckle as he watched his listeners trying to fathom out exactly what he meant, he added as an after-thought: 'I was born in the midst of so much history and so many historical puzzles in Derbyshire. I remember spending hours as a boy trying to find out whether an eleven-foot grave in the Church of St Michael of Hathersage really did hold the mortal remains of Robin Hood's lieutenant, Little John. They dug up a thigh bone which was thirty-two inches long, and what at one time was said to be Little John's bow was hung up inside the church. The bow was supposed to have a pull of one hundred and sixty pounds and that suggests an abnormally powerful man. But I never did solve the legend to my entire satisfaction. So, you see, history is not unlike the Intelligence game.'

Hathersage is only ten miles from where Oldfield was born at the village of Over Haddon, near Bakewell, on 16 November, 1915. This is the Derbyshire of the dales, of the River Derwent and its various tributaries, an ever-changing landscape of tree-covered peaks, wreathed in mist one moment and sunlit the next. Here, too, is a fisherman's paradise as well as some of the snuggest valleys in the whole country, ideal sites for the many villages which are sprinkled over a huge area.

But Over Haddon is different. It is a tiny village, situated two miles to the south-west of Bakewell on a rocky eminence some eight hundred feet above sea level, overlooking the exquisite Lathkill Dale. It comprises a mere cluster of grey stone cottages with a population of under two hundred. In winter it tends to be cold, wet and inhospitable, but in summer it comes into its own. Then, whichever way one looks, there are the most entrancing and romantic views to be found anywhere in the county, or indeed in any part of England. They are views which, once seen, are never forgotten. Not far away is Haddon Hall, one of the most perfectly preserved old manor houses in the whole of the United Kingdom. So immaculately has the Duke of Rutland kept this splendid edifice that, standing in its banqueting hall, one can imagine one is back in the Middle Ages with the lord and his retainers at the top of the table on the dais, the working folk carrying on with their duties in the body of the hall and the minstrels playing in the gallery.

To visit this part of the world, to start from Over Haddon and to explore the neighbourhood for some twenty miles around, is, in effect, to begin to understand Maurice Oldfield and his abiding love of the Derbyshire countryside. After only a few days spent in these parts one learns much about him from what his old schoolmaster, Dr R.A. Harvey, calls 'the interesting sites and physical features associated with him'. There is, first of all, a feeling that the people one meets not only have deep roots in the area, but are drawn back to it however far away they may travel. At Haddon Hall in a room adjoining the kitchen are some carved wooden cupboards – 'dole cupboards', which, in the Middle Ages, were used for keeping food specially prepared for passing travellers. Oldfield was throughout his life fascinated by the ideals of medieval charity and piety. Those 'dole-cupboards' at Haddon Hall may well have contributed to this viewpoint in the same way that the superb chapel at Haddon, with its ancient wall paintings and inscriptions, may have inspired his lifelong devotion to the Church of England.

Maurice Oldfield was the eldest of eleven children born to Joseph and Ada Annie Oldfield, of a family who had long been respected tenant farmers in the parish of Bakewell, of which Over Haddon is a part, for the best part of at least two centuries. The name Oldfield recurs in Kelly's and White's directories for 1857, 1881 and 1922.

Their small farm was concentrated almost entirely on dairy produce. It was an arduous occupation at the best of times, but in the twenties and thirties Derbyshire hill-farming was a long struggle and continual battle against the weather, poor pasturage and high prices. It demanded qualities of self-reliance and determination. All the Oldfield family in turn had to help with the innumerable jobs around the farm, and this produced strong family ties which drew Maurice back to Over Haddon at all stages in his life whenever circumstances permitted.

As the eldest son a great deal of responsibility fell on Maurice at an early age. He not only took his turn in keeping a watchful eye on his brothers and sisters as they came into the world, but helped on the farm in all manner of ways. Despite what he says, opportunities for solving historical puzzles must have been relatively few in the first ten years of his life. There were many chores to do before he went to the village infants' school attached to St Anne's Church of Ease in Over Haddon, a chapel which had only been built in 1880. At night those younger brothers and sisters had to be seen into bed before young Maurice could begin to study by the light of oil or candle, for neither gas nor electricity had come to the village at that time.

Perhaps one of the most important of all the various

turning points in Oldfield's career came in the autumn of 1926. Up to that date he had not been fortunate in his efforts to get a County Minor Scholarship which would take him to the Lady Manners Grammar School at Bakewell. Then the curate-in-charge of St Anne's Church at Over Haddon, the Reverend L.G. Evans, who was also history, divinity and games master at the grammar school, was appointed a Minor Canon at Llandaff Cathedral. This single event was not only to affect the lives of two other people, but to pave the way to a friendship which lasted for more than half a century. The curate's son had to surrender his free place at the grammar school and this enabled it to be passed on to Maurice Oldfield. At the same time R.A. Harvey, who had taught at Winchester and Norwich after serving in the Army in World War I, came to Bakewell to take over the teaching duties of the Reverend L.G. Evans.

'When the school re-assembled after half-term in the autumn of 1926,' Dr Harvey told me, 'two new arrivals were waiting to be received by the headmaster Ian MacDonald. I was the new master and Maurice Oldfield was the new pupil. We met, master and boy, outside Room "C", and from then on until his death Maurice and I remained close friends. At our school jubilee in October, 1976, I received the following greetings telegram: "Happy anniversary – shall we meet outside Room "C" – Love, thanks and all best wishes to you both [this was a reference to Mrs Harvey] – Maurice." '[1]

From that day onwards young Oldfield progressed rapidly. Yet his was no easy path to academic distinction. He still had to be up in time to feed the chickens and perform other duties on the farm before he set out on the two-mile walk to school. There was plenty of homework to be tackled, but again it was a question of waiting until all was quiet late at night before, by the light of lamp or candle, Maurice could develop his passion for 'the many cunning passages of history' and other subjects. The Right Reverend Kenneth Skelton, former Bishop of Lichfield, who was curate of Over Haddon during the war, recalls that 'the story was rife in the village about Maurice coming home from school and going to bed immediately, then getting up in the middle of the night to do his homework in order to get the necessary quietness in a four-room house with many brothers and sisters.'

Dr Harvey, who during his career at Bakewell taught no fewer than six members of the Oldfield family, was appointed to teach history, divinity and games, as had his predecessor, but he still claims that the 'real inspiration' for young Oldfield was his 'brilliant history teacher, Miss Olive Faber, of St Anne's College, Oxford. She made a tremendous impression on him.'

Lady Manners Grammar School has enjoyed a long record of academic success as well as having developed a remarkable communal spirit which has resulted in a flourishing Old Mannerians' Society. Founded in 1636 by Grace, Lady Manners, daughter-in-law of the celebrated Dorothy Vernon, it was endowed with a rent charge issuing out of four fields of land at Elton. Under the original terms of her endowment Lady Manners laid down that the 'Schoolemaister' should be unmarried and that if at any time afterwards he 'shall marry, or live disorderly or scandalously, then the said Schoolemaister shall have no benefitt by the said annuitie or rente charge, but shall be displaced from the said Schoole.'[2]

That the spirit of Lady Grace lived on well into the twentieth century is perhaps exemplifield by this verse from the School Song, composed in 1916:

'Ah! Lady Grace,
Thou proud of race!
Our hearts' ambition stir:
Make us to be thy progeny,
Teach us "Y Parvenir." '

Pour y Parvenir is the school motto, which, idiomatically translated, means 'Strive to attain'. Lady Manners School became a pioneer of co-education as long ago as 1896, when it was made open to boys and girls. It soon outgrew its early buildings and additional accommodation had to be added in various parts of the town, also acquiring a boarding house.

Today the school has been absorbed into the comprehensive system. Between 1976 and 1980 some 128 pupils went on to university.

In Oldfield's time there were just over two hundred pupils. A school of this size makes great demands on a small staff in providing all the subjects of the curriculum, but it has the advantage of more easily recognizing the inherent qualities of each individual and to harness these to the service of the school. Oldfield's first headmaster was Ian Pendlebury MacDonald, still alive and residing in Bath. He believed in breadth in education and demanded high standards of loyalty, manners and behaviour. Mr Mac-Donald had been an assistant master at Wellington and Oundle before coming to Lady Manners School in 1923. Somewhat of a folk hero with the boys on account of his prowess in the then relatively new sport of motor racing, he had had experience in the Ceylon Civil Service before joining the Punjab Regiment in World War I. He was succeeded by E. Leslie Wilks (1930), who had been wounded at Arras in 1917. A man of great charm, he tragically died two years after being appointed, largely as a result of his war service.

Young Oldfield was particularly fortunate in having such a versatile and distinguished teaching staff at his school. Collectively, they must have made an enormous impression on a country boy. But it was Dr Harvey who was perhaps Maurice's most enthusiastic patron and who early on saw the boy's potential: 'He was modest to a remarkable degree and achieved his successes effortlessly and almost unnoticed at first. If a photograph of a school group was ever taken, Maurice Oldfield managed either to be the boy on the edge of that photo, or to be the one who only half showed. His mind was so clear and quick that you could liken it to a photographer's dry plate, and he took in impressions at a glance. That is how fast his mind worked.'

Probably the one single talent which enabled him to overcome all other odds was that he was not merely a fast reader, but an extremely quick assimilator of what he read. This talent is borne out not only by Dr Harvey when talking

24

of Oldfield's boyhood, but by another close friend in nearby Darley Dale in later life, Mr John Brook-Taylor. 'I could pick up a book from my library shelf and hand it to him,' said Mr Brook-Taylor, ' and he would flick over page after page in a matter of a few minutes and then, astonishingly, make apt and critical comments on the whole book. One found it hard to believe he could have taken in all this in so short a time.'

Each Speech Day Oldfield was among the prize-winners, whether for a form prize, a specialist award for English, history or a language. This way he began to amass a small library of books, each one in those days embossed with the school crest and motto in gilt. An insatiable reader, he was often to be found in the school library which, even before the opening of a splendid War Memorial Library in his last year at school, was governed by exceptionally strict rules. A master and prefect were invariably on duty in the Library and one of the rules stated that 'this is not a refuge for chit-chat and relaxation'.

Maurice did not distinguish himself on the games field, but he was never one to shirk a challenge. He took part in athletics and on occasions found a place in the rugger fifteen. He was short and tubby and had no particular aptitude for cricket. It was also almost a family joke that he had a propensity for falling off horses. In other activities at Lady Manners School, however, the diffident boy showed considerable versatility. He was a prominent member of the LMSDS (the Literary, Musical, Scientific and Debating Society), which met on Friday nights. Afterwards he would walk all the way back to his home farm in the dark. His interventions in debate were always very much to the point and he was an all-round musician, not only playing the organ and the piano, but took his place as a violinist in the school orchestra and played solo numbers at concerts. Dr Harvey very much doubts whether Oldfield ever had any formal music lessons and was under the impression that he taught himself the organ. But his sister, Miss Renée Oldfield, says that he learned to play the organ from his father on a harmonium which had a prominent place in his home. Later he was able to practise on his own at the village school. In his last year at school he was organist at the nearby Monyash Church. Sometimes he played the organ at St Anne's Church, Over Haddon, as well. Throughout his life he loved to return to this church and enjoy the view from the graveyard in which, he would proudly tell friends, there were headstones bearing the name Oldfield dating back to 1879 – 'a year before the church was built'.

Other activities included writing articles for the school magazine, entering for and winning the Barker Memorial Essay Prize and producing plays. An interest in the theatre was stimulated by visits to the school by the Sir Ben Greet Shakespeare Company, which annually performed the play set for the School Certificate, and the English Classical Players. In the school magazine, *The Peacock*, in April 1931, Oldfield wrote of one of these visits: 'We had a fine production of selections from three of the world's greatest plays with the comedy especially living up to Dr Johnson's words concerning it: "I know of no comedy for many years that has so much exhilarated an audience, that has answered so much the great end of comedy – making an audience merry." ' The comedy was *She Stoops to Conquer*. Remarkably, the fifteen-year-old boy had actually read sufficiently widely to know what Dr Johnson thought about this play by Oliver Goldsmith.

Mrs Greta Nimse, of Ewell, in Surrey, who was a contemporary of Oldfield's at the Lady Manners School, says: 'I was in a lower form and had very little contact with such an elevated personage as the Head Boy. I remember him very well, nevertheless, as shortish and tubby, freckle-faced (very round fattish face!) and dark auburn, smooth hair. Always genial and, of course, a brilliant academic, liked very well by staff and pupils.'[3]

Maurice reached the peak of his career at school in 1933-34 when, as head boy, he obtained his matriculation and also Higher School Certificate. 'He achieved a distinction in divinity in the Higher School Certificate,' says Dr Harvey. 'In fact, he was the only boy I came across who ever obtained one during my time as a schoolmaster.'

At Speech Day in November 1934, the headmaster declared: 'The Higher School Certificate results were the best the school has produced during the last eight years, Oldfield's performance being specially praiseworthy. I have every confidence that Oldfield's open scholarship will stimulate others to achieve similar distinctions in the near future.'⁴

For in that same year, on the strength of his quite remarkable examination results, Oldfield was awarded a Jones Open Scholarship for History of £40 a year, a William Hulme bursary of £40 a year, a Hulme Hall scholarship, of £20 a year and a Derbyshire Education Committee training loan of £50, all tenable at the University of Manchester. The school was given a holiday in honour of his successes and, in wishing him many more, a citation assured him that he would be remembered as 'a most loyal upholder of the school's best traditions'.

'I often marvelled how he managed it all,' said Dr Harvey. 'It could never have been easy for him, yet somehow he made it seem easy. Those long walks to and from his home two miles away, those hours out of school devoted to extra-curricular activities, something simple for a boarder, but always requiring a special effort from a day boy. Not forgetting, of course, all those chores on the farm in the early mornings and at weekends. No doubt, too, he sometimes helped brothers and sisters with their homework.'

Perhaps part of the secret of his early success and how he never seemed to suffer from any sense of frustration – even at games he was able to laugh at himself – was a deeply held conviction of having firm roots, not just in his closely knit and united family circle, but in church, school and county. Especially for Derybyshire he had an abiding love. Years later a colleague called to see him in London and spent some time looking at Oldfield's bookshelves. There he noted a special section devoted to an unusual selection of relatively little known authors – F.C. Boden, Robert Gilchrist, W.K. Parkes, C. Porteous and B. Turnstall. The only name he recognized, commented the colleague, was 'Thomas Moult and that's because of his cricket writing. Why are these particular authors all set together?'

'They are all writers who have set their material, or most of it, either in the Peak District, or some other part of Derbyshire,' replied Oldfield. 'I started to collect them as a boy. Luckily I left them safely at home during the war, and I was able to add to the list afterwards. Alison Uttley was at my old school – long before me, of course. She was born at a small farm nearby.

'You could say that the farm was her universe. She's probably best known for her children's books, especially the *Grey Rabbit* series, but she turned out a number of novels about life on Derbyshire farms. Do you know that when she was quite tiny and attending the village school she had to walk four miles each way and that meant going through a rather frightening place called Dark Wood? She was quite a distinguished scientist as well and, what's more, she became the first woman to study physics at Manchester University.

'I often take a book from these particular shelves to refresh my memories. You see, there is something rather special about Derbyshire – not just to me, but to very many writers. Take Robert Gilchrist: he came from Sheffield and then spent several years in the High Peak, studying the country folk. George Eliot's *Adam Bede* is mainly set in Derbyshire. You just change the names in the book. Snowfield is really Wirksworth, while Stoniton is Derby. Then there is a post-war writer, Crichton Porteous, who has written at least three books about Derbyshire farm life. There must be something about Derbyshire farms that makes them more interesting than most others.

'You spoke of Thomas Moult: look at this book of his, *Snow Over Elden*. It's all about a Peakland farm and the bleak life out on the heights compared with the warmth and rather splendid quiet and loneliness of the dales.'

'The splendid loneliness?'

'Why, yes, even loneliness can be splendid. Of course it can be distressing, too. But, if one has absorbed the special loneliness of the dales and the moors, then loneliness is nothing to be afraid of, and there's much to commend it, provided you use it in the right way.'

2

Manchester – Paris – Berlin

It was in the autumn of 1934 that Maurice Oldfield took up
residence in Hulme Hall, Manchester University. In that
October he registered in the History School; he was
exceptionally fortunate as at that time the Manchester
School of History had such a high reputation. His
instructors included the late Sir Lewis Bernstein Namier,
Professor Ernest Jacob and a young don named A.J.P.
Taylor, who was to become one of the liveliest, best known
and most controversial historians of the period.

The influence of these men – particularly Jacob and
Taylor – was considerable. Oldfield first of all concentrated
on modern history in which both Namier and Taylor
specialized. It is noteworthy that Namier had been in the
Political Intelligence Department of the Foreign Office from
1918-1920, and 1929-1931 had been political secretary of the
Jewish Agency for Palestine. But it was Taylor, with his
talent for enthusing and stimulating his pupils, who
confirmed and strengthened Oldfield's passion for history
and the ways in which it could be extended into the whys
and wherefores of contemporary life. Taylor had spent some
time doing research in Vienna before taking up a lectureship
in modern history at Manchester, thus paving the way to his

work, *The Hapsburg Monarchy: 1815-1918*. The clue to Taylor's ability to cast a spell over his undergraduate audiences is perhaps best summed up in his own words: 'In my opinion the writings of an historian are no good unless readers get the same pleasure from them as he does himself.'[1]

Professor Jacob's influence manifested itself more strongly later when Maurice opted to specialize in medieval history. The late Ernest Fraser Jacob, one time Fellow and Librarian of All Souls College, Oxford, had spent his life lecturing in medieval history and for twenty years had been a member of the Church Assembly, serving on such Archbishops' Commissions as those on the Relations of Church and State, Canon Law, Church Courts and Crown Appointments. Both in his ecclesiastical interests and his choice of subjects in his writings, much of which concerned the legacy of the Middle Ages, it is easy to see how Jacob reinforced Oldfield's Anglo-Catholicism. Throughout his Manchester period, Oldfield continued to play the organ at various churches in the Bakewell district.

There was, however, nothing priggish or intolerant about his devotion to his Church. Quite a few of his friends at Manchester were atheists and it never made any difference either to him or to them. 'It was just never allowed to be an issue between us,' said one of them. 'He was very tolerant in an amused kind of way with unbelievers.' One of his overseas agents recalls: 'I remember once many years later in London walking with him from his flat to his church one Sunday morning. He stopped at the door, turned to me and said: "Why don't you come in for once? It would do you good." I didn't, of course, and he shook his head with a mock smile and said, "So often I seem to be surrounded by heathens." '

Sir Bryan Hopkin, a former senior Treasury officer, went up to Manchester in October 1936, to do post-graduate work in economics. 'Maurice was then in his third year, I think. We were both living in Hulme Hall, became friends and saw a good deal of each other during the academic year 1936-37,' says Sir Bryan. 'Maurice was religious, but he wore his religion lightly. There was nothing solemn about him. He was full of ecclesiastical jokes (and others). He loved music; we went together to the Hallé concerts. He had a serious interest in art and I learnt a lot about it from him. Not all his interests were elevated ones: when the Hall students assembled in the common-room to sing dirty songs, as they did from time to time, it was Maurice who played the piano.'[2]

One of Oldfield's closest friends was David Wiseman, an academic and writer who was at one time secretary of the British Institute of Adult Education. He and Oldfield registered together as students and, writes Mr Wiseman, 'we remained friends and kept in touch with each other almost up to Maurice's death.' Oldfield was best man at Wiseman's wedding and their last meeting was in August, 1979, when he joined the Wisemans to celebrate their ruby wedding.

'Maurice and I frequently discussed politics – with others, too, of course – but he did not commit himself to any narrow political viewpoint. He was a member of the Universities' League of Nations Union, but, to my knowledge, of no other political, or semi-political body,' adds David Wiseman. 'His ambitions and interests seemed to lie entirely in the academic world. I remember a conversation with him and a fellow-student just before our finals in 1937, when we all three attempted to forecast our futures. We had no doubt about Maurice: he was destined to be Professor of Medieval History somewhere.'[3]

That other fellow-student was Norman Dees, today Professor Emeritus of Glasgow University. He and Oldfield both resided at Hulme Hall and shared a room together in 1935-36. Just as Wiseman and Oldfield had a special bond and remained in touch throughout the latter's life, so, too, did Dees and Oldfield. 'We always kept in touch whenever possible,' said Professor Dees. 'We saw a certain amount of each other in 1938-40 and we attempted correspondence in 1942 when I was in the Eighth Army and Maurice was with the Intelligence Corps in the Middle East. After the war we met from time to time either at his Derbyshire home, or in London. He was godfather to my eldest daughter. The last time we spoke was by telephone just before he took up the Northern Ireland posting.'

While at school Oldfield earned the reputation of being an efficient and quick-witted pupil in French, and he had in fact spent an exchange visit at the Lyceé Janson de Sailly in Paris. Yet, though in later life he spoke French quite fluently, his proficiency was apparently not achieved without a struggle. Professor Dees says: 'In the matter of languages the study of *modern* languages was perhaps his weakest point as a student. French was a compulsory subject in the first year of honours history and Oldfield needed coaching along by friends. On the other hand, his grasp of Latin was firmer than that of most, and his skill in the interpretation of medieval Latin in texts was very high. He used to talk Latin in his sleep sometimes.'4

In 1935 Oldfield spent some time at the Hochschule für Politik in Berlin and began to speak German. His German, however, was never as good as his French, as his old friend, Dr Otto John, former head of West German Intelligence, was later to testify. But it was here in Berlin that for the first time Oldfield had a glimpse of the horrors which Nazi rule was already perpetrating. Hitler had become Chancellor the previous year. 'I was very glad indeed to have spent that short time in Germany before the war,' he told friends long afterwards. 'It certainly helped me when I joined Military Intelligence. But at the time one sensed the hidden horrors rather than experienced them. It was the atmosphere which was oppressive. Yet, while it enabled me to see at first hand exactly where Nazism was leading, it also gave me the chance to get to know some very fine Germans. I realized that there was a silent minority who hated Hitler and feared where he was taking them. They longed to make friends with us, but could see little hope that this would do them much good. Later in the Middle East this insight into the diversity and seeming contradictions of the German character was to prove invaluable in helping me to detect the potentially good German from the hopelessly bad.

'Intelligence, as I have always insisted, is about people. You have to study people and to weigh up your impressions with what you know of their national character, or even the character of their class. One of the secrets in spotting the potentially good German, I found, was to notice whether he had a sense of humour. If he had, then there was a good chance that he was potentially good. It was a test that worked more often than not. German humour, you see, is something rather special. One needs to study it. Some of the Germans I came across found it very funny to act as double agents. Whereas a Briton might do this with deadly seriousness and not a glimmer of humour, a German would react quite differently. Not all, mind you, and of course the problem was to make sure it wasn't oneself the German might be laughing at.'

Certainly his brief experience of life in Germany made him a critical observer of the contemporary European scene. On his return to Manchester he turned to the one cause in which at that time he most believed – that of upholding the pre-war League of Nations and its ideals. Oldfield believed fervently that the League could save the world. This might seem naive in the light of the depressingly inadequate and inept organization which today calls itself, somewhat incongruously, the United Nations. But the old League of Nations – surely a more honest title – at least offered some prospect of peace and hope for the world. To believe in the old League was not a mere pious aspiration, but an ideal worth sustaining at all costs. Even Sir Samuel Hoare, at the very beginning of Italy's invasion of Abyssinia, had as Foreign Secretary sounded what, to League supporters, seemed to be a clarion call for action when he urged 'steady and collective resistance to all acts of aggression'. True, having made that speech, Sir Samuel failed lamentably to live up to his own advice, but it was the kind of speech which would be unimaginable in the conclaves of the UN today.

To his delight Oldfield was elected president of the British Universities League of Nations Society. For the next year or two he devoted considerable time to this kind of work and to activities in connection with various international service organizations and conferences. In 1937 he acted as interpreter at the Pavillon de la Paix at the International Exhibition in Paris. He was keenly interested in all international friendship organizations, though wary of any that had purely party political motives, taking the view that the more such groups could be developed with the help of all Europeans in the form of camps and exchange visits, the more the cause of peace would be furthered. In the 1980s this might appear to be surprisingly unsophisticated, yet to those old enough to remember the 1930s it still appeared one way of helping to thwart the nightmare prospect of war. A feeling still lingered that the sanity of the majority would win in the end, that youth could keep totalitarianism in check.

These international contacts helped considerably to broaden Oldfield's mind. But while he was all for achieving a *modus vivendi* which would wipe out all the old antagonisms with which Europe was cursed, he never subscribed to any of the pacifist societies which sometimes sprang up out of international youth camps and among students.

During the 1936-7 period Oldfield, along with his friend David Wiseman, went to Geneva to a British Universities League of Nations Society conference. At the same time he attended the Zimmern School of International Studies. This was the foundation of Sir Alfred Zimmern, whose idea was to gather together from all countries of the world young people who were likely to make their mark in the years to come. No doubt he made some interesting contacts there.

Meanwhile at Manchester University he was generally popular in the Hall and made friends easily. 'I found him very sympathetic and stimulating company,' said Sir Bryan Hopkin. 'He was highly intelligent, good tempered, friendly and humorous. It was plain that he was a very serious student indeed, and was expected to do well.'

He continued to pick up various prizes with the greatest of ease. At the end of June 1936, he was awarded the Bradford History scholarship and a year later the Thomas Brown Memorial Prize in History. On 6 July 1937, Maurice graduated with first class honours in modern history. Out of some nineteen students who graduated in history he was the only one to gain a first. In October of that same year he secured a graduate research scholarship in history as well as a Hulme Hall scholarship and so was well set on the course of post-graduate research. The following year he was elected to a travelling scholarship at Geneva, tenable at Manchester University, and obtained his Master of Arts degree. The MA was the result of his research into the position of the clergy in Parliament in the later Middle Ages. In 1938 he was elected to a Fellowship and became a history tutor at Hulme Hall. The citation in the records of Manchester University states: 'M. Oldfield, Faulkner Fellowship (£100 for one year).'

In December of this same year an application was received from Oldfield for an additional grant for this Fellowship to assist him in 'carrying out research. Mr Oldfield has found it necessary to spend a considerable time in London working at the Public Record Office and at the British Museum.' An additional grant of £20 a year was made 'to assist him in carrying out historical research in London'.[5]

But by that time the shadows of war were closing in and not even such an optimist-idealist as Oldfield could believe in anything but a miracle to prevent the catastrophe which lay ahead. That he himself believed this to be inevitable by this time is clear from a letter he wrote to David Wiseman on his twenty-fourth birthday in 1939. War had been declared, Poland had been occupied, but the long period of inaction and uncertainty was lulling many into wishful thinking that peace might somehow come about by Christmas or the New Year. Oldfield was quite certain it would be otherwise. As a belated wedding present to Wiseman and his wife he sent them a copy of Langland's *The Vision of William Concerning Piers the Plowman*.

'I am sending you a book which will, I hope, bear witness to something we all have in common,' he wrote. 'The connection between myself and Langland is obvious and you can regard him as one of the first "socialist" thinkers in England ... Life here is very precious [he was still at Manchester University] – made more so by the fact that practically everyone wonders how long it can endure – it certainly heightens one's appreciation of an academic life. I am working very hard, hoping against hope to produce something worth while before I am sent to do the very opposite.'[6]

By that time Maurice had already volunteered for military service. 'We academics have no right whatsoever to expect to be able to do what millions of others cannot possibly do – to sit back in our ivory towers,' he once said at this time. He was also mindful of the fact that many of his teachers at school and fellow lecturers at Manchester had not only fought in the First World War, but that some, like Professor Jacob, had twice been seriously wounded. In many respects Ernest Jacob was one of his heroes.

Medieval history had claimed him in a very special way. The clue to his philosophy, his everyday outlook and even his religion lay in that reference he made to Langland. Oldfield could then and ever afterwards be summed up as a medieval socialist. This is not to say that he was a socialist in any political sense. Note the fact that he put inverted commas around the world socialist in his letter to Wiseman. What he imbibed deeply was the spirit of charity which abounded among so many people in the Middle Ages, and how the Church then took upon itself responsibility for the homeless. Charity as a way of life was what commended itself to Oldfield, and this he tried to practise himself, not in any ostentatious or priggish way, but in a modern interpretation of the word. This partly explains his interest in the Workers' Educational Association from which so many benefited in the thirties. Among the founders of the WEA were three men who could be called the high priests of medieval socialism – William Temple, later to become Archbishop of Canterbury, Charles Gore, Bishop of Oxford, and Professor R.H. Tawney, author of Religion and the Rise of Capitalism.

There can be no question but that Professor Jacob was the inspiration for Oldfield's passion for medievalism and for sustaining his youthful devotion to the Church. Professor C.R. Cheyney, who was at Manchester University at this time, says: 'A medieval historian myself, it did not seem strange to me that a young man trained by Jacob should be interested in the position of the clergy in the parliaments of the fourteenth-fifteenth centuries. This was what he told me he wanted to do in retirement when I met him years later for tea at the Athenaeum Club. When I knew him at Manchester he was doing research with Ernest Jacob and we met informally a good deal. He was, I think, like his teacher, Jacob, a devout High Anglican and I think he took an active part in the religious life of St Anselm Hall, the Anglican hall of residence in the university.'[7]

During this Manchester period Oldfield travelled around a great deal, not only in this country, but on the continent. Manchester University records show that in July 1939 he had been given a travelling grant to enable him to visit Canterbury and the County Records Office 'in connection with his research for the degree of Ph. D. on "Convocation during the 15th century." ' One of his Manchester friends, Elsa Dean, a music student, had a postcard from him, stamped 'Canterbury': 'I followed the Pilgrim's route part of the way,' it read, 'but only from Otford to Charing. Did you know that Geoffrey Chaucer was a JP of this county?'

At some time in this same year Oldfield visited an international students' rally in Boulogne and had been very depressed by the vehemence of the anti-war sentiments expressed there. 'It is one thing to shout for peace,' he wrote in a letter, 'but quite another to encourage the obvious enemy by saying in advance that you won't fight in any circumstances. It is frankly ridiculous to talk about capitalist wars. War, like peace, is indivisible, capitalist, communist, socialist or whatever. There was a very brilliant man at the rally, James Klugmann, who is secretary of the *Rassemblement Mondial des Etudiants*, a somewhat suspect organization which has its HQ in Paris. He has done research work at Trinity, Cambridge, and is a member of the CP [Communist Party]. A year ago he claims to have gone to China and met some of their party leaders. My assessment of him was that he is a communist first and foremost, not like some of our other friends who may be communists "third", but put home and country first and second, or second and first, if you prefer it that way.'[8]

Oldfield kept up his organ playing during his Manchester period, not only playing occasionally at Over Haddon and elsewhere, but also being the chapel organist at Hulme Hall. In December 1940, it was announced that he had secured his MA and the following month college records show that 'under the special resolutions of Senate and Council the following postponement of tenure has been granted – Maurice Oldfield, Jones Fellowship.'

But for the outbreak of war he would almost certainly have proceeded to a doctorate with the prospect of a long and distinguished academic career. When Sir Bryan Hopkin returned to Manchester in September 1940, having been posted there by his Civil Service department, Maurice was still waiting to go into the Army. 'I do remember going with him one afternoon in late December to hear the Hallé do Handel's *Messiah*,' said Sir Bryan. 'The same evening I shared with him the experience of the air blitz on Manchester. One thing I'm quite sure of is that at that time Maurice thought of himself as an intending academic once peace returned.'

Yet he would not have been content to allow his intensive, almost emotional, interest in medieval history to isolate him from the contemporary world. His work for the League of Nations Union and his wish to do something 'internationally useful' (his own phrase) would probably have propelled him into some form of part-time work in this field as well.

A unit such as the Military Intelligence Corps would have been an ideal first choice for Oldfield's wartime service. However, he was not one to wish to pull any strings, or to seek favours to get him the kind of posting he wanted, so he was content to take his chance like the majority of young people of the day, but registering a preference for the Army. Apart from this, early on in the war openings for the Intelligence Corps were not numerous as, in effect, the Corps was once again being developed from scratch. Though the importance of military intelligence had always been recognized in wartime, when peace came the various bodies previously formed to provide it had always been abolished.

After World War One military intelligence was allowed to 'dwindle until the Commandant, one other officer and one security policeman were all that remained and they finally departed from Wiesbaden in December, 1929,' declared the Colonel Commandant of the Corps. 'King George VI approved our actual formation on 15 July, 1940, with our badge and motto, and our own Colonel Commandant then, General Sir Bernard Paget, and it was due to him that after the war we were not again disbanded.'[9]

It might also be added that, had it not been for Major Gerald Templer (later Field Marshal Sir Gerald Templer), the Intelligence Corps would not even have been in the process of formation by September 1939.

So it was that Maurice Oldfield, at the age of twenty-five, received his call-up papers for the South Staffordshire Regiment in 1941. This was an infantry regiment which had always had a fair proportion of Derbyshire men in its ranks. He went to Over Haddon one night shortly after this to hold a farewell party with a few old friends at the Lathkill Dale Hotel, his favourite hostelry. One of his Manchester friends who accompanied him, the same Elsa Dean who had received the postcard from Canterbury, said: 'He was obviously very popular in his neighbourhood. Afterwards we had an impromptu dance and, to my amazement, Maurice, who had disappeared for a few minutes, returned with a violin which he proceeded to play as an accompaniment for our dancing! He was always ready to rally round in that way. I suppose he must have gone back home to get his violin.'

There was another farewell party for Maurice given by his university colleagues and others at the Royal George in Knutsford, and after this he left Manchester for the Trent Valley railway station at Lichfield to join the Army. It was, he used to say afterwards, 'probably the most decisive move I ever made'.

3

From Kantara To Beirut

At Wrottesley Block in Whittington Barracks at Lichfield Oldfield did his basic ten weeks' military training with the South Staffordshire Regiment. This must have been an irksome contrast to the relative placidity of academic life, even allowing for the fact that he was no stranger to hard manual labour on a farm and early rising. Squad drill and the usual monotonous chores of such basic training were, however, to some extent compensated for by Oldfield's facility for making friends very easily and quickly. He could also see the funny side of the absurdities which abound in the moulding of a recruit.

One such friend was David Potts who occupied the bunk below Oldfield's in Wrottesley Block, thus striking up a friendship which lasted for nearly forty years. Despite not seeing one another for most of this time, Oldfield always kept in touch with his old friend. David Potts would receive a Christmas card from him each year from various parts of the globe.

Speaking both French and German, Oldfield did not have much difficulty in qualifying for a transfer to the Military Intelligence Corps. From Lichfield he was drafted to the Field Security Police, the most junior branch of the Corps. It is believed that he had some specialized training in field intelligence and security and interrogation at the Intelligence School at Matlock, but there is no confirmation of this. He seems to have kept discreetly quiet about this short period in his career.

Very soon he was drafted to the Suez Canal Zone, joining Field Security Section 273 based on Ismailia. For a while he was a lance-corporal in charge of stores. Field Security Sections usually consisted of a captain and thirteen other ranks: they were primarily responsible for the security of military formations and installations. This made for a tight, comradely unit which was just as capable of operating independently as functioning while attached to a large unit. Sometimes such a section would be called upon for special intelligence work. It would also act in liaison between army commanders and staffs in the field and GSI (Military Intelligence) as well as cooperating with the civilian police.

There was always scope in wartime for a keen, enterprising linguistic corporal in Military Intelligence to obtain a commission – more so, perhaps, than in any other section of the British Army. Nor was such progress from the ranks limited only to scholars. The spy-thriller author, Ted Allbeury, who had started life as a foundry worker and taught himself French and German in his spare time by correspondence courses, volunteered for Military Intelligence on the strength of an advertisement in *The Times*. This asked for 'linguists to work with the Army: no possible promotion above lance-corporal.' Yet Allbeury finished the war with the rank of lieutenant-colonel in the Intelligence Corps. He recalls once meeting Oldfield (by then an officer) out in the Middle East, but not realizing who or what he was until sometime afterwards. Even in the Army Oldfield often managed to make himself inconspicuous.

But not all that inconspicuous. In September 1941, when Oldfield was stationed at Kantara, Major H.M. ('Monty') Trethowan arrived in Ismailia. Originally he had been posted to the Middle East as a trooper in Salisbury Troop 'A' Squadron of the Royal Wiltshire Yeomanry, which was part of the 1st (Horse) Cavalry Division. But by the time he was sent to Ismailia he was serving in the Intelligence Corps as Defence Security Officer (DSO), Suez Canal Area, working under the Defence Security Officer, Egypt, who in turn was part of Security Intelligence Middle East (SIME). It was Major Trethowan who first spotted Oldfield's talents and proposed him for promotion.

Egypt was then considered to be a 'home station' and therefore MI 5 and MI 6 operated in that territory. The Field Security Service, formerly the Field Security Police, was a separate intelligence organization which sometimes came under command of the local military commander and sometimes under SIME. Kantara in Arabic means a bridge, but at that time there was no bridge at Kantara and a ferry connected the railways from Palestine with the Egyptian State Railways. Oldfield was then in charge of the checking of passports at Kantara when Major Trethowan arrived on the scene. He was immediately impressed by Maurice's handling of this job.

'I congratulated him on his work,' said Mr Trethowan, now a solicitor living in Hampshire, 'and asked what he did in civilian life. He said he was a Jones Fellow in medieval history at Manchester University. Prior to coming to Ismailia I had been Field Security Officer in Greece, Crete and Syria. I was asked by the Commandant, FSS, to recommend a French-speaking NCO to act as liaison NCO at the Free French internment camp at Mieh-Mieh, south of Beirut, to work directly under the DSO, Syria. I recommended Maurice and he was promoted to sergeant and posted.'[2]

From then onwards Oldfield's steady and later rapid promotion was assured. But to understand his rise to influence one must appreciate the complexities of the Lebanon at this period and the position of the *Etats du Levant sous Mandat Français* from July 1941, until the mid-1940s. Once the Vichy French regime in the Levant had permitted German infiltration into this area, it was inevitable that sooner or later the Allies would have to intervene. Once they did so the major problem was the conflict of views between the British and the Free French. After the Allies occupied these territories the British Armistice Commission had ironically learned that it was easier to negotiate and talk with the departing Vichy administrators than with the Free French. One of the difficulties between French and British was their respective attitudes towards the Arabs. General Catroux for the Free French regarded the Arab Nationalist Bloc leader, Shukri al-Quwwatli, as an agitator who supported the Axis powers, whereas the British looked upon him as a nationalist who could be persuaded to cooperate with them provided he was given some promise of independence after the war.

In retrospect the Free French were probably being realistically correct in their hard line attitude whereas the British, who seemed incapable of frank communications, were, as so often, probably deceiving themselves with false hopes. But, curiously enough, relations between British and French in the sphere of intelligence were much better. The Free French claimed to be the successors to the French Government as the mandatory power and this position was confirmed by the 1941 Lyttelton – De Gaulle correspondence. The civilian law was unaltered and there was in addition French military law for matters such as espionage. Under General Catroux, the Free French administrator, was the Counter-Intelligence Section of the *Sûreté Generale aux Armées*, the head of which was Capitaine (later Commandant) Repiton-Préneuf. Catroux had been the only five-star general to rally to de Gaulle's side and both he and Repiton had de Gaulle's complete confidence.

From July 1941, when the Syrian campaign ended, onwards the Field Security Section initially and DSO, Syria, subsequently maintained good relations with the Free French. This was of inestimable value, particularly as at other levels relations were sometimes quite bad. Apart from clashes between Churchill and de Gaulle, General Spears, head of the British Security Mission, and General Catroux, head of the *Sûreté*, often failed to agree.

Oldfield on a much lower level and the Defence Security Officer at a higher level established an excellent relationship with their French opposite numbers. At first informally, and later formally, any arrest or security measure required by the

DSO was valid for fourteen days without French approval. Yet requests at other levels were often turned down. Although the informal arrangement was not secret, only the DSO, Syria, and Capitaine Repiton and his staff seemed to know of it.

From the viewpoint of obtaining intelligence this arrangement was vital for several reasons. Not least of these was the need to obtain information from suspected spies, for by this time it had been realized on the British side that it was better to try to 'turn' a spy and use him against his employers than to shoot him out of hand. It is greatly to the credit of the Field Security officers that they were gradually able to convince the French on this point. Four spies, two of whom came by submarine and two by parachute, had been convicted and shot under French law in the early part of the war. But from 1942 onwards no such person was executed or ill-treated for security reasons, largely as a result of persuasion by the British authorities.

Mieh-Mieh was a school a few miles south of Beirut which was converted into an internment camp in 1941. A French lieutenant was the commandant at Mieh-Mieh and Oldfield was the British liaison NCO, living at the camp and working under Major Irvine Gray. The latter, who in peacetime became Archivist to the Gloucestershire County Council, is now aged 81, living in retirement in London. He recalls Oldfield's arrival at Mieh-Mieh: 'He was a most unmilitary-looking character, but he soon proved to be very efficient and as an acting sergeant displayed an astonishing grasp of Lebanese politics. I had no hesitation in recommending him to our chief, Lieutenant-Colonel Douglas Roberts, as being worthy of a commission.'[3]

At this time Oldfield was billeted with a Lebanese family in Beirut. Professor Rames Azouri, a distinguished gynaecologist, and now of the American University in Beirut, was then a boy of eight, and he recalls 'Sergeant Oldfield, as he then was, being very kind to me. In those days he travelled to and from Beirut to the camp at Mieh-Mieh on a motor-bicycle. He was great friends with all my family and we kept in touch throughout his life. Though his army work kept him fully occupied, Maurice actually found time to do a history course at the university in Beirut.'

This was typical of Oldfield, never one to waste a single moment of his life. 'Once, when he was returning to London from Singapore many years later, he called in to see us in Beirut,' added Professor Azouri, 'and when he went to Washington he came to see me in Baltimore where I was studying at St John's Hospital. He had a great sense of fun. Once one of his female assistants was being posted out to Beirut and he said to her "you must see a very dear friend of mine when you get there. You had better take his name as you never know, you'll probably need him one day. He's a gynaecologist." '

Oldfield swiftly won the trust of the commandant and his opinions were highly valued by French as well as British. From a British viewpoint Mieh-Mieh was an important camp in that British Security had a say in the running of the place, whereas another internment camp near Damascus, where such politicians as Shukri el-Quwwatli were interned, had no British representative. It is interesting to record that at Mieh-Mieh, even under wartime conditions, there was only one death the whole time it existed, when an old man gave himself a heart attack by over-eating. The problem of dealing with large numbers of inmates was one of who should be kept and who released. In the early days some of the Palestinian police concerned with Mieh-Mieh had been singularly inefficient at distinguishing between enemy, neutral and friend. One typical example of their ineptitude was their arrest of some innocent traders running a Swiss patisserie just because some of their customers inevitably happened to be Germans and Vichy French.

'The decision as to who should be interned or released was usually a British one,' said Mr Trethowan, 'and Maurice's advice was usually wise and sensible. So far as those who were not released were concerned there were good military reasons for them being detained. Maurice became personal friends of nearly all of them and many kept in touch with him up to the time of his death. This he did without antagonising the Free French.'[4]

45

Mrs Jeanne Smith, of Illogan, Cornwall (in this period Miss Jeanne Groombridge, confidential secretary to the British Liaison Officer to the Free French in Beirut) recalls Staff Sergeant Oldfield, as he then was: 'He was well liked by the internees. Years later he was still receiving Christmas cards from some of them. Maurice was a very likeable, warm person with a boyish sense of fun and humour.'[5]

Major Trethowan was himself posted to Syria and the Lebanon in June 1942, as Assistant Defence Security Officer, under the then DSO, Lieutenant-Colonel Douglas (later Brigadier) Roberts, so that he saw something of Oldfield's work at Mieh-Mieh. It was not long before Oldfield had his name put forward for a commission by Major Robin Wordsworth, commandant of the Field Security Service in the Middle East.

Field Security NCOs were commissioned as full lieutenants in the Middle East without going to an OCTU (Officers' Training Course). They travelled to Cairo for a fortnight's parade ground drill with a regular regiment and a short intelligence course, after which they were gazetted full lieutenants. This is what happened to Oldfield. He was commissioned on 13 April 1943 and shortly afterwards was transferred to FSO 268 in Beirut, joining the DSO's staff. Soon he became part of Security Intelligence Middle East, more generally known as SIME. This organization, formed in 1939, was a joint-Service body responsible for coordinating the collection, evaluation and distribution of security intelligence throughout this theatre of war. It could be compared to MI 5 in Britain and its principal work was counter-espionage and counter-subversion on all British-held territory in the Middle East.

Yet SIME was very much more than that. Linked with 'A' Force under Brigadier Dudley Clarke, which made deception a fine art in World War II, it would be no exaggeration to say that in its own way it was a supreme war-winner, not only gathering intelligence, but helping in 'turning' enemy agents over to the Allies. Deception in the Middle East was far more successful than the over-publicized 'Double Cross' activities controlled from London, some of which were infiltrated by

Soviet agents. It was 'A' Force, with some help from SIME, which master-minded deception tactics to such an extent that the Germans lost the battle of El Alamein and were deluded as to the British plans for the invasion of Sicily and Normandy.

To read the official history of *British Intelligence in the Second World War* one could be forgiven for thinking that the war was won by a bunch of academics at Bletchley decoding intercepted enemy messages. Important as this contribution to victory undoubtedly was, it has been overstressed, whereas much less attention has been paid to the roles of the SIS, Force 'A' and SIME. In most histories touching on various aspects of World War Two the Intelligence Corps has rarely had even a mention. Yet the actual contribution of the force, which proudly boasts as its emblem the rose and the laurel, was considerable, if outwardly unspectacular. In August 1942, just four days before Montgomery took command of the 8th Army, a lengthy GC and CS Ultra signal to the C-in-C, Middle East, reached Cairo. It contained a complete summary of Rommel's intentions for his Alam Haifa offensive and the problems posed thereby. But without the essential back-up information from the Intelligence Corps on the spot such intelligence would have been far less useful.

The HQ of the DSO's staff in Beirut was on the top floor of a new office building a few hundred yards inland from the St Georges Hotel, which was occupied jointly by Field Security and MI 6. An adjoining similar building was occupied by the Spears Mission, later the British Legation. Cairo and Beirut were the only two stations in the Middle East which had both access to Enigma (the deciphering machine which enabled the British to read German messages) and the wireless and code facilities to communicate with London. It was a joint MI 5 and MI 6 operation. This gave SIME and DSO, Syria, considerable influence in security matters and enabled them to operate without much hindrance from political and military bodies. Both Cairo and Beirut were engaged in important deception activities closely connected with Enigma information. In 1943-45 the MI 6 officer for Syria and the Lebanon was Michael Ionides.

Most of the staff of SIME were people who had no connection with the Middle East and had no wish to stay there when the war was over. Certainly this applied to Oldfield who, while enjoying life in most places, disliked the Middle East as a territory. 'He really hated it,' said one of his colleagues, 'especially if he had to call in at any place there after the war. Yet he got on all right with the natives.'

A touching example of how his thoughts were never far away from Over Haddon and his family is provided by Mr Trethowan's story that 'as an NCO Maurice didn't get paid very much, but when he had saved up £50, he promptly sent it back home "to buy a cow". A long time afterwards I remember his saying "I've now got enough for two more cows." '

'A wealth of local knowledge was available to us, but Maurice's outlook was that every matter had to be dealt with as one would have dealt with it in Over Haddon, and you didn't do anything which you wouldn't have done in Over Haddon. Coming from an essentially countryside background myself, I could appreciate the commonsense of that.'[6]

This attitude might be criticized as being somewhat insular, but experience proved that it was often the wisest method, and certainly the most civilized. Imagination and a sense of humour were not missing in this seemingly parochial outlook. For example, there was an occasion when Oldfield and a colleague, Alan Cutbill, were given an old Austin 10, which had been painted up, to go on a secret mission. 'It looks like the English car it is and it's been badly painted,' Cutbill told Oldfield. 'It's sure to give us away.' To which the latter replied 'Not to worry. If we are questioned, all we need to say is that we pinched it.'[7]

Such missions were perhaps to form the basis of what experience Oldfield was ever to have of the work of an agent 'in the field'. But undoubtedly that experience in all its variety was to give him a useful insight into the problems which secret agents have to face. 'I got to know all the tricks in the Middle East,' he once said. 'I learned how easy it was, if one was so inclined, to build up a report into rather more than it was worth, and how some people would cover hours of fornication with some very dubious intelligence as the end product. I began to see how all-important was the job of the man at the desk, analysing it all. I also saw how vital it sometimes was to provide more material than was really necessary. It was the total output, the useless and the useful, which really helped the interpreter of intelligence in the end.'

Maurice came into contact with a wide range of personalities in the Middle East, some of them *Abwehr* agents whom he helped to 'turn' to the side of the Allies. His acute memory was as good on faces as it was on facts and figures, and a vital factor in his work in these early days. For most of the time he was very much a back-room boy, sharing an office, when he had the rank of captain, with Major Gray, sifting through reports.

In one letter home to his wife Major Gray, proved to be unerringly prophetic. 'There is a most remarkable person here named Maurice Oldfield,' wrote the Major. 'He is a lecturer in medieval history in peacetime, and one day he will be an eminent man, possibly in politics.' Well, not quite politics, but ultimately very much connected with them.

Only during the war period did Oldfield ever regularly drive a motor vehicle. Afterwards he confessed that he did not enjoy driving, though occasionally after the war he could be persuaded to take a turn at the wheel, usually to help out a friend. In the Middle East his excursions were merely as driver for a small team, but sometimes he went on lone intelligence enterprises with one other man such as Alan Cutbill. 'He was a serious driver, if you know what I mean,' said one of his wartime colleagues who later joined the SIS. 'That is to say, he took no risks and remained stone cold sober whenever he was due to take the wheel. We often had the fun, while he just waited to drive us back. Off duty, though, he developed a fondness for araki, that Egyptian liqueur which is made from the juice of dates. I remember going to his flat in London many years afterwards and I noticed a stock of the stuff. He could take it and remain clear-headed, but I often wondered how his guests fared if they ventured on it, for araki is certainly potent.'

Oldfield was generally popular, conscientious while at his desk, but a willing accompanist on the piano if there was a smoking concert. One such convivial occasion was a private party of members of the Corps and friends at the Lucullus Restaurant in Beirut on 16 July 1943, for which a special poster was designed, describing the affair as a 'Sub-Area Saga: An Epic of a Far-Flung Outpost of Empire, revealing little known secrets of 268 FSS Inactivity in Beirut for the past two years.' One rather pleasant feature of Military Intelligence Corps personnel was that, generally speaking, they lacked pomposity, never allowed the importance of their work to make them big-headed. Their happy knack of being able to debunk and satirize themselves is revealed in the programme for this party. Maurice Oldfield was billed as 'Lieut. Oldfield – Guest Star from the GUESTARPO', while his close colleague, Lieutenant Cutbill, was referred to as 'Alan Halberd, Blunderbuss, Platybus, Cutlas, Cutthroat, Billhook, Cutbill – Man of a Thousand Aliases'.

'So often we not only needed, but actually used aliases on our private mission,' says Mr Alan Cutbill, now a businessman in Chiswick. 'We were always pretending to be someone different. We had to do so, especially when we were combing the nightclubs of Beirut in search of information. One had to be an actor to do that, but I don't think Maurice was a very good actor. I remember once he posed as a lieutenant-colonel and was not too happy in the role. But perhaps he was worrying about keeping absolutely sober, as he was the reserve driver on that occasion. But Maurice was versatile and, if he was not a good actor, he certainly knew how to pump people for information.'[8]

Such missions could be both hilarious and provocative. One of the tasks of Military Intelligence in the Middle East was to screen the bordellos for potential spies. 'Our job was to spot the baddies,' was how one officer described it. 'If one prostitute chatted up a British serviceman and found out what his unit was, where he had been and where he was going, that might not tell a lot. But if she did this with scores of servicemen in the course of a week, it could build up into an accurate picture of army movements and strength. We had to establish a close relationship with some of the girls just to assess whether they could be acting as spies for the enemy. Maurice was particularly good in assessing our reports, sometimes with caustic criticism as to how we had acted, or what we had said. I remember once he asked me "couldn't you have stayed with the girl just a bit longer – until breakfast time, say? I'm sure she could have told you a lot more." Another time he commented: "This girl is too good to be true. Either she should be working for us, or she's one of the subtlest females in the service of the Germans." '

Maybe this was simply what might be called 'Over Haddon commonsense', but it was something which was expressed rather more neatly, if somewhat enigmatically in a song written for one of the Section's smoking concerts. Entitled 'Bachelors Beware', some of the verses relevant to this biography are as follows:

'O, dear, what can the matter be?
This was an office renowned for spy-catchery,
Now it's a matrimonial agency –
Who'll be the third one this year?
We once had a colonel who loved to disparage
The ancient and grim institution of marriage,
But he flew home on leave and got caught in the barrage
– He'll do no more flying, we fear.
Now there's old Captain O who looks rather monastic
(They say his conscience is made of elastic),
To get him a wife we must do something drastic
– There are lots of nice girls in Mieh-Mieh.
There's one pretty maiden who lives in Aleppo,
She came to Beirut for a *morceau de repos*,
But now she had better be watching her step-o
– They don't remain spinsters long here.'⁹

There certainly were 'lots of nice girls in Mieh-Mieh' and Oldfield kept in touch with some of them for many years afterwards, one in particular all his life. There were several Hungarian women who had been ejected from Turkey and interned at Mieh-Mieh. But Maurice corresponded with both male and female internees after the war.

Yet, outside of Mieh-Mieh, he developed and sustained friendships in Lebanon, notably with Farid Chehab, who had been the Lebanese Chief of Police under the Vichy regime. It was on Oldfield's advice that the British prevented the Free French from executing him. The Emir Farid Chehab (to give him his full title) was a member of a highly respected family of the Druze-Maronites, though the title of Emir seems not to have been used for some centuries. About 1768 the Chehabs became Christians and took up residence at Deit al Kamar, a Christian village in the centre of the Druze area of the mountains. After the war Farid Chehab became Chief of Police in Lebanon once again, and he and Oldfield kept in touch for many years.

More than twenty years later Oldfield was visiting Beirut en route to the Far East when he was given an invitation by one of the former internees at that wartime camp. 'Mr Oldfield,' he said, 'you must come and have dinner with us. We now have eight Mieh-Mieh men in the Cabinet and you must meet the others.'

The colonel mentioned in the mess song was Douglas Roberts, later to be promoted to brigadier in charge of Field Security for the whole of the Middle East. It was he who described Oldfield as 'the best counter-intelligence officer, both from the theoretical and practical point of view that it has been my privilege to meet. He is quite outstanding.'[10]

One of the strengths of the DSO organization in Syria and the Lebanon in the war was the excellent political reports it produced. Some of these were so important and of such a high quality that even today they form a part of the permanent Foreign Office records. A great deal of the information contained in them was collected by Oldfield from his Mieh-Mieh friends. Many of the names contained in those reports can still be heard of today in the troubled areas of the Lebanon and Syria.

Brigadier Roberts had had a varied and interesting career. Born in Odessa at the turn of the century, the son of a British consul in that city, he had served in the Royal Artillery in

World War One. For a time he was ADC to General Pierre Wrangel in the White Russian Army campaign against the Bolsheviks. After the war his experiences ranged from activities in the timber trade in Finland to working in Russia for E. and A. Harriman in their timber and manganese business. He was bilingual in English and Russian, spoke good French and had several prominent Russian friends. In between bouts of prolonged hard work, Sundays often included, the officers of the Intelligence Corps used to enjoy some very good parties at Brigadier Roberts' flat during the war. He used to sing Russian songs with tremendous verve, accompanying himself on the accordion.

When world War Two broke out he was sent to Istanbul as DSO, Turkey. There he contracted tuberculosis, but, after recovering in a Lebanese sanitorium, he became DSO, Syria, when the Allies occupied this territory in 1941. Eventually he became head of SIME, succeeding Brigadier Raymond Maunsell.

4

From Beirut To Cairo

Much has been written about the Special Operations Executive effort in Western Europe in World War Two. The truth is that SOE activities in the Western theatre of war were always subordinate to its objectives in the Mediterranean, the Balkans and the Middle East. In this strange world of double-cross and double-agents, of deception tactics and wooing the enemy over to one's own side, Oldfield learned the arts of intelligence in their most devious form. It gave him a glimpse of both spying and spy-catching, of men who might seem enemies, but who, with patience and care, might be turned into colleagues if not friends and, better still, be used to mislead the enemy.

His early experiences as an officer included the interrogating and screening of interned Syrian nationalists in Beirut. But he was also very much involved on occasions in sorting out not only the reports, but sometimes the hilarious love lives of some of the agents working for SIME. Occasionally it was a matter of deciding whether the love life helped or hindered the overall cause. Not always an easy question to answer either by Over Haddon, or any other standards, especially when one agent claimed he could achieve better results if provided with sufficient cash to extend his network of lovers.

Oldfield had promised shortly after he retired from the SIS to give some of his memoirs and anecdotes of his service in the Intelligence Corps to the Corps Museum and Archives in Templer Barracks, Ashford, Kent. Alas, first his sudden appointment to Northern Ireland and then his illness and death prevented this from being realized. But his observations on his experiences in the Middle East, though sparse and to the point and made informally in conversation with friends, are of some importance in relation to the history of the period. He was not a man who indulged in sensational statements in order to score a *bon mot*. Indeed, the reverse was true: the best of his wit was usually associated with his understatements. But he made the point again and again in private conversation that 'without aid from our friends inside the German *Abwehr*, we shouldn't have won the war quite so soon. And if we had heeded some of them rather more than we did, it is possible that we could have won the war much earlier and not ended up with another potential enemy, if not on our doorstep, at least not very far away.'

One of the aims of 'Double Cross' as practised in the Middle East was not merely to try to win allies from among Admiral Wilhelm Canaris' *Abwehr*, but to plant false information on the *Sicherheitsdienst*, the branch of German Intelligence controlled by the ruthless Himmler. This helped two ways: it pleased the *Abwehr* for the *Sicherheitsdienst* to be baffled, for these organizations hated one another, and it misled Himmler's men. Thus it came about that Force 'A', under Brigadier Dudley Clarke, a superb exploiter of the arts of deception, and SIME sometimes appeared to help the *Abwehr*, while occasionally the *Abwehr* seemed to go out of their way to help the Allies. Superficially, and to the uninitiated, this did not make sense. To those who were not at the time cognisant of the complexities and ambiguities of the rival German Intelligence Services, it was incredible.

The enigmatic Canaris could be ruthless, cunning and aloof, but as the war progressed it became increasingly clear that he was, if not an ally, at least something very like a friendly neutral at the top of the enemy's Intelligence Service and one who actually looked forward to the time when, with honour, he might once again be friends with the British. What was not realized until it was too late was the extent to which he was committing himself to the German Resistance against Hitler. For evidence in confirmation of this assessment there are these unequivocal statements: (1) 'During the whole of the war only one single "A" Force link with the *Abwehr* was either compromised or even under suspicion' (David Mure, a key officer in Force 'A'); (2) 'He [Canaris] served the enemy [i.e. the Allies] for many years' (General Jodl speaking at the Nuremberg war criminals' trials); (3) 'Canaris had never said a word to me about peace negotiations,' said Dr Paul Leverkuehn, the wartime German Intelligence Officer in Turkey, 'but I have no doubt now that he posted me to Istanbul to take up whatever threads might be put in my hand. He knew that one of my American friends of pre-war days was General William Donovan who became Chief of the OSS.'[1]

Deception and 'Double Cross' tactics in the Middle East, however, were not merely a question of winning over agents from the *Abwehr*, or other German Services. They also consisted of recruiting not only Allied agents to plant disinformation on the enemy, but in many cases creating fictional agents to provide misleading intelligence. Perhaps the most amusing instance of these tactics was the game played by a prostitute code-named GALA, who was actually in jail in Palestine, but for the purposes of misleading the Germans was portrayed as a *poule de luxe* in Beirut with a whole string of imaginary lovers, including Allied officers and an Air Force technician who was supposed to be preparing Turkish airfields for Allied occupation. Thus, through the darkest days in the Middle East (1940-42), the Germans were constantly being fed information to suggest that the British forces and defences were much stronger than they really were.

Two key members of the deception outfit were QUICKSILVER and PESSIMIST. QUICKSILVER was a former Greek Air Force officer who, when Allied resistance to the Germans collapsed in Greece, offered to act as a double agent. Having promised his services to the Germans in Athens, he turned himself over to the British Security Service in Lebanon on arrival there. PESSIMIST, the other double agent, known to the Germans as MIMI, was a radio operator. Both men were kept incommunicado at a villa on the main Beirut-Damascus road. It was nicknamed Q and P Hall after the two agents. The villa was chosen as an ideal centre from which to conduct radio traffic because it was essential that, while QUICKSILVER was transmitting from Beirut to Athens, it should appear that his colleague PESSIMIST was radioing from Damascus (where he was fictitiously established in German eyes) to Sofia.

'Sometimes Maurice would accompany us out to Q and P Hall,' said Major David Mure, who was one of the exponents of deception tactics. 'While the rest of us were out making inquiries, he would stay behind and keep the agents amused. This must have been quite a morale-booster for the agents and an unexpected bonus for them, as they were guarded day and night by East African personnel who spoke no known language.'[2]

Keeping the two agents amused was no easy task even when the authorities showed extraordinary benevolence by appreciating their need for some female company. On one occasion Oldfield had to report an appalling row had broken out at Q and P Hall. Two girls of easy virtue had been sent to the camp for the benefit of QUICKSILVER and PESSIMIST, but because they had insisted on contraceptives being used, the two agents had exploded with anger. 'This is an absolute disgrace,' both men shouted. 'It is wrong and insulting and we won't use them. This sort of thing is never done by decent people in Greece.' It was a long time before quiet was restored.

Gradually and logically, from regarding it as just an essential job to be done in wartime, Oldfield began to develop a positive liking for intelligence work. While consciously he had every intention at this time of returning to university life, subconsciously he had acquired the feeling that intelligence work was his real vocation, if he wished to do something truly constructive in life. He began to see such work not in the same cynical light as so many of his colleagues did – something rather underhand and shoddy – but as a patriotic duty of the highest order. This was not the patriotism of the unthinking jingo, but that of the humanitarian thinker. Experience had shown him that good intelligence could save lives, and it followed naturally that really first-class intelligence, maintained in peacetime, could probably either stave off wars, or, at the worst, end them more quickly. When arguments on the nature of intelligence work occurred from time to time, as inevitably they must among 'hostilities only' officers, this was the line Oldfield took.

'It makes much more sense to spend long hours patiently trying to "turn" an enemy into an ally,' he said to Major David Mure of SIME, 'than it does to launch some ill-planned military operation in which many lives are lost for no real gain – perhaps a mere fifty yards of territory. If we really take the art of 'turning' the enemy seriously, there is no reason why we shouldn't adopt the same tactics in peacetime with a view to preventing war.'

Few of his contemporaries thought that far ahead. One war at a time was quite enough to cope with. But the historian in Oldfield caused him to look at things differently, for the historian, paradoxically enough, is often just as concerned with the future as the past. His detailed knowledge of the past makes him wish to apply this to the future. It is significant that both Oldfield the historian and Irvine Gray the archivist and genealogist shared a belief that security work had something in common with historical research and genealogy.

Ancient history was in fact providing a lesson for the practitioners of deception tactics in World War Two. The Chinese sage, Sun Tzu, had pronounced in favour of such methods in his work, *Ping Fa, circa* 510 BC. His advice had been that it was not enough to recruit spies in enemy territory, but to convert the enemy's spies into one's own service and 'to induce them to carry back false information as well as to spy on their own countrymen.' These tactics were identical with those being adopted by SIME, but to

Westerners who knew nothing of Sun Tzu they were something completely new.

Oldfield's talents as an organist were sought after in August 1944, when 'Monty' Trethowan, now promoted to lieutenant-colonel, was married to Miss Flora Macdonald, who had also been working with SIME. The ceremony took place at the Anglican church in Beirut, which lacked an organ. Maurice played the harmonium instead. There was a touch of black comedy about the wedding celebrations. A specially ordered wedding cake had arrived at customs, but, as the icing sugar had turned grey, customs officials suspected it was being used as a means of smuggling in cocaine; consequently the cake was held up at the frontier for some time.

Mrs Jeanne Smith refers to Oldfield's 'deep religious convictions' which, she adds, 'he kept to himself. Nevertheless, on Christmas Eve 1944, we were celebrating and enjoying ourselves with a party of friends at one of the cabarets when he realized the time and asked me to leave the revellers and accompany him to Midnight Mass, which I did. I should perhaps point out that although this was a Catholic service and he was not a Catholic himself, I think it made an impression on him.'[3]

The Military Intelligence unit in Beirut was — again to quote Mrs Smith — 'more of a "family" than colleagues; we all got on extremely well.' She also cites a letter from Maurice Oldfield which he wrote to her from Cairo on 27 February 1945: 'I don't think any of us will ever find a happier office than that we had under Douglas Roberts in those days.'

Eventually Lieutenant-Colonel Trethowan was posted to Cairo as head of 'A' Section, which dealt with political and administrative matters, excluding Jewish affairs. Meanwhile Douglas Roberts had also been transferred to Cairo as head of SIME, having been promoted to brigadier. Oldfield was officially posted to Cairo at the beginning of 1945, when he replaced Lieutenant-Colonel Trethowan as head of 'A'

Section and in due course became Biigadier Roberts' right-hand man. By this time Oldfield had also been made a lieutenant-colonel.

In the early days of his stay in Cairo he was much more concerned with the problems of German prisoners, internees and even defectors than with Palestinian questions which were mainly dealt with by 'B' Section, which also handled counter-espionage. One of the *Abwehr* personnel in close touch with him was Johann Eppler, who had been a member of *Abwehr I H West* since 1938, and always on missions to the Middle East. He was a German born in Alexandria, but after his father's death his mother married a prosperous Egyptian lawyer named Saleh Ga'afer, so that from then onwards Johann was often known as Hussein Ga'afer. He went to a British school and spoke German, English and Arabic. As an *Abwehr* operative he travelled far and wide, visiting Rommel's headquarters in Libya, making three missions into Iran, which was full of Soviet agents at that time, and, finally, coming to Cairo in 1942, when he rented a luxurious house-boat on the Nile. One of the more amusing stories of World War Two, though it must have been anything but amusing to the person concerned at the time, was that the author Lawrence Durrell so resembled Eppler that he was suspected of being an enemy agent.

Eppler was, however, neither by temperament nor by conviction, a supporter of the Nazi regime in Germany. He is credited with having enlisted the late Anwar Sadat, ultimately President of Egypt, as an informant to the *Abwehr* when Sadat was a junior officer. Stories about Eppler's wartime activities vary according to the viewpoint of the person describing them. When he and his wireless operator arrived in Cairo, they established a direct link with Rommel's HQ from their houseboat on the Nile. Yet while it would seem that Eppler was a positive enemy, there was even before they arrived some suggestion that he might actually be eager to be taken over by the British. David Mure has stated that 'Eppler and his companion did not arrive until June of that year [1942], so barring an almost impossible coincidence, it would seem that "someone" wanted a rumour to get around Cairo via junior intelligence officers that there was a houseboat of German spies. As my experience had shown, there were several German sympathizers anxious to contact young British officers.'[4]

In other words, was there a plan by someone inside the *Abwehr* to ensure that eventually Eppler would help the British? There is perhaps nothing so difficult for an author as dealing with the subject of deception. Sometimes it is impossible to know where it all begins. Suffice it to say that Eppler appeared on a number of occasions to be more than willing to be 'turned', and eventually he was most effectively recruited to the Allied side.

In 1943 he was arrested in Cairo and brought in for interrogation. Long before this it is now clear that Eppler had become disillusioned by the way in which his reports to the *Abwehr* had been misused. Thus at the time of his arrest he was in a mood in which he might consider favourably any proposition put to him by his captors. Yet, clearly, there was a divergence of opinion as to what should be done with him. Ultimately the network he had operated was taken over by the British to make an addition to their own CHEESE network which was run by the 'turned' German agent, ORLANDO. A wealth of intelligence for the Allies resulted.

Having been in correspondence with Johann Eppler over a period of some years, I have found him a reliable witness on a wide range of subjects and particularly well informed on Soviet disinformation. Recently he wrote to me, saying: 'I remember Maurice Oldfield well. I practically owe him my life. Oldfield and Major Dunstun [sic], after my court martial with death sentence, tried very hard to cancel the sentence, otherwise I would have been executed. If I remember well, Oldfield was at this time in SIME, Central Security Detention and Interrogation Camp, Maadi, near Cairo. We often had long discussions after the sentence in my cell, or on walks in the compound with him and Captain Cecil Robson about politics and what could happen after the war.'[5]

Eventually Eppler and his wireless operator, Sanstede, were released from supervision by the British and returned to Germany. If before the war he was somewhat of a carefree playboy, afterwards he became a faithful adherent to the Western cause, settling in Paris. He has told his own story of the war years in his book, *Operation Condor*, published in 1977.

On 6 January 1945, Dr Sandor Rado, a Hungarian professor of geography whose real name was Alexander Radolphi, head of the Soviet-controlled LUCY network in Switzerland, was ordered by Russian Intelligence in Paris to return to Moscow. His network had been unmasked by the Swiss authorities who had discovered that he was secretly relaying information to Moscow by clandestine radio. Rado was accompanied by Alexander Foote, a Briton who had also been a member of the network. Both men travelled with Russian repatriation certificates.

This was the first Soviet plane to leave France after the liberation and, with the war still being waged in Europe, it had to be routed to Russia via Cairo. Rado was worried because the discovery of his radio transmitting stations was indirectly his fault: he had ignored a warning by Foote that there were probably two traitors in the network. When the plane stopped at Cairo, Rado took fright, believing that to return to Moscow would mean his ultimate execution. He walked out of his hotel, leaving his coat and luggage behind to avoid suspicion, having decided to seek sanctuary with the British. Meanwhile he cabled a friend in Paris who was in a position to corroborate that throughout the war he had pleaded with the Russians for cooperation with the British, but that his pleas fell on deaf ears. Foote himself stated on a later occasion that 'Rado suggested that the best thing for the network and himself would be for him to take refuge in the British Legation [in Berne] ...'[6]

Maurice Oldfield was one of Rado's principal interrogators. Johann Eppler says he 'well remembered the day when Oldfield brought Rado (code-named DORA) into the Maadi interrogation camp.' Oldfield was sympathetic and foresaw the advantage of further questioning of Rado, though at the time he sought intelligence on Germany rather than on the USSR. It would, of course, have been greatly in

British interests for Rado to be given sanctuary for not only could he have given details of the Soviet set-up in Switzerland, but of that inside Britain, too.

Oldfield was unable to take action independently without referring the matter first to the SIS in London. Back came the answer that Military Intelligence in Cairo should ensure that Rado was sent on to Moscow forthwith. So he was handed over to the Cairo police who had him extradited to Russia. There he served ten years in a Siberian labour camp.

'Even if they were not interested in Rado's fate,' wrote Arthur Koestler, a fellow-countryman and friend of Rado, 'they ought to have prevented his illegal extradition to the Russians, as Rado was not a Soviet citizen, but a Hungarian, and his repatriation papers were faked ... Alex Rado, the gentle, lovable, scholarly master-spy was one of the victims of the Occident's guilty ignorance and homicidal illusions.'[7]

Leopold Trepper, the mastermind behind the *Rote Kapelle* Soviet network in Occupied Europe, who later went to live in Israel, asserted that the British official responsible for Rado's extradition from Cairo was none other than Kim Philby.[8] After seeking guidance from his Soviet controller, Philby instructed Military Intelligence in Cairo to make sure that Rado was sent on to Moscow. But both Donald Maclean, that other traitor in the Diplomatic Service then in Paris, and James Klugmann, then operating in the Balkans division of the SOE in Cairo, played a part in advocating the 'repatriation' of Rado. Oldfield was unfortunately outgunned by the pro-Soviets inside British officialdom.

This was a decision which Oldfield anguished over for many years afterwards. The more he pondered on the affair the more he thought that this instruction from London was senseless by any standards. But it was only when he made other discoveries that he began to think Philby might be a mole in the service of the Russians. A chance query from Beirut to Cairo caused him to make some inquiries into the case of Dr Erich Vermehren and his wife who, early in 1944, had approached MI 6 in Istanbul and asked for protection. This was provided and eventually the pair reached the safety of London. At this stage H.A.R. ('Kim') Philby, head of

Section V of the SIS, came into the picture. He suddenly took the keenest interest in the Vermehrens, even offering to lend them his mother's flat in Drayton Gardens. But, instead of keeping silent about this case of defection, the British authorities, presumably on the strength of advice from someone in the SIS, actually publicized the affair in a statement – fatal publicity which led to the downfall of Admiral Canaris, head of the *Abwehr*.

By the early months of 1944 Oldfield was already inclined to believe that Admiral Canaris was a vital, if not easily explicable factor in the Allies' favour: in short, here was one man who could yet not merely shorten the war, but see Hitler overthrown. What disturbed him – though it was a mere suspicion at the time – was that some people inside the British Establishment were either wittingly or unwittingly anxious to see Canaris isolated to such an extent that he could no longer work for a negotiated peace.

Hitler was so infuriated by the news of the Vermehrens' defection having been publicized by the British (Dr Vermehren had been recruited into the *Abwehr* by Canaris himself) that on 12 February 1944, he had ordered the absorption of the *Abwehr* by the *Sicherheitsdienst*; a week later Canaris was dismissed. The last hope of a key German figure of stature to assist in any negotiated peace had been destroyed overnight. This incident puzzled Oldfield for a long time. As far as the British were concerned, it didn't make sense. The Vermehrens had defected in the Middle East: after Istanbul they had been taken to Cairo. Had they been kept under arrest, or in safe custody, it might have been possible for them to be used in a new deception operation. By publicizing their defection all the British did was to sign Canaris's death warrant. A year later he was arrested and garrotted by the Gestapo on Hitler's orders.

Philby's role in the Vermehrens' defection and later in the case of Rado were the first danger signals to concentrate Oldfield's acutely analytical mind. But the whole story of Admiral Canaris fascinated him. Had the Admiral actually helped the Royal Navy to sink the *Bismarck*? Oldfield took the trouble some long time afterwards to check up on rumours that this was the case. He found what he believed to be the answer in the report not of an SIS operative, but an NID (Naval Intelligence Division) agent who recorded that on one of his wartime trips to Algeciras when Canaris was dropping hints about possible secret talks with Royal Navy personnel, the Admiral told the agent:

'If your people care to look up your records, you will find that you obtained some very important intelligence in Stockholm from a Hamburg source that led to the sinking of the *Bismarck* and you very nearly ignored the true purport of this.'

The same NID agent admitted that 'Canaris talked in riddles like this. One was often left guessing. Once he seemed to be warning us of a Soviet agent high up in the British Secret Service. Of course we didn't believe him. But our biggest error was to pass this information on to the Iberian Section of MI 6, where, of course, "Kim" Philby was in control.'[9]

Oldfield was installed in a flat in Cairo, not far from the Maadi internment camp. He spoke very little Arabic, but always seemed able to make himself understood in an emergency. Mrs Elizabeth Roberts, widow of Brigadier Roberts, recalls one day when her husband was away and a terrible row, with threats of violence, broke out among the male servants. 'I telephoned Maurice who came over to our home at once and sorted things out surprisingly quickly.'

With the war in Europe virtually at an end, there remained chiefly the problem of what to do with the prisoners-of-war and, often much more difficult, the Germans who had served as agents in the British deception game. But gradually the vital issue became the future of Palestine and Britain's relations with Egypt and other Arab states as well as the problem of the Jews. These were all urgent questions, but a war-weary Britain both at governmental and administrative level in the Middle East was displaying a singularly unimaginative and rather blindly optimistic attitude in tackling them.

Despite the fact that the Jews had provided excellent intelligence as well as serving in the British Army in the

Middle East and elsewhere during the war, there appeared to be a prejudice against some of them. While the War Diaries of the period show there was a general feeling that the Army had been working hard not to appear to be taking sides, it was stressed that 'there were quite a number of Jewish personnel stationed with the Army in Palestine and quite a number of them seemed to have been regarded with suspicion. It was felt that all Jewish personnel should be replaced as soon as possible with other serving soldiers – possibly from one of the Indian regiments.'[10]

Although the British had few friends on either side on the issue of Palestine, reports in the War Diaries show that many officers were going to social gatherings given by the Arabs, and that 'most particularly the Army officers seem to have a great deal of admiration for the Syrians and the way they were running their army.'[11]

At that time the illegal immigration of Jews into Palestine from Europe and elsewhere was occupying the minds of the Intelligence Services. Yet it is clear from most official War Office and Embassy papers of the period 1945-46 that Egypt was given a much higher priority in policy-making at the time. The British were worried that Egypt might use the peace conference to press for the annexation of the Sudan, and it appeared from the records that they were busy equipping the Sudanese as well. By the end of the war the British were closely involved in running Egypt. At one point there was even a discussion that they should actually take it over. Certainly there were several discussions in private on a takeover of the Egyptian army, if any problems should arise.

On the advice of the British Ambassador in Cairo, Lord Killearn, the numbers of Jewish personnel in Cairo were reduced. In a message to the Foreign Office in London Killearn said: 'Jewish personnel should be removed from Egypt in the largest possible numbers in the shortest possible time.' He expressed the opinion that the British Army was 'playing with fire in having people likely to be loyal to the [Jewish] underground in their midst.'[12]

Not until fairly late in 1945 did Oldfield have any responsibility for, or much connection with Jewish affairs.

In so far as he was associated with them he was very open-minded. There was nothing in his background, or in his academic life, to make him in any way an Arabist, though the influence of Namier had enlightened him on the Jewish question generally. Without being in any way hostile to the Arabs, as time passed he became markedly pro-Jewish. Mr Alastair Horne, of St Antony's College, Oxford, who served in Intelligence in the Middle East at the end of the war, says: 'Maurice took some risks in keeping close friends with some Jews during this very tricky period, but in the long term and light of experience I think this almost certainly paid off. I do not, of course, suggest for one moment that he took any security risks.'[13]

No doubt any tendency Oldfield had to guard and sustain Jewish friendships and connections in this period can also be explained to some extent by the fact that both Force 'A' and SIME were aided in their tactics of deception by some extremely clever manipulation of German agents by the Zionist secret society, Haganah, which, in effect, provided a vital nucleus of what eventually became the Israeli Secret Service, or the Mossad. One of the most important of these agents was code-named ORLANDO. He arrived in Cairo in the latter part of 1940 and was understood to be a German agent with extensive business connections in the Middle East. In truth ORLANDO was an Austrian Jew and a member of Haganah and, when he reached Cairo, he reported not to his pro-German contacts, but to SIME. What he proposed to SIME was that he should use his contacts to penetrate Axis espionage in Egypt and report back to the British. Fortunately SIME accepted his story after having carefully checked his past history. All ORLANDO asked in return was that after the war he should be given British citizenship and protection of his real identity. Not only did he recruit a radio operator who could pass on disinformation to the Germans, but he helped to develop the 'Double-Cross' system from inside Egypt. Oldfield was always mindful of the highly skilled ploys and sophisticated deception tactics which Haganah on more than one occasion provided. He felt that the Allies owed a debt to those Jews who, often stateless, offered their services to the Allies in the Middle East, sometimes at risk to their lives. This, too, may explain why in later years he occasionally showed untypical impatience and some exasperation with what he called 'Arab-temporizing' policies in the British Foreign Office.

Such policies, he argued, both in 1945-46 and even in the early 1970s played into the hands of the Russians. In 1945-46 there was no doubt that some hostility on the British side more or less forced some of the Zionists to try to win the support of Russia, something which Ernest Bevin, as British Foreign Secretary, feared above all else. He need not have had this fear because the Zionist leaders were under no illusions about the Soviet Union, knowing that in the past the USSR had condemned Zionism as 'the tool of British imperialism and a bourgeois movement'. Ben Gurion had always expressed his doubts about getting any genuine support from the Russians. As early as March 1945, he had said: 'we must also be prepared for a negative decision, either through the absence of a decision, or through a specific decision by the USSR.'

When the Jewish underground began a campaign of terrorism against the British administration in Palestine, the British-controlled Palestine Police were hard pressed to cope with the situation. Indeed, they were overwhelmed and lacked secure facilities in which to interrogate captured terrorists. As Oldfield shrewdly commented: 'They lacked the know-how of interrogating whether they were dealing with Jews or Arabs. It was inevitable that they should turn to Military Intelligence.'

In 1946 Oldfield was involved in discussions which gave the Palestine Police permission to use the Combined Services Detailed Interrogation Centre (located in the Suez Canal Zone) for the in-depth questioning of a number of captured terrorists.[14]

The official War Diary records for February 1946 mention Oldfield's name in Item 3 of a document covering 'Policy-Palestine Detachment': 'A suggestion was put forward by HQ Palestine that the Palestine Detachment should not operate until a full scale operation developed.

After consultations with Lt.-Col. Dewhurst (GI[I]), Brigadier Roberts and Lt.-Col. Oldfield (SIME) it was decided there were no security objections to the immediate operation of the detachment, and that Major Sedgwick (OC CSDIC MEF) should go to Palestine to consult GSI [SIME] and CID with a view to immediate operation.'[15]

This apparently led to a meeting on 19 February 1946, between Sedgwick, Lieutenant-Colonel Martin Charteris (now Lord Charteris) and Mr Catling (now Sir Richard Catling) during which it was agreed that the Palestine Detachment of the CSDIC should start work as soon as possible. Following this Oldfield spent some time in the Defence Security Office in Jerusalem.

Mr Teddy Kollek, the Mayor of Jerusalem, a friend of Oldfield's over many years, recalls the time when he was maintaining a liaison with British Intelligence in Cairo on behalf of the Jewish Agency during World War Two and immediately afterwards: 'I knew Douglas Roberts, Maurice's superior. Through him I met Maurice who introduced himself as a pupil of Lewis Namier which created a close connection between us. I came to know him fairly well on my frequent visits to Cairo. Our main topic of conversation was Jewish terrorism which worried the British very much, particularly after the death of Lord Moyne, and to which we were totally opposed.

'I arrived at his office late one evening. Office hours lasted until about 8 pm after a four hour siesta because of the heat. Maurice showed me a cupboard which, on an inspection tour, he had found not securely locked. In it, to his great surprise, he found the detailed report of Aaron Aaronson to the British when he left Turkish Palestine, with handwritten comments by Hogarth and Lawrence [T.E. Lawrence "of Arabia"]. Maurice let me sit and read it but – regrettably – he did not allow me to steal it. All subsequent efforts on my part, even to obtain a photocopy, were in vain.

'Maurice came regularly to Israel in later years and even though I no longer had any connection with Israeli Intelligence, we often met and he took a little time to let me show him around Jerusalem.'[16]

This was typical of occasional markedly independent actions by Oldfield in the course of his work. In other words he always knew exactly when to bend the rules while furthering the long term cause. The Aaronsons were a wealthy and extremely cultured family greatly respected in their own community in Palestine. In World War One, convinced that the Allies could win, Aaron Aaronson offered to set up a spy network for the British. He promised to keep them posted on Turkish troop movements, while making it clear that his family wanted no financial reward for their services. His aim was to win British support for a Jewish home in Palestine. A botanist, who had an experimental station at Atlit on the Palestinian coast, he had set up his spy network there, calling it Nili, an acronym of the Hebrew words for 'The Eternal One of Israel does not Lie'.

Aaronson's brother and sister were also in the network which provided a steady stream of invaluable intelligence for the British. Unhappily, Sara Aaronson was eventually suspected of spying and was arrested by the Turks, tortured and died – probably by her own hand so that she would not give way under torture.

Oldfield undoubtedly had good reasons for showing this dossier to Mr Kollek and he made a number of similar gestures to win the goodwill of Palestinian Jews. He maintained at the time and for ever after that many of the Jewish terrorists could have been recruited to the British side long before if there had been a little imagination on the part of the authorities, and that it was a grave error to make illegal immigration such a major issue. 'Many, if not most of those Jews were escaping from the horrors of Nazi-dominated Europe and some of the rest were escaping from Stalinist anti-semitism,' he declared.

In a report from the Middle East Department of the Colonial Office in December 1946, it was stated that 'without Jewish personnel the Force [the Palestinian Police] must be handicapped. The introduction of more Jews would be dangerous, but on balance the case for increasing the number of Jewish personnel seems well founded if they can be obtained. But it has been constantly stressed that rates of pay are far too low. If it is agreed that more Jewish personnel will be of assistance in dealing with the existing situation the question of increased emoluments should receive favourable consideration. This would lessen the excuse for graft, which is said to be widespread and not altogether confined to Palestinians.'[17]

Another interesting point in the report made by Sir Charles Wickham on the Palestinian situation as a whole was that 'as few hindrances as possible should be placed in the way of political personnel obtaining at short notice funds from the Secret Service for the adequate reward of informants. The promptness with which payment is made and the adequacy of the amount are important factors in retaining their services. I believe that district officers are severely restricted in the amounts which they may disburse under this head on their own authority.'[18]

5

Desk Officer In R 5

At the end of 1946 Oldfield, a major with the temporary rank of Lieutenant-colonel, was made a Member of the Order of the British Empire for his war services. By this time he was overdue to leave the Army and seriously concerned about planning his future.

The idea of returning to academic life had become less of a certainty and rather more of a personal dilemma. There had been no pressure on him to stay on in the Service, but it had been impressed upon him, especially by Brigadier Roberts, that he was doing a highly important job. He began to renew acquaintanceships with old friends, especially some of those with whom he had been a fellow-student at Manchester University. One of these was Professor Norman Dees, who had been serving with the Eighth Army. He always listened carefully to any advice which Dees might give him. 'Why he stayed on in Intelligence work after the war is a many-sided question,' says Professor Dees. 'I think you are right in supposing that a sense of Christian duty was strong, but I think that it worked just as much as a set of moral imperatives to *restrain* him from opting for what constantly *tempted* him, namely the continued study of history (which he never gave up) in a professional way within a university.

Finally, he once told me that he found the business of interpreting evidence in the intelligence world not very different from dealing with medieval documents.'[1]

Undoubtedly, however, the chief influence was that of Brigadier Douglas Roberts. Oldfield had proved over and over again in conducting interrogations and in analysing the results of these that careful, patient and intelligently conducted interrogation could result in valuable information and, occasionally, a new ally. Much of the interrogation work conducted in Cairo prior to the establishment of CSDIC, and sometimes independently of it afterwards had been lamentably lacking in the kind of talents required for skilful interrogation. Sir Charles Wickham's report had made it clear that 'many of its [the CID] personnel are far from efficient. The Force had only a small proportion of men with more than three years' service, and the trend seems still to be for very many of its members to leave it when their initial three-year contracts expire. Besides, the type of intake since 1938 appears to have been in many cases unsatisfactory.'[2]

Brigadier Roberts had been highly regarded in intelligence circles outside SIME, and in London it was noted that he was one of the very few men engaged in this work who was not only an authority on Russia, but had lived and worked there. He had met Lenin and one or two other of the Bolshevik leaders and had several prominent Russians among his acquaintances, including Stanislavsky. So it was not surprising that he should be asked to join the SIS in London as head of R-5, the Counter-Espionage Directorate, which included the Russian desk and the investigation of communism. Equally, it made sense that Roberts should invite his own most trusted and admired intelligence officer, Oldfield, to accompany him. He wanted someone he knew and understood among his senior desk officers.

As the two men had worked so well together, this was probably an important factor in persuading Oldfield to give serious consideration to this proposition. It was not an easy decision to take and it was some time before he made up his mind. Those closest to him believed that he felt he might be able to win over some adherents from the Soviet regime in the same way that he had helped to 'turn' one or two *Abwehr* agents. Certainly he was very conscious of the parallel.

From this time onwards his career came to be marked by that degree of anonymity which work for the SIS confers on its members. Officially, his employment from 1947 consisted of a series of so-called diplomatic appointments, often merely being noted as 'attached to the Foreign Office'. And from 1947-49 he was so attached in London, but actually working in the old Secret Service offices in Broadway as deputy chief of R-5.

First of all there was a happy return to his family and friends in Derbyshire. After seeing his family he went with one of his brothers to the Lathkill Arms Hotel in Over Haddon. Maurice was in mufti, as he did not want to flaunt his rank in front of old friends, but his brother was in Army uniform and revealing that he had a sergeant's stripes.

'Where are yer stripes, Maurice?' asked one of the locals. 'Yer brother's got 'is stripes up and yet you, 'oo's bin to university and all, 'ave got nowt!'

Maurice always relished telling this story against himself. By this time he had developed into something of a Pickwickian figure to look at, but, says one of his friends, 'that would depend as much upon the mood of the man observing him as the man himself.' He was small in build, slightly stocky, with large cheeks and heavy spectacles, but always with a benign expression. 'He was so obviously friendly to everyone, yet in an unconspicuous way,' was how another colleague put it. 'One always felt he understood about things without his needing to spell them out.'

For many young men who had served in exotic, distant places while in the Forces in World War Two it was not always easy to adapt to the old life of dull routine, especially that of a small village. But to Oldfield it made no difference at all. He entered completely into the spirit of life at Over Haddon, whether at home, on the farm, in the pub, or just walking around meeting people. Mr Phillip Whitehead the former MP for Derby North, has described him as pottering about his father's farm unnoticed, adding that the casual stroller who found his way up from the valley of the Lathkill to Over Haddon would not give a second glance to the 'rumpled, homespun figure in transit between farmhouse and cowshed. The face is not bucolic; behind the owlish spectacles it almost has the look of Sartre, transposed from *Les Deux Magots*.'[3]

In due course the inevitable question was put to him time and again by villagers and friends: 'What exactly are you doing now, Maurice?' To which he would usually reply: 'Well, it's really to do with the security of embassies.' He looked wise, declined to elaborate on his statement and proceeded at once to tell one of his innumerable stories. His talent for playing himself down, for blending into the environment of his local village and being popular with all was something which enabled him to look upon Over Haddon as an ever-desirable retreat from the pressures of London. Apart from this he continued to take a keen interest in the family farm. The village postmistress, Mrs Philomena Elliot, who lived close by the farm, said: 'Maurice never changed either after university or the war. His success never went to his head, and that is why we were all so very proud of him and his success.'

Just how seriously he took his new work in London can be judged from the fact that, when he spent his weekends at Over Haddon, he always made a point of returning by train early on a Sunday afternoon. When one of his Bakewell friends, John Carrington, asked why he did this, he was told: 'Oh, I always go straight into the office before going back to my place. That way I can see what there is to tackle and can be ahead of my work schedule for the following day.'

There is some evidence that Oldfield suffered from a degree of homesickness when he had to live in London for his new post with the SIS. Fortunately, he was able to counteract this by living with old friends for several months. Sir Bryan Hopkin writes: 'After the war ended, Maurice was our lodger in our flat in North London for a time. I cannot date this precisely, but it must have been sometime between early 1947 and autumn 1951. Nor can I remember exactly how long his stay with us lasted, though I am sure it was months rather than years. I think that when he left us it was to go to Singapore. We then had two small boys, and I do remember Maurice as being very kind with them. He was always very interesting to talk with, and as concerned with human beings as with public events.

'He developed at this time the habit of playing bridge once a week with some close neighbours of ours, and he must have enjoyed it because he kept it up after he left us, travelling a fair distance in order to do so.'[4]

The new assignment that confronted him and his chief was indeed a formidable one. It was increasingly made more difficult and arduous by the development of the Cold War. But to Oldfield himself it must have seemed a sphere of work in which the Over Haddon commonsense outlook was no longer applicable. The whole world of intelligence had been sent into a non-stop spin on both sides of the Atlantic. In the meantime the village boy who had made good was snared into an intelligence stable where Eton counted more than Lady Manners' Grammar School and membership of White's rather more even than Eton, while Oxford and Cambridge had preference over Manchester University and belonging to a Guards' regiment meant more than experience in the Intelligence Corps. Quite a few of the old school eyebrows were raised prejudicially at the newcomer.

Some time before the end of the war the senior staff of the Secret Service began to make plans for their future priority targets for intelligence after the war was ended. By this time it was quite clear that the next potential enemy would be Soviet Russia. As a preliminary step it was decided to create a small section of MI 6 which could study this problem both in the light of past experience and what were likely to be future requirements. Inevitably, there were discussions about this with representatives of MI 5.

This was probably the biggest mistake which MI 6 chiefs made at this time. By the last year of the war MI 5 had already been infiltrated by the Soviet Union in more than one department. Thus any discussions between MI 6 and MI 5 on the subject of the new Soviet-probing section were liable to be exploited by the infiltrators, not only in passing on information to Moscow, but in influencing the choice of personnel for the section.

At the time it seemed highly likely that the head of this new section of MI 6 would be Colonel Felix Cowgill, a former officer in the Indian Police and a high-ranking figure in the Secret Service. The new section was then to be named Section IX, though it was later referred to as R-5, partly because, in the interests of economy, there was a plan to merge the old Section V (the Iberian Section) into the proposed Counter-Espionage Directorate. Now at this time the head of Section V was still Kim Philby, so he took part in these various discussions at a very early stage. In his memoirs Philby states: 'My Soviet contact asked me if I would be offered a senior position in the section. I thought I probably would. But could I be certain, he persisted? To that question I could not possibly give him a categorical affirmation.'[5]

The Soviet controller, however, practically ordered Philby to ensure that he got the job of head of Section IX whether or not it had merged with his own Section V. From that moment the situation developed into a battle for power between Cowgill's allies and his enemies inside MI 6, with Philby, of course, quietly gaining support for himself from the enemies. While all this office in-fighting was going on, Stewart Menzies, the current 'C', stayed aloof, and, as far as can be judged, had not the slightest suspicion of what lay behind the various intrigues. Nor could he hope for much support or worthwhile advice from MI 5, even on the highest level. Sir Percy Sillitoe, the ex-police chief who was the new head of MI 5, was himself kept in the dark about the true state of affairs by Philby's main ally in 5 – the shrewdly and quietly ubiquitous Captain Guy Liddell, deputy head of the counter-espionage organization. In short, Philby had ensured that MI 5 would put forward no arguments against his projected new appointment.

Thus Philby was made head of the new section, which gave him enormous powers, including liaison with MI 5; he moved from Ryder Street in London to the rabbit warren which comprised MI 6's offices in Broadway. With the re-organization of the SIS at the end of the war, Section V was abolished. If Philby had been in any way apprehensive about the risks of his new appointment, he was soon to have a sharp reminder. One day he was called into 'C's' office and told about a certain Constantin Volkov, a Soviet vice-consul in Istanbul, who had not only asked for political asylum from the British for his wife and himself, but had claimed to know the names of three Soviet agents in Britain, two inside the Foreign Office and one in MI 5.

This must have come as an acute shock for Philby because, though this information did not seem to point directly to him, it certainly indicated that some of his friends were implicated. But an even greater shock must have been his chief's intimation that the man he proposed to send out to Istanbul to investigate the Volkov allegations was none other than Brigadier Roberts, then home on leave from Cairo. 'C' pointed out that Roberts knew Istanbul, had worked in collaboration with Turkish Intelligence and spoke fluent Russian.

Later the same day 'C' called Philby back into his office and, according to Philby, said that Roberts had 'an unconquerable distaste for flying ... He had made his arrangements to return by boat from Liverpool early the following week [presumably en route to Cairo]. Nothing the Chief could say would induce him to change his plans.'[6]

Brigadier Roberts was at this time still working for SIME and had no obligation to carry out 'C's' request. His duty was to return to Cairo. But it should also be mentioned that Philby's allegation that he would not go to Istanbul because he hated flying is grossly inaccurate. Before World War Two Roberts had been an enthusiastic amateur flier, frequently piloting his own plane. It was not that he was afraid of flying, but that a lung damaged by tuberculosis made flying inadvisable. Nevertheless, as he was often to agonize in later years, this decision of his not only let Philby off the hook, but sealed Volkov's doom. For Philby went out to Istanbul instead, and, having tipped off Moscow, ensured that Volkov was promptly liquidated by the KGB before he could make his revelations to the British.

Towards the end of 1946 Philby was told that his time had come for a tour of duty overseas and that he had been selected to take charge of the Secret Service station in Istanbul. Ironically his successor in charge of R-5 was none other than Brigadier Roberts, who had just given up his post as head of SIME. It was an imaginative and sensible choice as not only had Roberts achieved many successes in SIME, but he was in every respect well equipped to help launch a Russian department. Philby has this, again totally unfair and snide, comment to make on his successor – that Roberts' 'firmest claim to fame as head of R-5, was his success in persuading Maurice Oldfield, an officer of high quality from SIME, also to join SIS. Within a few weeks of his installation as Roberts' deputy, Oldfield had earned the nickname "Brig's Brains".' [7]

The attempt by Philby to play down the importance of Brigadier Roberts, and to suggest that he was below par for the job, can only be interpreted as an attempt to smear those people in the SIS who were top Soviet-watchers. What Philby hides is that during his period as head of R-5, with Oldfield as one of his desk officers, Brigadier Roberts achieved quite a few successes, though the credit for these has sometimes been attributed to other people.

Oldfield knew practically nothing about the wartime SIS, though occasionally he had had to work in collaboration with some MI 6 officers, most recently and notably in the case of Sandor Rado. But in the beginning of 1947 he was joining a service which had the task of adapting itself to peacetime conditions. The Secret Service was faced with a very different world from that in which the war began. The British Empire had begun to crumble, the overseas possessions were slowly to disappear. Inevitably, some of the old rivalries between MI 6 and MI 5 sprang up again and, more disturbingly, there had been a renewal of the personal animosities and vendettas between some of the MI 6 senior staff. After the team-work and *ésprit de corps* of Military Intelligence, all this must have been both puzzling and hurtful to Oldfield.

Probably for the first time, except for some marginal experience in the Middle East, he was learning about Soviet subversion tactics. However he never, even at this stage of his career, allowed himself to be completely departmentalized. He retained a keen interest in Middle East affairs, even though he had been glad to leave these. He had absorbed so much of the political history of the area, especially of the Lebanon, Syria and Egypt, that he was often called upon for advice and comments by other sections.

The Foreign Secretary, Ernest Bevin, had opposed the creation of an independent Jewish state largely because he feared it might give Soviet Russia a bridgehead in the Middle East. At that time Russia was playing a devious game which suggested to some – quite wrongly as it turned out – that the USSR would establish a special relationship with Israel. Only much later did Bevin realize that this was a totally wrong interpretation largely wished on him by a few Arabists inside the Foreign Office. But once the state of Israel was created Bevin had concurred in the setting up of a Secret Service station in Tel Aviv; it was agreed that relations between the SIS and Israeli Intelligence (the Mossad) should be encouraged and developed.

'Oldfield played a small part in this,' a retired Mossad officer has commented. 'It may only have been a small part at the time, but he used some of his wartime experience not only to help begin to build a good relationship – no easy task at that time – but also to give some very good advice to us. He passed on to us quite a bit of information on the persecution of Jews inside the Soviet Union and even went out of his way to indicate some escape routes and people who might help organize rescue attempts. He also wanted to know from us of any dissident Jews in Soviet-controlled territories, how best they could be helped, how rescued and, naturally, what they had to tell. I think he had a genuine humanitarian interest in all this, apart from a professional concern.

'Anyhow, he was one who helped to get SIS-Mossad relations off to a good start. They continued to be quite good for many years, even when relations between the British government of the day and the Israeli government were not so good. There will be some people who will tell you that Oldfield was soft and easy-going. Don't believe a word of it. Appearances could be deceptive. When necessary he knew how to be ruthless and, if there was unpleasant work to be done, he never shirked it.'

One of the first clandestine operations with which Oldfield was concerned was that of infiltrating agents into Albania to set up an information-gathering and resistance network. The agents were Albanians recruited from displaced persons' camps in Greece and Italy. Trained at a British establishment in Malta, they were taught to use parachutes, codes and operate radio transmitters. Eventually, operating under British control, the agents were parachuted into an area in central Albania called the Mati, where there was believed to be a small group of people loyal to the Albanian monarchy. At that time the Albanian regime was more Stalinist that Stalin himself, almost regarding themselves as the sole custodians of orthodox Marxism.

The SIS aim was to encourage, if not to foment, an anti-communist rising in Albania. Between 1946 and 1951 scores of drops were made by parachutists and after that date the whole operation was largely taken over by the Americans, who were called in to discuss the situation by the SIS. It was finally and abruptly brought to an end a few weeks before Easter 1953.

'In the early stages this operation was a well-kept secret and produced some worthwhile intelligence,' declared an Albanian who took part in it and is now living in London with British citizenship. 'But it soon became apparent that somebody had tipped off the Albanian authorities and that they were ready waiting for us when we landed. Some of the parachutists managed to get in and out all right, but those who were landed by sea were all arrested on arrival. Much later I was interviewed by Maurice Oldfield who wanted my opinion on how the leakages of information had occurred. I felt he was suspicious that someone in his own organization had given us away.'

This member of the Committee of Free Albanians was

under the impression that Oldfield was very unhappy about the whole operation and feared it was almost totally counter-productive. At no time, he insisted, was Philby's name mentioned in the course of his interview with Oldfield, but long afterwards he felt sure that Oldfield had Philby in mind.

Just how much Oldfield had Philby in mind at this time is still a matter of conjecture. It must be remembered that Oldfield was not only a newcomer, but, by SIS standards, somewhat of an outsider in the late 1940s, and that Philby himself was highly regarded in the echelons of the Service. Added to this was the disadvantage that Oldfield understood, though he did not go along with, those of his own generation who were anti-establishment and pro-Soviet. He appreciated the motives of at least some of them, people he respected. It may have been a serious error to respect such motives while disagreeing with them, but in the somewhat confused situation of the period it was at least excusable.

In any event, however much Oldfield might have doubted Philby, he would have been up against tremendous opposition within the SIS, largely because Philby had secured for himself one invaluable alibi. When he was posted to Istanbul shortly after the war ended, Philby began to exchange confidences with the Russians with, as far as can be ascertained, the tacit understanding of the SIS. In other words, to some extent – it will probably never be known how much – he was allowed to play a double game, but one which was intended to help the SIS in the long run. The fact that he had been working for the Soviet Union for several years was, of course, unknown to the SIS. But this liberty to play a double game was one reason why Philby was able to brush aside any allegations made against him during the fifties. Whenever MI 5, or anyone else, raised the issue of treachery, the SIS would come to Philby's defence and indignantly reject such pleas, explaining that what he was doing in Istanbul, and elsewhere for that matter, was carried out with their full approval.

This, of course, is a perennial risk for all secret services.

Once any of them gives the go-ahead for one of its own agents to play the role of a double-agent, there must always be doubts. History shows that the risks rarely justify the results.

What disturbed Oldfield rather more than anything he had then learned about Philby was information he obtained first hand on Alexander Foote, a member of the LUCY Soviet network in Switzerland. Foote, who had travelled to Russia on the same plane as Rado, soon realized that, though a member of a Soviet spy network, he was suspected of working for the British and trying to 'retard the advance of the Red Army'.

The statement made by Alexander Foote was as follows: 'I was recruited into the *Razvedka*, the Intelligence Service of the Red Army, towards the end of 1938, on my return to this country after almost two years' service in the International Brigade in Spain. Until the outbreak of World War Two I was active in Germany, subsequently operating from Switzerland against the Axis powers until my arrest by the Swiss Federal Police towards the end of November 1943. Because of the geographical situation of Switzerland, entirely surrounded by Axis powers, it was not possible for the Soviets to reinforce their agents in the Swiss anti-Axis network, and I had swift promotion, being at the time of my arrest in charge of the sole remaining communications between the Soviet General Staff in Russia and its sources of information "in the heart of the German High Command".

'I was subsequently released by the Swiss and arrived in Moscow in January 1945. Owing to a peculiar set of circumstances it then appeared to the Soviets that I had in fact been "got at" by the British Intelligence Service, and that certain actions on my part *since* my release by the Swiss in September 1944, were construed in Moscow to be British inspired with the object of "retarding the Red Army". I was cleared of this suspicion only after a lengthy scientific interrogation and a check-up on the spot in West Europe after the end of the war.

'At the beginning of 1947 (still in Moscow) I was informed that I was to be entrusted with the rebuilding of a

Razvedka network in the USA from an HQ that I was to establish in Mexico. I was told that all Resident Directors of Soviet espionage had been withdrawn from activity in the territory of Russia's co-belligerents in June, 1941, and that numerous dormant sources of information in the USA were to be reactivated.

'My arrest by the Swiss as a Soviet agent had made it impossible for me to work again whilst living under my own name and I left East Berlin to establish a German background for a new identity.

'In mid-July, 1947, I announced myself to a British Intelligence HQ in West Berlin, and subsequently, in Hanover, made a report to a certain Mr —— who, I understood, had flown from London to interview me.

'Mr —— adopted a rather unfriendly and sceptical attitude towards me and more or less limited himself to taking down notes of statements that I volunteered. Although I had for the previous two years been in regular contact with high officers of one of the Soviet Union's most important agencies, little interest was evinced in what I had to say or what I had learned. Mr ——'s first action on meeting me across the interrogation table was to produce a packet of Senior Service cigarettes and light one. As an afterthought, he asked me if I would like to smoke and on my affirmative reply contemptuously tossed me a small packet of Woodbines. He then informed me that I should not take it for granted that I should be allowed to return to England. In short, my impression was that Mr —— wished to antagonize me into saying as little as possible.

'During the interview I reported the names of two of my former colleagues, "John" and "Sonia" [Leon and Ursula Beurton] who had, since 1941, been living in England. I mentioned that although I had been told in Moscow that they had been dormant during the war, it was obvious that some contact with the Centre in Moscow [had been made], for it was known there that the couple had recently had a child. Also towards the end of 1941 I had sent Sonia (by means of Post Office jargon telegramme) to see the London Soviet military attaché on organizational matters.

'I spent a total of about ten weeks incommunicado as a "guest" of MI 5, one month in Germany and six weeks in a flat in Hammersmith. My release coincided with my trial "*in absentia*" before a Swiss Military Tribunal, where I was sentenced to three years' imprisonment, fifteen years' expulsion, 8,000 francs fine and the confiscation of my property.

'Some time later I met a sister of Sonia (a certain Brigitte Kuczhinsky, onetime secretary of the Hampstead Communist Party) who had knowledge of my collaboration with her sister in the Swiss network. At this time she did not know of my defection and she confided in me that John and Sonia had had a very narrow escape. On the very day before they were due to go to an important secret rendezvous the police questioned them and searched their home on the pretext that their marriage was illegal. I learned later that both John and Sonia had fled to East Berlin.

'I would point out that if I at the time of my defection had been persuaded to continue my work with the Soviets, with the secret cognizance of British Intelligence, very possibly the latter would now be in the possession of facts and information about *Razvedka* activities, which at present they do not have. Also if the couple John and Sonia had been put under lengthy surveillance instead of alerted by precipitous police action, their contacts with sources of information in this country would ultimately have been disclosed.

'I am deeply conscious that in affairs of espionage and counter-espionage what superficially may appear to be blunders or worse can have a totally different aspect when assessed in the light of the full facts of the case, and for this reason I have until now rejected all offers to publish the story of the treatment of my affair by the MI responsible. However, in view of recent events in this country it appears to me to be in the interest of security that the reason for the apparent failure of our Intelligence to draw any benefits from my defection should now be studied by the Committee of Privy Councillors set up by the Prime Minister.'

Alexander Foote went on to compare the very thorough

questioning he had by the Swiss with the 'interrogation' by Mr ——, 'who did not appear to have very profound knowledge of the Soviet espionage system – questions, if any, were sketchy and unplanned ... This is a striking contrast to the Soviet procedure of thoroughness and the elimination of possibility of error when it is really desired to arrive at the truth.

'I would also mention that my successor in the Hammersmith flat and "guest" of MI 5 was a certain defecting Soviet colonel. This individual after only a short stay preferred the risk of death by deciding to return to the Soviet Union. To obtain his repatriation he left the flat and created a public scandal in Olympia. It is reasonable to suppose that this colonel was in the hands of the same people, and had been subject to the same cynical treatment that had been accorded to me.'[8]

So at this time Oldfield's doubts were more about the methods of MI 5 than those of MI 6. Those doubts continued for many years until very much later he became convinced that MI 5 had been thoroughly infiltrated by the Russians. He stubbornly clung to the view that this infiltration had been made long before the Second World War, before Burgess or Blunt. When the allegations against the late Sir Roger Hollis were made after the death of that head of MI 5, Oldfield was convinced that this was a Soviet-inspired plot and smear to detract attention from the real villain in MI 5. That villain, he was quite sure, was none other than Captain Guy Liddell, the deputy head of the organization under Sir Percy Sillitoe. Towards the end of his life Oldfield was asked by a close friend what he thought about Liddell: 'best forgotten and soonest mended' was his reply.

Perhaps because in many respects, especially by training, Oldfield was *par excellence* the counter-intelligence agent, he must have seemed an odd man out in MI 6. In fact what MI 6 largely lacked was an appreciation of the value of a counter-intelligence expert in their own ranks. He soon developed a professional admiration for the successes of the KGB's agents who penetrated the intelligence services of other powers. When in retirement he discussed this subject with Phillip Knightley of the *Sunday Times*, Oldfield posed this question in relation to Rudolf Hess, Hitler's deputy who flew to Scotland on 10 May 1941, to try to persuade Churchill to end the war: 'Did you know that Hess had his own intelligence service and that the head of it was in reality a KGB agent [to be strictly accurate it would be a NKVD or GRU agent at this time]? Consider this: was this KGB agent behind Hess's flight to Britain? Is this why the Russians are so intent on keeping Hess in jail until he dies?'[9]

The implications behind these questions posed by Oldfield are still of some importance. For example, if Hess had succeeded in his quest of a deal for peace, did the Russians hope that the Nazi-Soviet pact would still be honoured and that Germany would not invade Russia? On the other hand was the KGB agent actually operating on behalf of yet another nation's intelligence service? Was he a double agent?

In the middle of 1949 Philby was recalled from Turkey and given the post of representing the SIS in Washington and collaborating with the newly-formed CIA. 'My briefing on the counter-espionage side also aroused grave anxiety in my mind,' said Philby. 'This was given me by the formidable Maurice Oldfield, and included a communication of the first importance. Joint Anglo-American investigation of Soviet intelligence activity in the United States had yielded a strong suggestion that there had been a leakage from the British Embassy in Washington during the years 1944-45, and another from the atomic energy establishment in Los Alamos. I had no ideas about Los Alamos. But a swift check of the relevant Foreign Office list left me in little doubt about the identity of the source in the British Embassy.'[10]

From this time onwards Philby not only worked in collaboration with the CIA in Washington, but actually sat in at the Special Policy Committee meetings which directed the Anglo-American joint efforts to infiltrate anti-communist agents in Albania. It is not surprising that shortly afterwards Oldfield began to have grave doubts about Philby.

6

Sojourn In The Far East

In 1950 Oldfield was given his first overseas tour of duty in the SIS when he was appointed to the staff of the Commissioner-General for the United Kingdom in South-East Asia, at that time Malcolm Macdonald who, since May 1948, had combined the post of Governor-General for the British territories in Malaya with that of Special Commissioner.

It was an appointment which appealed to Oldfield personally as he had long nursed a desire to explore that part of the world, and, though stationed in Singapore, he had the opportunity of travelling over the whole area, Hong Kong and Bangkok included. Nevertheless the assignment was far from comfortable at that particular time. The situation in this part of the world was anything but stable, with Malaya, as it then was, caught up in a prolonged guerrilla war conducted by the Chinese communists and with uncertain political conditions prevailing in other parts of South-East Asia.

The overall situation had not been helped by the fact that the SOE (Special Operations Executive) in the Far East during World War Two had not exactly covered themselves with glory. The courage of their operatives in the jungles was often wasted by the inefficiency of their directors and an appalling muddle in the distribution of inadequate and sometimes unworkable equipment. Apart from this, the area was one in which the SIS urgently required reconstruction.

A major problem for MI 6 in the early post-war years was its relations with MI 5 in Commonwealth territories overseas. Traditionally, MI 5 had always operated in colonial areas, but it was realized that this would be highly undesirable once these territories were granted independence, or even a limited form of self-government. In Singapore not only were MI 5 and 6 both represented but in addition a Psychological Warfare Section was attached to the South East Asia High Commission. MI 6 was directed by James Fulton, a former Army Intelligence officer who was head of station, with Oldfield as his deputy. MI 5 was headed by Keith Way, whose main links were with the Malayan Police. It was a peculiar situation in that effectively MI 5 and MI 6 shared responsibilities, MI 5 for such British possessions as at that time were Borneo, Sarawak and Malaya, while, officially at least, MI 6's brief was to concentrate on the neighbouring non-British territories of Burma, French Indochina (as it then still was) and to some extent Indonesia and Thailand.

MI 6 needed to operate with considerable tact and understanding, for not only was there the question of maintaining good relations with the local police and Military Intelligence, but liaising with MI 5 on the one hand and the infant CIA station on the other, not to mention keeping some links with the French. It called for skill and diplomacy and, generally speaking, this is what James Fulton provided, ably understudied by Maurice Oldfield. Kim Philby's sneering picture of the British Secret Service in the Far East having been run by only one man for many years is a gross misrepresentation. Certainly there was a need for an overhaul of the whole system of intelligence-gathering out there, but this was mainly due to the changed conditions after the war. One major difficulty early on was that Anglo-American relations in the sphere of intelligence were not as close or as effective as in the Western world.

In these trying two years Oldfield learned the value of the 'softly-softly' approach to the gathering of intelligence and maintaining equable relations with those who were supposed to be on the same side, but often treated their allies as enemies. In other words, much of his time was spent in damping down local rivalries, encouraging team work and trying to persuade the Americans that the British were not what Joseph Smith, the CIA station chief in the area, had called 'a bunch of supercilious snobs'.

Sometimes Oldfield's inquiries ranged far beyond his normal territory. 'He was not one to be put off by the fact that this place or that was just outside his own patch,' said one of his agents in the field. 'If it made sense to inquire in Hong Kong about something which was of vital importance in Singapore, then he would do it. One such case was the smuggling of wolfram in match-boxes. Early in 1950 wolfram, like penicillin in post-war Vienna, was almost as good as a currency.'

Hong Kong was a centre for this racket and not all the operators were Chinese. Some were renegade Americans, others were Russians masquerading under the title of 'White', while their trade was 'Red'. Much of the wolfram was finding its way into China and Russia. Wolfram is the ore from which tungsten is derived, and tungsten was what was needed to make a hundred articles from armour-piercing shells to electric light bulbs. Hong Kong was then a fruitful source of supply for this precious ore. The hills of the colony abounded with it, and its chief attractions to smugglers was that it fetched as much as one pound for a match-boxful, which at that time made it a profitable and easily negotiable commodity.

Oldfield soon amassed evidence that buyers across the border in Red China were offering such a price and that hundreds, if not thousands, of illegal miners were daily digging wolfram out of the gullies where alluvial deposits had collected. He also learned that Russian technicians were directing operations. Once Hong Kong had been one of the main wolfram ports of the world. Most of it had gone to the USA. But in the early 1950s hardly a trickle remained and the United States had noted the lack of it. Shortly after Oldfield made his inquiries it was reported that major staff changes were to be made in the import and export offices at Hong Kong as part of the new Colonial Secretary's (Oliver Lyttleton) shake-up in South-East Asia. This was a positive response to the fact that quantities of wolfram urgently needed in Britain and the West were being smuggled into China and Russia.

'Oldfield was able to establish quite a useful new relationship inside the CIA on the strength of a bit of swapping of intelligence on wolfram,' said his agent. 'That single incident proved to be the beginning of improved links with our American friends who had been very suspicious of our motives in the Far East, chiefly because the State Department had taken a strong anti-colonial line. In due course the CIA began to trust us rather more than their own State Department when it came to matters of policy in the Far East. Not always, of course, as from time to time there was a clash of interests when the Americans deployed their Clandestine Services Division in ways which did not exactly help us with our own colonial problems.'

Wolfram was, of course, merely one of literally scores of subjects with which Oldfield had to deal. Intelligence-gathering in the Far East was, and perhaps still is, one of the most exhausting tasks for any secret service. It is not so much a question of combatting disinformation, or misinformation, but of probing what one agent dubbed 'masked information'. Very often the truth would be wrapped up in mystery and obscurities and the real problem was how to interpret what one was told. 'Think of medieval documents,' said Oldfield, 'and then one begins to come to terms with how to analyse such ambiguities as oriental intelligence.' Those first two years of his SIS career in Singapore were especially difficult in that the government of the day had not come to grips with the problem of guerrilla warfare in Malaya. By 1951 the situation had become so bad that nearly 7,000 Chinese and Indian workers on fourteen rubber estates had refused to go to work because terrorists had threatened to nail them alive on trees they tapped. Yet while the SIS was fully aware of a rapidly worsening situation, partly due to administrative inefficiency and a police force which was singularly inept, this was not their responsibility. They needed to have their own intelligence on the situation, yet there was little they could do about it. In such circumstances it is easy to understand how rivalries and animosities between MI 5 and MI 6 developed. Not until shortly afterwards was General Sir Gerald Templer (later Field Marshal Templer) appointed High Commissioner in Malaya.

MI 6 could help best by supplying intelligence on supplies and finances reaching the Chinese guerrillas in Malaya from outside the territory. The border with Thailand posed one such problem. Indonesia, to a lesser extent, presented another, not least because of Soviet supplies and finance being provided for that country. It was not until the mid-1950s that Russian equipment reached Indonesia in large quantities, but quite early on Oldfield was able to report that what was being sent in by the USSR was mainly material ten or more years old and much inferior to the equivalent type of material being used by European forces. Ironically Britain's own intelligence reports only induced complacency and a policy of effecting economies at the expense of improving the armed forces' equipment in Far Eastern colonial outposts. SEATO (South-East Asia Treaty Organization) was always treated as very much the poor relation of NATO.

Singapore was in this period almost as useful a listening post from an overall intelligence viewpoint as Hong Kong. Here Oldfield quickly made a number of friends in the Chinese colony, and he decided to study their language. As with his other friendships, he maintained these new ones over a long period, and a few of his Chinese friends he first met in the 1950-52 period of service later settled in London and actually attended his memorial service. Mr Peter Ellis, son of another former SIS officer of lengthy experience, the late Colonel 'Dick' Ellis, writes that 'Oldfield picked up Cantonese and he sometimes used greetings in that language in letters to my father, who had learned some Mandarin Chinese while stationed in the Far East.'[1]

Travelling around as he did, however, Oldfield took an interest not only in the language of the Far East, but in the various dialects, too, with special emphasis on the subtle meanings contained in some of them. He took a special interest in the speech of Laos which was a dialect variation of standard Thai rather than a distinct language. This was undoubtedly because he became extremely fond of Laos and its people: 'Laos is one of my favourite countries in the whole of the world,' he told John Carrington, an old Bakewell friend to whom he also confided his eagerness to study Chinese astrology. 'He even worked out my combined Chinese-cum-Western zodiac horoscope reading.'[2]

A complex subject to which Oldfield had to turn his attention while in the Far East was that of the secret societies of the Chinese. The problem was finding out who controlled them. In early 1951 it was reported that some 179 entirely new secret societies in Singapore had applied for exemption from compulsory registration by the authorities. Registration had been introduced to curb the activities of criminal gangs. Politics and the Tongs, as the societies were known, had been indivisible down the centuries, though this did not apply to all of them. Sometimes the basest of the Tongs would masquerade under the title of a friendly society. For many years Malaya's Chinese population had been terrorized by the strangely named Peace by Land and Water Society, which trafficked in women, ran gambling houses and brothels and smuggled opium as well as engaging in blackmail.

It was, of course, well known that some of the secret societies had teamed up with the Kuomintang, Chiang Kai-shek's nationalist army, against the Communists. In this respect Chiang had emulated Sun Yat-sen, who had also developed branches of the Triads (not the same as Tongs, but originally oriental versions of the medieval guilds in the West, tending to be anti-Establishment) for intelligence-gathering purposes. After the establishment of the People's Republic in 1949 the celebrated '14-K' Triad had been resurrected and rejuvenated in Canton by the Nationalist General Koi Sui-heong, who operated it as a secret intelligence agency for the Kuomintang. It was known as '14-K' because its original address was 14 Po-wah Road, Canton.[3]

Up to the end of World War Two the Triads had been rather more like the Masonic movement than, say, a gangster organization such as the Mafia, into which category they gradually degenerated. Chiang had some success initially with his development of the Triads as a source of power and influence, but this was never absolute. Occasionally, despite the oaths of loyalty, the Triads actually worked against the Nationalists. On the other hand there was some evidence that, emulating Mussolini when he clamped down on the Mafia, Mao Tse-tung had driven the secret societies out of the People's Republic of China.

Oldfield soon concluded that the political implications of the secret societies were not only minimal and that their only whole-hearted aim was making money, but that they were by their very nature against all forms of government. 'They might well become enthusiastic about destroying a government, anybody's government, if it suited them,' he once told a colleague, 'but that did not mean they would continue to support whatever government was put in its place. My advice to you is always beware of any Triad member who volunteers his services to you. Be sure the true aim of any such person is to mislead, to provide misinformation and, above all, to mask the real motives and organization of the Triads.'

This same colleague told the author: 'Oldfield was at that time helping to re-build our South-East Asia network – no easy task after the war and in the rapidly changing circumstances of the period. He made it almost an order that contact with Chinese secret society members was to be kept to a minimum and that any information gained through them was not to be acted upon before it was double-checked.

'He had learned through contacts with the Americans that the FBI (Federal Bureau of Investigation) had been sometimes dangerously misinformed by taking on informers in the Chinese communal colonies in the United States from among members of the various Triads. Oldfield had also discovered that the revelation of such an astonishing number of secret societies applying for registration in the 1949-50 period was itself an example of the desire to mislead the authorities – masking information once again. While the bureaucrats were making painstaking inquiries about each of these societies, several of them were secretly planning mergers, and it was from these mergers that they became more powerful and eventually spread their influence all over South-East Asia, later setting themselves up in Europe, too, first in Amsterdam, then in London and Liverpool.'

The American OSS (Office of Strategic Services), the predecessor of the CIA, had, it is true, learned the hard way during World War Two that collaboration with so-called representatives of the various Triads could lead to disaster. At that time there were no fewer than four rival secret services in China all working against each other. They were, first, the Secret Police and Personal Intelligence Service of Chiang Kai-shek; second, the small but rapidly improving Communist Secret Service; third, the Wang Ching-wei organization (belonging to the man who joined forces with the Japanese in 1939 and became head of the puppet South China Government); and, finally, the anti-Kuomintang branch of the Triads. Yet, despite such wartime lessons of the Americans in the Far East, it was the British Secret Service which was the first to arrive at the correct deductions to be drawn from all this. Oldfield put the matter succinctly when he opined that 'when the Communist menace in South-East Asia declines, a new menace will appear, as the Triads will take over in the vacuum areas left by the Communists. One problem will replace another.'

There was some disputing of this observation at the time. A few felt Oldfield was exaggerating, but it is worth recording that in December 1953, the Acting Secretary for Chinese Affairs in Malaya reported that it was becoming increasingly evident that the more the Communist menace receded, the more the *Wah Kee* (a secret society) engaged in unlawful activities.[4]

In these first two years in the Far East Oldfield was learning fast, though often to the point of exhuastion, as he mined all seams of information. He had to assess the relative strengths of both Chinese and Soviet influence in this vast area. It would have been a hard task for someone permanently resident in the region, but for a newcomer the work involved must have been exacting in the extreme, especially in a climate so different from even the Middle East. But Oldfield was not keeping to a work schedule: he toiled day and night, travelling around by day and attending to office work while by night he studied, sometimes reports, sometimes languages and frequently that most intriguing of all oriental works, *I Ching*.

'He really overdid things where work was concerned,' says Air Commodore Sir James Easton, who had been his superior officer in London at one time and had taken a special interest in Oldfield. 'He worked himself to the point of exhaustion. When this happened, he always developed psoriasis which, in his case, seemed linked solely to overwork, but maybe worry as well. He did a wonderful job in Singapore where, eventually, he came into his own. Once, though, on my suggestion he was given three months' paid leave on the understanding that he just rested. It was not only necessary, but well worth it in the end.'[5]

It is perhaps sensible at this stage to ignore the strict chronological order which, generally speaking, a biographer should maintain. But Singapore and South-East Asia are really a complete chapter in Oldfield's life and it would be distracting if, at this stage, one suddenly followed his trail back to London in 1953-56.

When he returned to Singapore in 1956 it was with the rank of First Secretary and as head of station for MI 6. At this period he was in effect in control of MI 5 and MI 6 for Malaya and he came into his own as a powerful figure behind the scenes, one who was as at home with Malcolm Macdonald, the Commissioner-General for South-East Asia, as with Lee Kuan Yew, who eventually became Prime Minister in Singapore. The break back in London had fully refreshed him and he entered his second sojourn in this area from 1956-58 with a quite surprising gusto, revealing much greater self-confidence and his old zest for life.

He had a large house in Singapore with a garden and a tennis court on which he occasionally played, though as he and his friends would admit, rather badly. But he was a great party-goer as well as a party-giver, and if he gave nothing away on such occasions, he probably learned quite a lot. 'It helps me in assessing characters,' he once confessed. Such asides as this were made almost apologetically, never as points to be scored. Not surprisingly, he did not neglect his love of organ playing. This was regularly indulged at St Paul's Church, Upper Sarangoon Road, Singapore.

While in Singapore he met another old boy of Lady Manners School. This was Professor John Purseglove, a specialist in agriculture, botany and zoology, who had even had a previously undiscovered plant specimen named after him – the *Trifolium Purseglove*, a clover from Uganda. Professor Purseglove was Director of the Botanic Gardens in Singapore. He had undertaken plant collecting expeditions in Sarawak, sometimes in little-known country, occasionally staying in Dyak log houses and in uninhibited forest. 'Maurice came to our house in the Botanic Gardens on a few occasions, but I had no idea he was in MI 6. When we were about to leave for Trinidad, he very kindly offered us the use of his flat in London when we were on leave, but we never went there. We had been at school together, but he was three years my junior and we were never in the same form.'[6]

By the time Oldfield had returned to Singapore the collation of intelligence by the Combined Intelligence Staff had produced most encouraging results after the disasters of the earlier period. This was not a matter of direct concern for the new chief of station, but naturally he was anxious to learn what he could from the new techniques. Importantly, the greatly improved Intelligence papers provided an evaluation of the government's strengths and weaknesses as well as an analysis of the guerrillas' organization. General Templer had created a new and highly professional intelligence-gathering system, aiming to get a great deal of extra information from the ordinary public through a device known as 'the whisper box', into which anybody could drop a report or message.

But Oldfield's really vital work consisted of keeping a close eye on such distant areas as Korea, Vietnam, Laos and, above all, obtaining an accurate picture of what was going on in the People's Republic of China. In this connection perhaps it should be stressed that this was not aggressive espionage, nor could it be compared with Russia-watching. It was conducted as much in a spirit of seeking possible friends as watching potential enemies. Nor was there any desire to indulge in the kind of hostile covert operations which in the 1950s the CIA sometimes conducted in a clumsy and counter-productive style. One of the enigmas for intelligence-gatherers in the Korean War had been that of infiltrators who caused considerable trouble behind the lines. They specialized in spreading disinformation and, in some instances, actually setting out to destroy the characters of certain Allied military and diplomatic personnel. Nor was this purely a temporary problem. The results of some character-smearing by Soviet and North Vietnamese agents only surfaced twenty years afterwards in some instances, when they often did more harm than anything which occurred in the Korean War.

While General Templer was concerned with intelligence-gathering inside Malaya, Oldfield was keenly interested in ascertaining what aid the Malayan Communists were getting from outside the territory. For years successive colonial administrators in Malaya had insisted that stories of such outside aid were exaggerated. Eventually it transpired that something like £18 millions a year had been swelling the coffers of the Malayan Communist guerrilla army in the years immediately preceding Templer's arrival. One can only assume that in these years there was a lack of coordination of intelligence between the SIS and the colonial and military authorities. Much the same happened in other parts of the colonial empire. Subsequently it was believed that some of these millions were intercepted and siphoned off by the Triads.

The vast majority of this aid came in the form of supplies, much of it from across the dense 130-miles long jungle border with Thailand, but some by small craft navigating narrow creeks by night. The Communists also prospered whenever rubber prices boomed. They gained considerable sums each month by extorting money from the native rubber tappers. In addition each tapper was expected to leave a small percentage of his daily tappings in an agreed hiding place for the guerrillas to pick up. All this changed in the early fifties. The tapper who had previously given some of his earnings to the bandits (for that is what the guerrillas really were) now acted as an informer against the Communists. The real turn of the tide came when the creation of Malayan-Chinese associations all over the territory was speeded up.

What provided Oldfield with a subject for much careful analysis at this time was keeping watch on the career of K'ang Sheng, the Director of Intelligence of China under Mao Tse-tung. Perhaps this personal interest in a foreign intelligence officer was stimulated by the fact that for Oldfield any person who was inspired by ancient history or literature was a suitable case for study. For K'ang Sheng the Commentaries of *I Ching*, which originated some time between 1200 and 1100 BC, were the supreme source of distilled wisdom. This work (*The Book of Changes*, to give it its western title) was the only book which was not condemned to be burnt by the Emperor Ch'in Shik Huang Ti. It was honoured and consulted by statesmen and scientists and under the Ch'in and Han dynasties its teachings emerged as a formalized philosophical system and an almost compulsory source for consultation. Ultimately *I Ching* has been used frequently even in modern times for seeking interpretations of intelligence.

To Oldfield there was a parallel between the modern Chinese respect for *I Ching* and his own regard for medieval teachings. 'There is one thing about *I Ching* which may not only explain many seemingly inexplicable moves by the Chinese Communists, but also contain a warning for some of our own aggressive intelligence chiefs in the West,' Oldfield told the late Morgan Goronwy Rees. '*I Ching* says that success lies in being able to retreat at the right moment and in the right manner. Then it goes on to add that "this success is made possible by the fact that the retreat is not the forced flight of a weak person, but the voluntary withdrawal of a strong one." '

Oldfield made this comment in 1979, when he was at All Souls, Oxford. The point he went on to make was that K'ang Sheng had throughout his life followed the *I Ching* precept on the arts of retreat. In the 1930s K'ang Sheng had moved into the French concession in the then international city of Shanghai so that he would be safe from Kuomintang interference. He operated from a 'secret house' in the concession and used this as a hiding place for other prominent Communists. He also acquired a knowledge of French intelligence methods and even made friends with some French Intelligence officers.

What interested Oldfield most about K'ang Sheng was that from the very moment he had arrived in Russia to study security and intelligence techniques before World War Two he had convinced himself that in the long run Soviet Russia would exploit China if given the opportunity. Apparently Oldfield had read my book, *A History of the Chinese Secret Service*, and he had mentioned this to Goronwy Rees, who had been Bursar at All Souls at one time. Goronwy told me that 'Maurice Oldfield would very much like to meet you. He says he was interested in your diagnosis of K'ang Sheng. He claims that it was K'ang Sheng who eventually convinced Mao Tse-tung that the Russians in the early 1950s had obtained control of the Chinese Institute of Mathematics and that by doing so they threatened to acquire total control of Chinese technology and make the People's Republic entirely dependent upon the USSR.'

This, in 1979, was not an indiscreet remark on Oldfield's part, for, while K'ang's attitude to the USSR may have been carefully masked in the early 1950s, on his last visit to Moscow in 1960 as leader of the Chinese 'observer' delegation to the Warsaw Treaty Political Consultative Committee, he made it publicly clear that China disagreed strongly with Soviet policies towards the West, especially on the subject of disarmament. What is significant through other and earlier sources is that Oldfield was one of the first intelligence officers in the West to detect K'ang's antipathy towards Russia. Most of such officers had allowed themselves to take an opposite view because in 1933 K'ang had been sent to Moscow to study Soviet security and intelligence techniques.

Not only did Oldfield manage to strengthen and improve the still somewhat slender network of British intelligence-gatherers in the Far East, but greatly to improve relations with the Americans. He got on well with Americans and most of them got on well with him. Mr Ray S. Cline, former Deputy Director of the CIA, recalls first meeting Oldfield in Asia – 'probably in Singapore or Hong Kong in the 1950s, when we traded views mainly on the Chinese and their posture in South-East Asia. I honestly do not remember if he shared my (not very widely held) view that the Chinese Communists are overrated as a national power, but might in the twenty-first century be more menacing than the Russians, who are not so clever or hard-working.'[7]

In fact Oldfield very much shared this view, though he would have expressed it rather differently. He once made the comment that 'we still tend to think of the Russians as though the year was back in 1917. In some ways that is not altogether an inaccurate picture of them. But to understand the Chinese we really need to peer into the future to see what they will be like in 2017.'

Mr Cline was based in Taiwan from 1957-62 and inevitably some quite grave issues arose from time to time to discuss with the SIS man in Singapore, though such meetings as they had were usually at other places in the Far East. One of the main problems for China-watchers at this time was what action the United States might take if the People's Republic of China invaded the offshore islands of Quemoy and Matsu. A Department of Defense (USA) memorandum of 18 March 1955, stated that in such an event the United States planned 'no military action except to defend Formosa [Taiwan].' Emergency plans for the defence of Taiwan were developed and revised over the next few years. As late as 22 October 1959, a top secret United States Department of Defense memorandum mentioned that

Taiwan was seeking US support for an invasion of the Chinese mainland.

'Maurice preceded me in going back to Washington,' said Mr Cline, adding that in that period when he was stationed in Taiwan, 'we would have talked electronic intercepts, agent penetrations of the China mainland, overflights of hostile areas and Asian politics.'[3]

On his second sojourn in Singapore Oldfield was much more relaxed than on his previous term of duty. He was popular with his staff, especially the women. One who feels he owes Oldfield a great deal for his influence and support in this period is the Reverend Gerald Buss, chaplain of Hurstpierpoint College, Sussex. 'I was very young at the time, having recently left school and being unable to take up a place at Oxford owing to a domestic tragedy. So, not very happily, and feeling extremely lonely and unwanted, I went out to Malaya to take a post in commerce. Oldfield was like a father to me. He helped to change my whole attitude to life and paved the way to my eventually taking up a place at Oxford University.'

Eventually, too, it was Maurice Oldfield who nominated Gerald Buss for ordination in the Church of England.

Oldfield's principal fault in his work emerged about this time. Until he arrived in Singapore in charge of the Far East station it was a fault which did not matter very much. But at last it showed to those who watched him. This was a reluctance on his part to delegate important work. Often he took on jobs, even missions, which others should have done. He was only really happy when he was personally supervising a job and he never said 'no' to any task offered him, sometimes when he had more than enough to do already. Doubtless there were many occasions when the Service actually benefited from this fault in that they got a better service than if he had delegated a particular job. But it was a fault which irritated a few within the Service, especially the high-fliers who felt their capabilities thwarted.

Mr L.A. Choong, one of his friends in Singapore in the

1950s, talks of Oldfield's interest in Chinese astrology. 'He was fascinated by it and he studied it in great detail, always seeking out which system was the most applicable to assessment of character. I remember his saying once that this approach to a study of character was just as important to the average individual as to those who wished to analyse other people's characters. "It is no use applying it simply to others, if one doesn't apply it to oneself," he used to say. "Don't let us forget that it can enable us to study and guard against our own weaknesses. I have personally found this quite helpful, though I don't talk about it much to my friends." '[9]

It was the astrological system known as Nine Star Ki which Oldfield ultimately adopted as the most accurate of all oriental methods of interpretation of astrology. Nine Star Ki dates back to antiquity, but has been modernized by more recent astrologers and scholars, the latter playing a part because the system is linked with *I Ching*'s trigrams and what is known as the Five Transformations, which covers methods of healing, acupuncture and what is called 'creative communication'. Mr Choong comments that 'Maurice could absorb such complex subjects astonishingly quickly. What is more he was able to single out exactly what was important to him and to concentrate on that. It was character analysis that he was interested in and I could never succeed in making him realize that Nine Star Ki was a way of life, something which could be extended to improving one's life style and health. Yes, he was politely interested in such details, but he would not allow these to detract him from his own special interest. I did not realize at the time that he must have been thinking in terms of intelligence for the simple reason that I never knew what his work was.'[10]

A young female friend of Oldfield used to discuss astrology with him. 'He taught me most of what I know about Chinese astrology, which he appeared to have studied in great detail. He even gave me books on the subject as birthday presents,' said Miss ——, who prefers simply to be known as 'Sandie'. 'We first met when I was a university student and he was spending a quiet holiday on the Isle of

Wight. I remember that he actually worked out my horoscope very quickly while we were having a drink in a hotel in Ventnor. Of course at that time I had no idea of who he was, or what he did, and, as I was somewhat sceptical I asked him why he was so interested in the subject. He replied that he had been in the Far East and had discovered that the Chinese had taken it seriously for many centuries and relied on it for character analysis. I don't think he paid much attention to any claims that astrology could enable one to predict the future. I was already interested in astrology – the western kind – before I met Maurice, and he helped me by applying the Nine Star Ki system to western astrology and so combining the two. This way it made it much easier for me to follow. Maurice was marvellous at simplifying what is complicated.

'We kept in touch and we met on various occasions when he was in this country. But it wasn't for many years that I realized who he was and what he did. He gave me the impression that he was an academic who specialized in studying Chinese history and customs. When eventually I told him I had put two and two together by reading the newspapers several years later, he just smiled and said: "Well, I hope this doesn't mean the end of a beautiful friendship. But, now that you seem to know so much, I will show you my Chinese horoscope reading. You have known me for some years now and it should make you take notice. I'm very anxious to know your verdict on the reading." '

Oldfield showed her a mass of hieroglyphics and writing in Chinese, beside which were some pencilled notes (in English) made by him. Then he gave her a verbal translation of the reading. After giving details of the date and time of his birth, this reading noted that Oldfield was born in the Chinese Year of the Rabbit (1915), that he was a 'Wood Rabbit', wood being the vital element in relationship to his birth, while in terms of a combination of western and oriental astrology he was a 'Scorpio Rabbit'.

All this may seem an irrelevance to the main theme of this book, but few (either of his critics or his friends) would deny that the character reading for Oldfield is astonishingly accurate and perspicacious. It is as follows:

'This person enjoys tranquillity above all else. He may enter the battle of life with quiet determination and never shirk a challenge, but in the end it is tranquillity he seeks. His speech is soft and quiet, sometimes excessively quiet, but he has wit and a sense of humour. Occasionally, he may be moody, but this is usually disguised by his innate courtesy and natural good manners. When he is in this frame of mind he will give the impression of being totally detached and objective. He prefers to resolve all problems by quiet discussion and never over-presents his case. Sometimes this will make him appear slow and unable to make up his mind. But that is because he is essentially cautious and wants to be sure he has heard and understood every argument. This will irritate some people, who may accuse him of wasting time. But usually he will prove to be right in the long term, and only occasionally will his critics be right.

'Self-discipline is his strong line. It is this which gives him his greatest strength and his authority. This trait also gives him one priceless asset — the gift of inscrutability. He gives nothing away as to his innermost thoughts, except to a very few persons, and it is not easy for others to assess his inner thinking. One facet of his personality is that he can put his many friends and acquaintances into separate compartments so that some of them are always ignorant of all that he is and all that he means. Those in one compartment would see him as a somewhat different person from those in another compartment.

'Perhaps his chief fault is to take too many problems on his own broad shoulders, and that can sometimes lead to health problems. Overwork is the factor he will need to watch, for he drives himself hard. While he can be tender and benevolent to his friends and those he loves, there is a latent ruthless streak in him which sometimes surfaces. Then one needs to beware, if one has anything to fear, because one might find oneself deep in his clutches. He can dig in his claws when he wishes.

'But these are the exceptions. They are exceptions created by the tasks he sets himself, or others set him. By and large he is friendly, liking to make permanent friends and with a great regard for good manners towards all people, high and low.

'He is generous towards very many people and especially understanding of other's problems. He will even see the best side of his own enemies. But while he has some ambitions, these are not obvious to others, and he has a tendency to avoid using his authority and to make allowance for other people's mistakes, partly because he dislikes rows, but also to maintain a spirit of conciliation. Some will in consequence tend to take advantage of him on such occasions.

'This particular Rabbit is essentially one of a team and he will tend to give of his best working in a large firm, or organization, in which, almost inevitably, he will rise to the top, or very near the top. He may hesitate about making a decision which involves hurting someone unduly, or may seem to set a dangerous precedent for the future. If, in such circumstances, he declines to take sides, or sits back and takes no action, he may injure himself more than others. But that is the way he is made. It is a fault which can sometimes be a virtue, but at others a vice. But those who try to take advantage of this Rabbit at such moments should not think they will get away with their own misdemeanours for long.

'He will revel in putting confused reports, or rumours, or gossip, or concepts into order and this may astonish some of his colleagues. When a problem seems insoluble, he will be at his best. He loves to be on his own to think things out, to take long walks while pondering problems and to seek the delights of oblivion. He likes to escape from the real world for brief spells, though he is essentially gregarious.

'He will always be popular with most women, not least because he is undemanding and seems to give the impression of being inaccessible. But when he so desires, he can converse with them in a manner which they not only understand, but which makes them wonder why other men cannot do likewise. Yet the odds are he will end up without finding a permanent female companion.

'His powers of tenacity are tremendous and he can face crushing blows which would be ruinous to others, but inwardly this causes him to suffer both mentally and physically. An idealist, essentially humanitarian, he will constantly seek to do the right thing by his own high standards, even at a cost to himself. But he has a passion for secrecy and things secret. The very idea of something being secret enthralls him. Though straightforward, he has not only a love of secrecy, but of intrigue, too. He might find his true vocation in something of this nature, not in anything criminal or of doubtful morality, but as a diplomat or as one who has to deal in secrets of a kind important to the state, or the community.'

'Sandie' had this to say on this oriental horoscope reading for Oldfield: 'I obviously did not know him as well as many of his close friends, so I cannot speak for the whole of the character assessment. But much of it seemed to be absolutely spot on. I gather the reading was given to him by a Chinese sometime in the early 1950s.'

'Sandie' says: 'I'm sure his interest in Nine Star Ki was not just a casual one, but that he felt it was of some professional value. I once asked him what he really thought about Kim Philby, and he replied that he would rather not discuss that, but that, if one had studied his horoscope, much that wasn't clear would become much clearer. He was a Capricornian Pig, which is a most complicated personality.'

In the Queen's Birthday Honours List of 1956 Oldfield was awarded the CBE. Within two years he had added to his reputation as being generally acknowledged the best all-rounder in Intelligence in the Foreign Service with a remarkable memory and an outstanding and far-ranging understanding of South-East Asia in all aspects. He had also extended the frontiers of his territory to maintain close links with the Australian Security Service. The value of the Australian link was fully justified about the time that Vladimir Petrov, a Soviet diplomat in Canberra, defected in 1954, even though Oldfield was not actually in the Far East at that time. But he was able to help clear up some of the many questions raised about a vast Soviet network in the Far East and the Pacific Ocean areas which the de-briefing of Petrov raised.

In all the time he spent in the Far East Oldfield built up a large circle of friends in the Chinese community. He also, in his own unobtrusive way, did much good. There are for example at least two refugee Chinese for whose education he paid; one of them today occupies a high position in a Commonwealth country.

7

London And Washington

Oldfield did two stints of duty based on London during the 1950s – in 1953-55 between his two postings to Singapore, and again in 1958-59 after his final return from the Far East.

During his spells of duty in the United Kingdom he spent as much time as he could in Over Haddon, where he still took a keen interest in the family farm, doing everything he could to increase its efficiency. Indeed, he helped his family to take over the freehold of the land. At the Lathkill Arms Hotel in Over Haddon, his favourite local hostelry, he normally drank bitter ale, but occasionally switched to vodka and tomato juice, 'not that he ever called it a Bloody Mary,' said one barmaid who served him. There was a gurgle of delight among the customers at the Lathkill Arms when Maurice was first mentioned in *Who's Who*, and much mirth when they read that he had cited 'farming' as his recreation apart from organ playing.

Yet this was a fair observation. Dr R.A. Harvey says: 'I knew the boy, I also knew the man, perhaps better than anyone living. Farming in that healthy altitude was a complete change and getaway. Maurice helped his brothers, was the "Lord of the Manor" of Over Haddon and overseer in his modesty of the whole domain and demesne.'[1]

One of his brothers was the postmaster at Bakewell, but three of his other brothers helped run the family farm. Maurice always took care to keep up his image as 'one of the boys' in his relations with people in the Bakewell-Over Haddon area and various villages in the district, too. He once signed a local visitors' book: 'Not Lieutenant-Colonel Oldfield of the Foreign Office, but Maurice Oldfield of Over Haddon.' It was a neat way of spelling things out. Until the railway line between Matlock and Bakewell was closed down he made a habit of calling in at the Wheatsheaf public house in Bakewell before going on to Over Haddon. This pub was conveniently near to the station.

Much of his time was taken up by travelling to various points of the globe, not only the Far East and Middle East, but to Latin America as well, an area in which he developed some surprisingly good contacts, despite his superficial knowledge of the territory. The truth was that he made such contacts fairly easily wherever he was, but he relied a great deal on friendships and acquaintanceships of earlier years. Mrs Jeanne Smith says: 'In later years, after the war, when his duties took him to Germany and other parts of Europe, Maurice met again quite a number of the French officers he had known in Beirut, and their wives, and he kept me posted as to their news and messages to me. He followed the Algerian uprising with personal anxiety and interest as some of the military involved were mutual friends.'[2]

Because of his Middle East experiences Oldfield was frequently consulted during his 1953-55 period in London on questions concerning the area. Though his instincts had been to view sympathetically the problems of the new state of Israel, these tended to take a more positive form during the mid-1950s when he was sometimes irritated by the devious manner in which some of his colleagues played off intelligence received from the Mossad to try to buy off Egyptian contacts. Oldfield not only felt this was a betrayal of confidence, but that in the long term it could be disastrous.

In 1953 Mahmoud Khalil was appointed Chief of Intelligence of the Egyptian Air Force and not long afterwards was recruited as an informant to the British Secret Service. The idea was that Khalil would form a secret group of Egyptian Army officers who would attempt a coup against the current regime and restore the monarchy in Cairo. To finance all this Khalil was given a sum of money equivalent to £1,000 at a secret meeting in Beirut. As he would need to make fairly frequent journeys outside of Egypt to make his contacts, his SIS controller promised he would be given secret intelligence on Israel and, to prevent his superior officers being suspicious about his travels, he could say that these were to meet his informants on Israeli affairs.

Relations between Britain and Israel were very good at this time and so, too, were relations between the SIS and the Mossad. It is probable that the Mossad knew something of this devious and dangerous game, but whether they were kept fully in the picture by the British is not so clear. What is clear, however, is that Oldfield not only expressed grave doubts about this operation, but actually condemned it on the grounds that it could upset relations with the Mossad and ultimately play right into President Nasser's hands. 'You don't realize,' he said to a colleague, 'that to ask an Egyptian to spy against his own country's government is in itself taking a big risk. When I was in the Middle East I had occasion to study the Egyptian *Book of the Dead*, which was found in the Egyptian tombs of the Twenty-Eighth Dynasty. One very significant passage in this book sets out the doctrine of resurrection and is in fact a guide-book to the hereafter. Now this work makes it quite clear that espionage is a major sin and that to indulge in it is to endanger one's soul. So don't be surprised if conscience overcomes greed and ambition in this case.'

Whether this proved to be correct in Khalil's case one does not know. But despite receiving sums of more than £150,000 and various promises, he betrayed the British and the whole plot was uncovered. On 23 December 1957, when Oldfield was back in Singapore, Nasser made a speech in which he made it clear that the so-called 'Restoration Plot' had been discovered and that Khalil had all the time acted with his full permission. It was a blow for the SIS, made worse shortly afterwards when some sixteen people were arrested in Egypt charged with being British agents.

Nasser's speech need not be taken too literally. Obviously there was a strong element of propaganda in it. But when he was asked afterwards if he was serious in citing *The Book of the Dead*, Oldfield replied: 'It is always worth while understanding the other person's religious background, what he thinks and feels, or indeed if he has no such thoughts at all. Intelligence is about what people think and feel. Somebody might have found out whether Khalil came into this category. The probability is that he did.'

MI 6's chief in Singapore must have been relieved that he was now away from London and in no way associated with these Middle East operations, some of which were pressed on the SIS by none other than Anthony Eden, then British Prime Minister. Even the Foreign Office seemed to be obsessed by events in the Middle East at this time and therefore tended to neglect reports from other areas. The SIS network in Eastern Europe had already indicated that a rising against the government in Hungary was imminent, yet nobody inside the FO gave such reports any credibility or predicted the insurrection in Budapest on 23 October 1956, which subsequently spread throughout the country. Just over a week later the Anglo-French invasion of Egypt began and Hungary was relegated to the bottom of the Foreign Secretary's agenda.

Normally, the British Foreign Office is supremely good at playing down a crisis and smoothing away the causes of trouble. In this instance it seems to have failed in the case of Egypt and, worse still, ignored the situation in Hungary. Possibly one clue to this lies in a statement made by Sir Frederick Hoyer Millar in evidence to the Select Committee on Estimates: 'The Permanent Under Secretary,' he declared, 'always tries to avoid having to tell the Minister that half the Foreign Office thinks this and half thinks that.'[3]

A spectacularly successful operation with which Oldfield was indirectly associated was that of Operation 'Boot' to destroy Prime Minister Mohammed Mossadegh and restore the Shah in Iran in 1953. This whole operation marked the excellent relationship formed in that period between George Young, then deputy chief of MI 6, and Maurice Oldfield. Oldfield had always regarded the Persian Gulf as being a supremely important target for intelligence-gathering, so indeed he believed that all oil-producing countries should come into this category. Over the years he established a personal relationship with the late Shah, not only meeting him on various occasions, but actually advising him on intelligence matters. Nor did he take such a harshly critical view of the much condemned SAVAK (the Iranian Secret Police) as many of the Western world's liberals. In fact he helped in an indirect way to encourage and support links which the Israeli Military Intelligence established for cooperation between the Aman (Israeli Military Intelligence) and SAVAK, thanks largely to Oldfield's personal relationship with the Shah. This was no mean diplomatic feat, because the Israelis, who had their own special links with the French in Iran, had come to the conclusion that the Shah did not altogether trust his own secret service. As one shrewd Israeli commented: 'If the Shah could make a deal between Israeli Intelligence and his private Secret Service, doubtless he would feel better able to keep an eye on SAVAK.'

In the operation against Mossadegh, chiefly known in US code terms as Operation TPAJAX/Boot, American and British intelligence services cooperated admirably. Mossadegh had declared Iran neutral in terms of the Cold War and set out to nationalize the chiefly British-owned oil wells and refineries. MI 6 planned the initial details of the coup; interestingly, a future head of MI 6, Sir Arthur Franks, was Second Secretary in Teheran at this time, and himself involved in the operation. In the early stages of this dispute the Americans had shown a strong disinclination to become involved, believing that Britain might be branded as an aggressor at the United Nations. However, despite this, the SIS strengthened their links inside Iran, and, in pushing ahead with the plan, both George Young and Maurice Oldfield played useful roles. Inside Iran a key man in the

British planning was Shapoor Reporter, a Parsee who had originally been attached to the India Office and then became oriental secretary in the British Embassy in Teheran. He had almost grown up with the Shah, and was in his confidence as well as that of the British.

Though the initial planning for the coup to restore the Shah was entirely in the hands of the British, it soon became evident that to succeed there needed to be full cooperation with the recently formed CIA. The CIA station chief in Teheran was Kermit Roosevelt, a grandson of President Theodore Roosevelt. The operation succeeded brilliantly, even though the number of CIA operatives in the area was not more than forty at this time. The beginning of the end of this coup came when Mossadegh's chief of police, General Ashfar-Tus, was kidnapped and pro-Soviet agents inside the police and army were removed.

When he returned to Britain in the late fifties Oldfield set about rebuilding some of his former contacts with the Mossad, cautiously at first as he was not sure how much harm had been done by the intrigues of the 'Restoration Plot'. Fortunately for all concerned, he was able to help towards paving the way to some twenty years' of invaluable links between the SIS and the Mossad. This was especially useful in relation to intelligence not only on the Middle East, but Russia as well.

'There was a real need to re-establish something like a genuine trust between the two Intelligence agencies once again,' says a retired Mossad agent. 'Maurice knew that he had to prove himself worthy of this trust before he could achieve much. But he worked very hard at doing so, and much goodwill was built up on his various missions to stations overseas. One knew that if Maurice promised to do something, he did it himself and never relied on anyone else to do it for him. At least, that was my experience.'

On Speech Day, 1959, Oldfield presented the prizes at Lady Manners Grammar School in Bakewell. 'Life,' he declared on that occasion, 'could be regarded as a series of concentric circles moving from the individual at the centre through the family to school, the district and then outwards

114

to the world. All should be governed by the same principles of honesty, enthusiasm and loyalty.'

When in London one of his favourite places for lunch was Rules in Maiden Lane. Perhaps it was the Victorian club atmosphere as much as the quality of the claret which appealed to him here. Yet his tastes were versatile: he sometimes drank beer at the Athenaeum just as he would back in Over Haddon, and occasionally he would not only delight in taking friends to a Chinese restaurant of his choice, but in ordering the dishes in the Chinese language. 'Sometimes it seemed that he spoke better Chinese than the Chinese waiters,' was the comment of Mr John Brook-Taylor. The New Friends' Restaurant in the East End and Loon Fung's in Gerrard Street were two of his favourites.

The general consensus of opinion is that while Oldfield may have acquired a smattering of Chinese, he was never fluent in the language. But he had a talent for making the best possible use of a smattering of several languages and using this to make friends easily. In much the same way, though never shining in any sport, he never shirked taking part in the occasional game, whether of tennis or bowls, even if he knew beforehand he would be the inevitable loser. It was friendship which counted with Maurice, not winning. He had that supreme quality – possibly one which is essential in a first class intelligence officer – of always knowing exactly what he couldn't do and, paradoxically, taking strength from this to tackle many awkward problems which he felt he *could* do, even if others baulked at them.

Only very occasionally did he go on holidays alone. Sometimes he went to the Isle of Wight, Austria, and Italy with Brigadier Roberts and his wife. Mrs Elizabeth Roberts remembers that in Italy he 'astonished the waiters and others by speaking to them in Latin.' At that time, she says, he spoke no Italian, but he got through on his Latin. Often, by way of relaxation, he would help Italian peasants with hay-making and the Roberts family took snapshots of Maurice hay-making both in Austria and Italy. Just as he could read books at a phenomenal speed, so he could take in marathon-style sight-seeing. 'Once, travelling from Lake

Garda to Verona,' says Mrs Elizabeth Roberts, 'Maurice and I actually visited thirteen churches before lunch.'[4]

'Sandie' remembers him in the Isle of Wight 'being something of a chain smoker – innumerable cigarettes – and he would pace about while smoking. Later he switched to panatellas. I think he realized the dangers of smoking and wanted to escape from them.' She also recalled his friendship with Sir Max Aitken, Lord Beaverbrook's son. The two frequently met both in London and the Isle of Wight. 'They had very much in common in a surprising way as they came from such different backgrounds. I always had the feeling that between them they could have moved mountains ... how shall I put it? They could have solved so many problems that now seem insoluble.'

Though during this period the United States was often publicly urging Britain to take the lead in developing a policy of independence for colonial peoples,[5] there was also evidence of their gratitude for liaison on intelligence matters. Secretary of State John Foster Dulles sent a confidential message on 26 August 1955, thanking Britain for cooperation 'with the Alpha project in the Middle East'.[6]

On the question of East-West relations Oldfield had his own strongly held view, one he did not alter as the years went by. He always said that he perfectly understood (though not agreeing with) the view some people took in the 1930s that they were prepared to betray their own country for a much broader and internationalist view of things, but that in the light of events after 1945 it should be equally clear that people in the Soviet Union and the satellite countries of Eastern Europe were entitled to take the same view – that they, too, could betray their country in the common cause of a humanitarian-minded Free World. This, and possibly this alone, was the power engine behind Maurice's thinking. Unquestionably it inspired his zeal for his work.

By this time he had established himself in a secure position in life. He was at his prime and still unmarried. Why? Without doubt one reason was the work he had undertaken. He often hesitated as to whether it was suitable for married status. As the years passed, as he ultimately became a target for terrorists, this query was probably accentuated. But there were other reasons for his doubts. One was the fact that he suffered from recurring psoriasis, made worse by pressure of work. It is true that this ailment proved an irritation to him, but it need never really have been a source of embarrassment. The real problem was that Maurice Oldfield had begun to apply to the subject of marriage the same kind of questions that he would have put in an interrogation. When it came to matrimony, he might well be the odd man out. He had by the nature of his work changed so much that he felt even a choice of wives might be not easy to make. In other words he had moved a long, long way from Over Haddon.

In this period he had many female friends, but at no time did any of these seem to bring him closer to marriage. There was Janet Wadsworth, daughter of the editor of the old *Manchester Guardian*, who used to drive him around the Derbyshire countryside. She had joined Granada Television through a personal contact with Sidney Bernstein, and became Granada's educational adviser. Eventually she introduced the first sex-education series after a great fight with the authorities. Miss Wadsworth died from cancer in 1974.

Sir James Easton recalls a younger woman of whom 'Maurice was rather fond. I think he was rather slow in popping the question, and in the end she married someone else.'

In the latter part of the 1950s Sir Dick Goldsmith White, a former head of MI 5, had become chief of MI 6, and under his regime the Service became much more professional. During this time Oldfield's chief asset was that he had proved his worth not only in the world of intelligence, but of counter-intelligence, too. Increasingly, his views on possible suspects within the two services – MI 5 as well as MI 6 – were sought on an informal basis.

When a vacancy for an SIS senior officer to liaise with the CIA in Washington occurred towards the end of 1959 Oldfield was in every respect ideally suited for the task. He was, as one of his colleagues put it, 'an ideal link between the past and the present, and yet sufficiently part of the acceptable present in the SIS to be viewed favourably in the United States.'

The job demanded a man who was as *au fait* with past history of the Service as he was with its current activities, for at that time both the CIA and the FBI were very much concerned with previous errors in British Intelligence and the harm wrought by Philby and others. They wanted reassuring not simply in honeyed words and sweet promises, but by dealing with a man who could answer their long list of questions on the subjects of operational errors and the presence of traitors in the ranks. Relations between the United States and Britain on the subject of intelligence were somewhat uneasily maintained and considerable doubts and suspicions lingered in the USA that either Britain had not learned the lessons of the past, or that too lenient an attitude had been shown to some suspected traitors. These doubts and suspicions had recently been exacerbated by the revelations of certain defectors from behind the Iron Curtain to the United States. In almost every case the finger of suspicion was pointed at even more traitors in the British camp.

Though Oldfield was fully aware of the difficulties of the task which faced him, he had no doubts about accepting it. By this time he had acquired a zest for tackling difficult problems and he had the advantage of being able to get along very well with Americans. He had proved this in the Far East.

Thus from 1960-1964 Oldfield stayed in Washington with the official title of Counsellor. His dealings with the CIA were, of course, primarily with the operational side of the Agency, but he did not allow this to limit his scope for rank talks and exchanges of views on a much wider range of subjects. He had his links to the State Department, the NSA (National Security Agency) and the FBI.

'I took a bet with myself that the names of Burgess and Maclean would be mentioned to me within a month of my arriving in Washington,' he told a colleague in London. 'So I

118

had taken every chance to study all reports concerning those two. I wanted to have all the answers. Sure enough within two weeks I was shown a memorandum of the American Joint Chiefs of Staff, which stated that regarding inquiries into the affair of Burgess and Maclean "in 1955 little or no action has been taken to prevent repetition of these mistakes". To which Admiral Arthur Radford had added his own comment that Burgess and Maclean "were apparently protected by others in high places, some allegedly still in key positions." [7]

It was pointed out to Oldfield that all United Kingdom codes and possibly some American codes and ciphers used until 25 May 1951, were probably in Soviet possession and of no further use. Furthermore a tripartite (US, UK and France) group of inspectors had made a report in June 1951, mentioning certain deficiencies in the British security facilities, especially that of personnel clearance. Suggestions for improvement, he was told, were not well received.

'That was nine years ago,' said Oldfield. 'I think you will find we have made many changes for the better since then. But may I just point out that we have both had our security problems of a similar nature. I think if you look up your files, you will find that your own Security Office of the CIA unearthed what appeared to be a communist colonization of a section of the Office of Strategic Services, your own predecessor, as early as 1942.'

To the amazement of his CIA inquisitor, Oldfield then cited a memorandum from Sheffield Edwards, Director of Security of the CIA, to J. Edgar Hoover, chief of the FBI, dated 12 May 1955. This confirmed what he had just asserted. 'Let's admit one another's errors and really get down to helping one another, and cut out the recriminations,' he added.

Washington was then, as it still is, the largest British diplomatic post in the world, significant of the special relationship that exists between the two English-speaking powers. Despite all setbacks and occasional bouts of mistrust and suspicion on one side or the other, this special relationship had been extended to close cooperation between

119

MI 6 and the CIA right from the inception of the latter organization. Indeed, in the early days of the CIA immediately after World War Two, MI 6 had helped and advised the Americans in establishing themselves in the intelligence world. And, as the years passed by, the Americans had more than repaid this debt by exchanging information and collaborating in certain joint operations. Thus the post of liaison officer with the CIA in Washington was not simply a reward for Oldfield's good work in London and the Far East, but a testimony to his tact and skill in dealing with people in what was possibly the most sensitive post of all – in some ways as important as that of 'C' himself.

In the early 1950s the CIA in London had agreed on an exchange of their NIE (National Intelligence Estimate) material with the British, the latter giving in return their own JIC (Joint Intelligence Committee) evaluations. This system has continued ever since, amounting to a regular, but informal exchange of intelligence evaluations between London and Washington. But apart from this the CIA also have their own off-the-record and totally unofficial contacts with MI 6. To an outsider this may seem an erratic method of conducting business in a highly sensitive area, but this is exactly where the special relationship between the two countries shows itself at its best. While a certain degree of informality, or clandestinity, as some would call it, exists, there are also strict rules of protocol. This Oldfield was soon to learn. His normal contact when in Washington was with Richard Helms, the OPS chief. But surprisingly enough the British Embassy had their own channels of communication to the Deputy Director of Intelligence (CIA), quite separately from Oldfield. The DDI and his analytical material tended to go direct to London, while OPS was mainly run through contacts in Washington.

Luckily, Oldfield understood this complicated procedure from his experience in London, though as he wrily said once: 'It seems to work, yet I am never quite sure why. The procedure always seems to encourage that dangerous practice of the left hand not telling the right hand what it is doing.'

Mona View, Over Haddon, Oldfield's birthplace.

above Over Haddon village. Mona View is the house on the right.
below Dr R.A. Harvey, Oldfield's schoolmaster and one of his oldest friends.

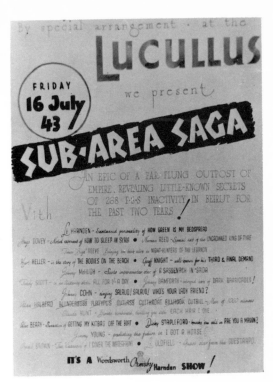

above Poster for a Military Intelligence smoking concert in Beirut, which Oldfield helped to compose.

below Field Security Section Christmas party in Beirut, 1943. Oldfield is second on the left in the front row.

above Maurice Oldfield in the mid-1960s: an informal portrait.
below Gathering hay in Austria while on holiday.

above President Kennedy discussing the Cuban crisis with General David Shoup and Admiral George Anderson, Chief of US Naval Operations.
below left Julian Amery MP: one of Oldfield's favourite ministers.
below right James Angleton of the CIA: Oldfield and he clashed on the subject of Penkovsky's evidence.

above Oleg Penkovsky on trial. His espionage for the British and the Americans helped to end the Cuban missiles crisis.

below Articles displayed at the Moscow trial of Oleg Penkovsky. The Soviet authorities claimed that he used the transistor radio to 'receive instructions' from British Intelligence.

above left Sir Maurice Oldfield, outside Buckingham Palace after receiving his knighthood in 1975.

above right Alexander Foote, a spy who came in from the cold and fascinated Oldfield.

below left Anthony Crosland, Foreign Secretary 1976-77. Oldfield described one meeting with him as 'the loveliest moment I've ever had with a foreign secretary.'

below right Dr David Owen, Foreign Secretary 1977-79, was a great admirer of Oldfield.

above Cartoon of 'Maurice the Mole' in Northern Ireland.
below Stormont House, Belfast, where Oldfield had his offices when working in Northern Ireland.

Mr Ray Cline, who had known Oldfield in the Far East, did not become Deputy Director of the CIA until 1962. 'Maurice and I talked many times, but my main contacts were with Sir Dick White, Sir Kenneth Strong and Burke (later Lord) Trend.

'Maurice was so unpretentious a man in both bearing and appearance that he looked as if he had been invented to deflate silly Ian Fleming caricatures of the British secret agent. Maurice remains in my mind a slight, inconspicuous figure with scanty hair and dandruff on the lapel easily setting the suspicious or fearful at rest by looking and acting somewhat like George Smiley and not at all like James Bond. He spoke with the typical Oxbridge understatement in normal conversation, not likely to leave a deep impression on first contact. This quality of course, is an excellent thing in the trade.

'On closer contact and with mutual confidence established, Maurice was a fascinating person with whom to exchange observations on world affairs. A little donnish, with a wry rather robust sense of humour, he had the customary sceptical view of princes and potentates as well as the prospect for sensible decisions in government. I suppose I liked him most because he did not let his realistic view of the way the world wags prevent him from trying to strike small blows for liberty in the Anglo-American value system and do in the KGB if possible. A mixture of modest expectations and subtle appreciation of useful things to be accomplished in the national security field is the characteristic of the better intelligence officers I have known.'[8]

This last sentence of assessment of Oldfield's qualities is perhaps best illustrated by Oldfield's insistence that one must never be too optimistic in seeking intelligence. 'One is bound to collect an awful lot of rubbish in the course of one's work, but it is no use trying to take a short cut and ignore some of it, nor must one get depressed by the sight of it. The only worthwhile method is to go on collecting, rubbish and all, and then let the analysts sift the wheat from the chaff.' He never worried about using clichés.

His first six months in Washington were spent rather

more in listening than in talking; his natural talent for getting people to talk freely came into its own. Sir Robert Thompson, the British expert on jungle guerrilla warfare, recalls meeting Oldfield in Washington shortly before he went out to Vietnam with an advisory mission in 1961. 'I only met him once with Fitzgerald of the CIA. From what I remember the latter did most of the talking.'[9]

Repairing the ravages wrought in the Anglo-American intelligence relationship not merely by Burgess and Maclean, but by other of the then unmasked traitors in the British ranks, was not an easy task for a newcomer. This was especially the case throughout Oldfield's term of office in Washington from 1960-64, when the CIA were getting disturbing reports about the infiltration of British security services from defectors from the USSR, culminating in 1963 with the flight of Philby from Beirut to Moscow and the unmasking of Anthony Blunt.

The United States had, of course, suffered from similar cases of treachery in their own ranks some twenty or thirty years earlier, but what often caused them doubts about their allies was the unfortunate British habit of appearing to take too casual a view of intelligence assessments. In 1947 Britain and the United States had agreed to monitor together the electronic, coded signals of other nations. Britain's GCHQ and the American National Security Agency had since then worked in collaboration. But in 1950 there had been a considerable difference of opinion between Britain's Joint Intelligence Bureau and the CIA on their respective estimates of intelligence. This had led to some American intelligence chiefs, supported by some senior US Army officers, asserting that Britain was not taking the Soviet threat to the Western world seriously enough.

Oldfield was able to show that this was an unjust view, though he agreed that probably British understatement was to blame. 'I do it myself sometimes,' he added ruefully, and then went on to tell the story of how a small British military unit in Korea, hard pressed to hold out against the North Koreans, had answered an American query as to what the situation was by the brave but inept comment: 'It's rather dicey up here, but we're holding on.' 'Of course,' explained Oldfield, 'what they really meant was it's bloody awful up here and we do need some help.' Needless to say they didn't get it on that occasion.'

However, while conceding the point that sometimes British understatement was misleading and even dangerous, he stressed that it did not mean any weakness or lack of endeavour. 'Sometimes you people can go too quickly in pursuit of an idea,' he warned the CIA, and he cited the case of how in 1950 the CIA had wanted global cooperation between the intelligence agencies of all non-communist countries. 'I think you will now agree that at the time we were right for once, while you were wrong in making that suggestion. We took the view that your plan actually threatened the security of our own Secret Service, especially if you had certain foreigners (I won't say which ones) sitting on a steering committee. But we said we would be happy just to work with you alone. Well, our plan won the day, we have worked together and, I hope, we are still reasonably happy.'[10]

My American informant on Oldfield's dissertation on differences between the two countries said that 'Maurice had this remarkable gift for telling an apt story against himself, or even his country, and then proceeding with another story or example of how good you Brits can be. It was a very effective talent of his. The stories were invariably apt, intended especially to appeal to an American, and in the end one felt that one not only understood him, but Britain as well. But he always insisted that intelligence assessments were useless unless one understood something of the make-up of the man, or men who made them. That's the way to understand what they mean. 'Always suspect some bureaucrat who writes in a report "As you will well understand", urged Maurice. "It probably means he hasn't a clue as to what it means himself." He had a dry, cynical sense of humour when he liked, though he was a kindly chap.'

On 11 April 1960, Joseph Oldfield, Maurice's father, died at the age of seventy-five. Not only was his son out of the country, but unable to attend the funeral, something which he always regretted. This is perhaps some indication of the pressures of work he was undergoing at that time, as he was still deeply concerned about his family in any domestic troubles.

Most British intelligence officers in the United States had found it more difficult to get along with the FBI, the counter-intelligence agency, than with the CIA. To some extent this was because since the Burgess-Maclean case the FBI had at times been paranoically suspicious of British newcomers. One FBI officer had heard that Oldfield thought the polygraph lie detector was 'a lot of nonsense' and made the comment that 'this is an easy way out for any rogue who funks the test.'

This comment was reported back to Oldfield who, to the great surprise of the CIA, actually volunteered to undergo the test. He took the view that his own opinion of the lie detector did not matter, but if by undergoing the test he could destroy any suspicions, that was all to the good. Somewhat sadly he smiled and said: 'However heterosexual we may be, we bachelors today are always suspected of being homosexual just because we aren't married. Maybe they will now agree I have no such problems.'

Nevertheless, having taken the test, Oldfield remained highly sceptical of the lie-detector whether for positive vetting or any other purpose. Although the 1,500-strong American Polygraphers Association had claimed that it provided up to 95 per cent accuracy, some American academics and even Government officials had taken a different view. Notwithstanding, all CIA personnel had to undergo this test, and even up to this day the official CIA view is that Britain should have adopted it several years ago, if only as a part of their vetting and security procedures, especially at places like GCHQ, Cheltenham.

The polygraph measures breathing, pulse rate and skin moisture, and a belt around the examinee's chest monitors respiration; a blood-pressure cuff is applied and electrodes around the first and middle fingers measure sweating. The readings taken are transferred electronically and appear as lines on a graph paper. The basis of the test is to measure reactions to various questions, some relevant, others irrelevant.

Having undergone the test, however, Oldfield felt free to express his own doubts about it. He strongly urged the view that there were two equally powerful objections to the lie-detector. The first was that someone quite innocent, but unduly nervous, could be victimized unfairly by it, and the second was that the Soviet Union had for years been working on experiments designed to withstand brain-washing and to beat the lie-detector. He urged the CIA to do some research into what exactly the Russians were doing in this respect. In the light of what Oldfield suggested in the 1960s it is worth noting that in 1983 Dr John Beary, health director of the US Defense Department, stated in a Pentagon memorandum that 'increasing reliance on lie detectors to protect its secrets will make it easier for Soviet "moles" to penetrate the Pentagon. The polygraph endangers national security rather than protects it because the Russians know how to beat the tests designed to determine whether a person is lying. I am told the Soviets have a training school in an Eastern bloc country where they teach their agents how to beat the polygraph.'[11]

Dr Beary went on record as saying that not only did the polygraph not work, but its hypothesis was scientifically unsound: 'there is no physiologic response unique to the cognitive state of lying. No psycho-physiologist has been able to identify such a unique response.' Whether Oldfield's suggestions actually contributed to some new thinking in the CIA ranks is not certain, but a CIA paper listed under the heading MKULTRA Projects, released from classification in August 1977, is of some interest. Unfortunately no date for this paper is given, but one can assume it was possibly at least ten years earlier than the date when it was declassified.

The paper states that recommendations for improving the polygraph had been made. Some of these were obviously censored still, but the aim of one recommendation was 'to improve the polygraph, create an ideal biographic file and research methods of artificially established positive identification – i.e. the use of radioisotypes implanted in the body or anti-bodies alien to the area of operation.' There was a note that this was 'for establishing and substantiating the *bona fides* of agent/and/or staff personnel through techniques and methods other than interrogation, especially to determine if agents are the same people, or have been "substituted".'[12]

No doubt Oldfield would have been amused to read this memorandum. Yet in 1983 the American Bar Association *Intelligence Report* stated that two members of MI 5 were shortly to visit the USA to undergo training in the use of the lie-detector at the Polygraph Training School in Alabama. Oldfield maintained that the polygraph gave the wrong answer about one time in three, a view which has been shared by Dr David Lykken, of the University of Minnesota.

Apart from the revelations of Americans about Oldfield's doubts about the lie detector, one of his friends in London can verify this. Mr Fred Bardwell, a member of the Parochial Church Council at St Matthews's Church, Westminster, where Oldfield attended, says that 'he was always dubious about the polygraph, arguing that a bare-faced liar could probably lie and not give anything away emotionally, even convincing himself he was telling the truth, whereas someone telling the truth might be nervous and therefore adjudged to be a liar. He kept a black box which was marked M.O., his own initials, but he called it his Modus Operandi. He liked to use this to try it out on people and debunk the polygraph. If you were asked a question and answered to this box, sometimes a red light and sometimes a green one would go on. That box about sums up Maurice's views on lie-detectors.'[13]

Another colleague of Oldfield's also recalls the apparatus described by Fred Bardwell. 'Oh, yes, I know what you mean,' he replied when I asked if he had ever heard of it. 'Maurice used to call it his "Worry Box". It was specially made for him by those of our people who construct such things for the trade. It had two standard answers – "true", or "false". Maurice had no end of fun pulling people's legs with this gimmick, literally shaking his box with glee. It was intended to cock a snook at the lie detector.'

Oldfield, however, would never let a difference of opinion on an issue such as the polygraph cause him to halt in his pursuit of closer and better relations between the SIS and the CIA. His own view was that the exchange of intelligence secrets between the two nations was all important and he succeeded brilliantly in winning back the confidence of many Americans in key positions who had hitherto been either lukewarm towards cooperation with the British, or openly critical of the latter's security arrangements. 'We had been pressing your MI 5 and MI 6 to adopt the lie-detector for some years,' says one CIA officer. 'We never had much luck. Our view was that, while it had its defects, it was invaluable in speeding up security checks. For example, at one time at Cheltenham GCHQ there were only twelve security officers to check a staff of 7,000. No wonder Prime got away with it. Our point was, and still is, when you have large numbers of people to deal with, the polygraph does provide a chance to weed out. The doubtful, or unproven cases can always be re-vetted. Oldfield accepted this argument, while quietly stressing the hazards of the polygraph about which he seemed to be singularly well informed.'

8

The Cuban Missiles Crisis

So whole-hearted was Oldfield in his quest for Anglo-American cooperation that some of his critics later unfairly accused him of insufficient criticism of the CIA during the time he was in Washington.[1] His answer would undoubtedly have been that maybe the Americans had not been sufficiently critical of some of Britain's own shortcomings in the field of intelligence and security. With the Cuban missiles crisis slowly clouding the political horizon in the autumn of 1960, this was no time for recriminations, or quibbles on methods between the respective Intelligence Services of the two countries. A report reached the CIA in late October 1960 that Nikita Khrushchev had told delegates from the Soviet satellite countries earlier that month that the USSR had a formidable store of nuclear rockets, two hundred of which would destroy the United Kingdom, France and West Germany, while three hundred would knock out the United States. 'We have so many of these weapons', boasted the Soviet leader, 'that some of them are being melted down and made into tractors.' This was a typical example of Khrushchev allowing his rhetoric to get the better of him.

Yet in December 1960 the CIA had another report which

strongly suggested that the USSR would not risk war with the United States and that therefore there was no need to worry about rockets being sent to Cuba. Fortunately, nobody in the White House, the State Department or the CIA took the latter report too seriously. But some ministers and bureaucrats were inclined to this viewpoint. Oldfield was very quick to detect the divergence of views inside the administration and elsewhere on the question of a direct Soviet threat to the USA and the possibility of Cuba being used as a siting-place for Russian missiles. He also developed a growing admiration for President Kennedy's grasp of and handling of intelligence affairs.

This perceptiveness was fully justified after the Bay of Pigs fiasco in 1961, when Kennedy set about re-planning the upper hierarchy of the CIA. It was he who appointed John A. McCone as the new director of the CIA, a move which led to much tighter control at the top. Resulting from this reorganization, Ray Cline was brought back from the Far East to become deputy director. He and Oldfield, while not in constant contact, shared very much the same broad views on the tasks of intelligence and the role of intelligence operators and analysts in decision-making. Oldfield believed that MI 6 officers were better in clandestine operations than the Americans, but expressed his envy and admiration for the resources the latter could call on, especially when devoted to research and analysis.

In this epoch, when the United States faced the imponderables of how far the USSR would seek to extend their power and influence in the Caribbean area, Britain held one or two trump cards in terms of intelligence. But Oldfield, as well as a few others on the British side, soon realized that those cards needed to be held until the psychologically right moment. For United States thinking on the Russian threat in the Caribbean was by no means based on all-round agreement of Department of Defense, State Department, CIA and the Services' intelligence network. The director of the CIA was then in a minority in thinking that Russia was actually sending missiles to Cuba. But what also perturbed Oldfield was that Robert McNamara, the Defense Secretary, might succeed in damping down President Kennedy's persistence in getting at the truth of reports that Russia was sending weapons to Cuba.

To succeed Oldfield had to play more the role of the skilled diplomat than an intelligence officer. Step by step he had to ensure that his allies were working in the right direction, that nobody would feel there was any British coercion in pressing one point more than another. The months before the Cuban missiles crisis suddenly developed were not merely fraught with danger, but with a psychological minefield into which one careless move could be ruinous – even among allies.

Fortunately, from the viewpoint of Anglo-American relations the British played their cards particularly effectively at this time. For once there wasn't a single joker in the pack. At least the Foreign Office and the SIS were working together in perfect accord in their relations with the United States and this simplified the whole operation of joint intelligence analysis. There were three aces who contributed a great deal – 'C', Sir Dick Goldsmith White, in London, and Oldfield and Thomas Brimelow (now Lord Brimelow) in Washington. Educated at the universities of Michigan and California as well as at Oxford, Sir Dick White had a good understanding of American methods and requirements. Brimelow was a man of very wide experience who had already served in New York, Moscow and Havana and been head of the Northern Department of the Foreign Office. He also held the rank of Counsellor in Washington, where he was a straightforward member of Chancery for liaison with the State Department on Soviet and Eastern Europe affairs. He was too the Washington representative of the British Joint Intelligence Committee, and in that capacity maintained liaison with the 'overt' side of the CIA, chiefly the sections dealing with National Estimates and Current Intelligence. He also presided as chairman over a weekly meeting of those concerned with current intelligence in the Embassy – Navy, Army, Air Force and Oldfield.

But the trump card in all talks with the Americans at this time was undoubtedly Colonel Oleg Penkovsky, the mole in the Soviet camp who was supplying a vast quantity of scientific and technical intelligence on Soviet weaponry to the British. 'The answer to a prayer,' was how Oldfield described Penkovsky. 'What he provided seemed like a miracle, too. That is why for so long he was mistrusted on both sides of the Atlantic. It seemed incredible that he could take such risks – not merely photographing top secret documents, but actually giving us the original documents in some instances.'

Penkovsky, a GRU (Soviet Military Intelligence) officer, supplied the British Secret Service with invaluable information about Russian military technology and the deployment pattern for nuclear missiles sites from the early days of 1961 and the late summer of 1962. The risks which Penkovsky took in contacting the British, sometimes on missions outside the USSR, not unnaturally caused him to be regarded with some suspicion at first. It seemed probable that he was being planted on the British as a disinformer.

Oleg Penkovsky was born in the North Caucasus in 1919, and he joined the artillery school in Kiev, passing out as a lieutenant in 1939. He fought in the Soviet-Finnish war, joined the Communist party and at the end of World War Two was a lieutenant-colonel. In 1955 he was appointed assistant military attaché in Ankara, at which time he was first marked down by the British Secret Service as a potential defector or informant. No move was made by the SIS, but from then on he was closely watched. It was noted that for some curious reason Penkovsky would sit alone drinking in pavement cafés.

A clumsy attempt to make contact with the Americans in November 1960 had been rejected because it was suspected this might be an attempt at provoking trouble by the Soviet police. Meanwhile Penkovsky had been appointed to the State Committee for the Coordination of Scientific Research, where he became deputy head of the foreign department. The full details of how Penkovsky was eventually recruited by the British may well remain a secret for all time, not least because there were other recruits from the Russian side who were able to substantiate Penkovsky. Various stories as to how contact with him was first made have been circulated and published, but some of these are almost as fictional as factual. Incontrovertibly, however, Penkovsky was finally accepted as a supremely important informant on an official visit to Britain in April 1961.

From then on he turned over to the British a wealth of intelligence, not merely about Russian military technology, but the deployment pattern for missile sites. He revealed how Khrushchev's 'secret weapon' had blown up on the launching pad, killing the chief of the Soviet missile forces, Marshal Nedelin, and three hundred officers. He revealed that the USSR was in no position to make good its boasts of being able to threaten the United States. This had called for careful analysis by scientific experts as well as by SIS officers. It was so vitally important to the whole of the Western world that it was essential for the British to convince the Americans that Penkovsky was genuine.

The Americans had had experience of bogus defectors planted on them by the Russians. They were also very wary of the British in view of the infiltration of the latter's Security and Intelligence services by the Russians. The great doubter in the American ranks was that brilliant chief of the CIA's counter-intelligence division, James Jesus Angleton. He was for a long time convinced that Penkovsky was a double agent deliberately sent to contact the British so as to spread disinformation.

Thus this particular ace in the British pack was not an easy one to play. Much of Penkovsky's information was highly technical and before it could be passed on to the Americans it needed to be analysed by scientific experts in the Ministry of Defence. The most vital part of the intelligence he supplied comprised some five thousand photographs of documents and sketches taken with a miniature camera. His information on deployment patterns of Soviet missile sites enabled American air reconnaissance to spot the setting up of missiles in Cuba much more easily. So what Penkovsky had to contribute was not merely a warning of future dangers, but at the same time an assurance that all was not as bad as it seemed because the Soviet Union could not then attack the USA with inter-continental-ballistic-missiles. It was as essential to stress the good news as the bad, to help curb any panic reactions as well as to stress the need for vigilance. This was no easy task, especially as there were doubters in the British ranks, in Washington and in Langley, Virginia.

To counter these problems all Penkovsky's material was carefully edited and annotated in London before being passed to the USA, and the CIA also decided that the distribution of what they received from the British should be restricted to a small group of trusted analysts. From April 1961, when Penkovsky paid a visit to London, right up to the October of the following year was a period of strain and tension for Americans and British alike. On each side were the hawks and the doves, though their motives were not always the same. It was to President Kennedy's credit that he was an eager listener to both sides, anxious to learn and to test out the various theories. Some nervous types in the Pentagon had whispered in Kennedy's ear that Soviet missiles were being hidden in caves in Cuba. Confirmation of that sugestion might well have given the hawks the political ammunition required. Luckily, Ray Cline was able to check with the ORR (Office of Research and Reports) and found that the CIA had a card index on every known cave in Cuba, with indications of the size of the entrance and the suitability for the storage of weapons. The file stated that only a very few missiles could possibly fit into or get through the entrance to these caves.[2]

Cuba was eleven thousand kilometres from Russia and at that date the Soviet Union's sea and air communications were not strong enough to make an attack upon the USA feasible. Khrushchev was bluffing wildly when he suggested that he could launch such an operation, though some politicians on both sides of the Atlantic were apt to believe what he said. In retrospect it is probably true to say that at most times from 1961-62 either the SIS or the CIA were ahead of the politicians in making positive and constructive suggestions.

It is now clear that the British role in the Penkovsky case

was more crucial than public accounts to date have indicated. Oldfield's own part in all this, how he not only obtained personal access to the President to stress the value of Penkovsky's evidence, but ensured that Kennedy had an independent scientific opinion and interpretation of the situation from the British side, was absolutely vital. It was Oldfield who was able to counteract the mistrust of Penkovsky as put forward by Angleton and others. For, while Kennedy listened, he had to choose between those in his administration who wanted an air strike to wipe out the missiles on Cuba and those who contemplated doing nothing at all, playing a waiting game in the hope that Khrushchev might back down. It was not easy for the President to make an early decision because the right policy lay somewhere between these two extremes.

Much of the really valuable intelligence which Penkovsky passed on to the British has still not been revealed and is highly unlikely to be available for public inspection for many years to come, if ever. Some of this concerned Britain alone; for example Ivanov, the Russian diplomat who became involved in what was known as the Profumo Affair, was a KGB agent. At least two traitors in the British Intelligence Services were pointed out as well. Once the Americans had been convinced that Penkovsky had access to intelligence of the highest possible level it was unfortunate that pressure was put on the British and Penkovsky himself to supply more information in the weeks immediately preceding October 1962. Such impatience may have partially contributed to his exposure to the Russians. For by this time Penkovsky himself was in no doubt that he was being watched closely by the KGB, and that he had to operate with extreme caution.

Yet in looking back on this crisis period, what is truly frightening is just how two natural allies, speaking the same language and enjoying the same cultures, found it necessary on a political-diplomatic level to try to deceive one another. They had a common enemy, their true views were identical, yet both the United States and British found it difficult to spell out the truth through some of their spokesmen. On the

American side this was no doubt through fear that the British would object to any action which carried the risk of war, while on the British side there was a feeling that the Penkovsky revelations were so impressive that reservations had to be placed upon them. The Macmillan government, containing quite a few doubters, not least among its advisers, hampered by a divided Foreign Office, never gave to the Americans anything remotely like the solid backing which some historians of the period have suggested. President Kennedy secured much greater moral support from General de Gaulle than ever he did from Macmillan.

In many respects the situation in October 1962 may be compared to that in August 1914, when the two warring factions in Europe were not merely deceiving one another, but deceiving themselves. The difference was that in 1962 the secret services of the allies actually prevented the kind of misunderstanding which could have led to war.

Ray Cline has this to say on the subject: 'I happened to have Strong [Major-General Sir Kenneth Strong] and Trend [Sir Burke Trend] both on my hands during the week of 15 October 1962, for a Quadrennial DDI conference which I hosted. I misled them all week into thinking my obvious preoccupation with business was about Berlin, not Cuba, and only got permission from President Kennedy to brief Strong and Trend orally before their departure on Friday, 19 October. My exercise in deception was totally successful because these British friends took several occasions during the week to argue with me that the Russians would never put missiles in Cuba because of the risk to their interests in Europe. When I refused to dismiss this as an outside possibility (knowing full well they were there!), Ken Strong in particular chided me for making the American error of overrating the importance of Cuba because it was so close.'[3]

When allies have to indulge in double-talk, one begins to wonder who needs enemies. In this instance it is rather easier to understand and appreciate the American viewpoint of the need for some deception and secrecy, but very much less easy to know quite what the British on this level were attempting to say. Something very similar occurred again twenty years later over Grenada: one hopes some day the right lesson will be learned from all this. Whatever the British motive was in talking in this way, not only was the reason obscure, but the manner in which it was expressed could have been positively dangerous if taken literally.

It cannot, however, be too strongly stressed that the one vital link in those months and weeks leading up to the Cuban missiles crisis was Maurice Oldfield and arising out of this the friendship which sprang up between him and the US President. It was his advice, his steadfast advocacy of Penkovsky and his ability to get speedy answers to Kennedy's persistent questioning on technical matters which more than anything else enabled the Cuban threat to be dealt with in the most practical manner. The militants of the Kennedy administration, led by Acheson, urged an air attack to wipe out the missiles, while McNamara, the Defense Secretary, was not simply against this, but often gave the impression of merely hoping that something would turn up to change the situation. Oldfield was able to score by showing the President, through Penkovsky's testimony, not only where to concentrate for air pictures of the installation of Soviet missiles in Cuba, but even more importantly to stress that Khrushchev's bluff could be called by an ultimatum.

Rather more difficult was the task of proving Angleton wrong in thinking Penkovsky a Soviet plant. A great deal of superficial evidence suggested him to be just that. Penkovsky was a complex character with a streak of vanity in his make-up allied no doubt to a feeling of contempt for his Soviet masters. His motives for passing information to the West at such great risk to himself and sometimes in what would seem to be a highly amateurish and dangerous manner still remain to some extent a mystery. Many SIS high level personnel could have been forgiven for doubting him; so, too, could many counter-intelligence officers on both sides of the Atlantic. Perhaps it was because Oldfield had had experience of both intelligence-gathering and counter-intelligence that he was able more easily to grasp the importance of Penkovsky.

Mr Alistair Horne, of St Antony's College, Oxford, declares that Oldfield insisted that Penkovsky was the most important defector and discovery as an informant for the West since World War Two. When, a few years later, the *Penkovsky Papers* were published in the United States with the apparent blessing of the CIA, many critics both in America and Europe cast doubt on the authenticity of the material. Mr Horne had done a favourable review of the book for the London *Sunday Telegraph* and this was queried by the editor, the late Donald Maclachlan. 'You seem to be in a minority,' said Maclachlan. 'Are you absolutely sure?'

Mr Horne replied that he was convinced he was right, although he was almost alone among the critics in praising the book. 'I did not reveal my source, but I got the answer in an oblique form from Oldfield before I wrote my piece.'[4]

Eventually, of course, to some extent helped by Penkovsky's pin-pointing of what to look for, the CIA secured an aerial photograph of a medium-range missile site being built at San Cristobal in Cuba on 14 October 1962. When the Soviet ships were heading for Cuba and the deadline of 24 October 1962 was approaching (the time set and the quarantine line drawn for the missile-carriers to stop), all manner of suggestions were put forward. One such was that, if the Soviet ships sailed on, the United States should use weapons only to destroy the propellors of the vessels heading for Cuba, and not to sink them.

President Kennedy's gratitude for the advice he had been given by Oldfield when Khrushchev's bluff was called and the Soviet ships turned back from Cuba by the deadline given was passed back to London. Shortly afterwards Sir Dick Goldsmith White called his staff together in Century House and stressed the Americans' appreciation of the role played by the SIS in exploiting Penkovsky's intelligence to the fullest extent.

Both the Foreign office and the SIS, however, shared the view that the most vital service provided by Penkovsky and developed by Oldfield was to convince the President of Russia's inability to attack the USA with ICBMs. Indeed, it could be said that on this occasion the Intelligence Services of the two countries had preserved the peace and checked brinkmanship on both sides. Kennedy's handling of the crisis was praised at the time, but in retrospect it looks as though he failed lamentably to take full advantage of his diplomatic victory. The President could have insisted upon a neutral, disarmed Cuban, but he made the fatal error of agreeing that Fidel Castro could be left alone.

Quite apart from the Cuban missiles crisis, Oldfield could hardly have chosen four more exciting years in which to be stationed in Washington. On the intelligence front there were constant upheavals, reappraisals and such controversial issues as the unmasking of Philby, Blunt and others, the quest for a mole inside the CIA, the long-running argument as to who was the most important defector – Anatolyi Golitsin or Yuri Nosenko, and, finally, the question of who killed President Kennedy in 1963. They were exhausting years for British diplomats in the USA, but much more strenuous for those concerned with covert intelligence. Oldfield himself was once heard to mutter that 'the situation here is much more like *Alice in Wonderland* than anything Lewis Carroll could have thought up. There must be several candidates for the role of Mad Hatter.'

Yet he found time for other activities, even though he had to confess that sometimes he needed to make himself 'the original Invisible Man' to avoid any unwelcome publicity. He lived at Waterside Drive, Washington and was a member of the Metropolitan Club, while he covered the cocktail party circuit with immense skill. One distinguished Washington corespondent on a British national newspaper told me: 'I saw him at these parties and I talked with him there. But for the life of me I can't think of anything he said. Yet he talked all the time.' A diplomat put it more trenchantly: 'Maurice would talk very softly and wisely and he knew perfectly well that at a cocktail party few would often hear what he said, let alone remember it. He was an absolute genius for giving the impression of having said the right thing without anyone remembering what the hell he had said. All part of the act.'

He carefully picked the nearest High church he could conveniently attend. Lady Brimelow recalls that 'one wintry morning at a church on Massachusetts Avenue Maurice Oldfield took up a spade and cleared the snow from the steps.' A CIA officer, learning that Oldfield could play the organ, once invited him to try out a harmonium in his home. 'To my astonishment he agreed to show that traditional jazz could be just as effective on this medium as any other music. But he was very insistent that this was "just a private whim".'

Oldfield had made a point of keeping in close touch with the late Shah of Iran ever since the joint Anglo-American coup which had restored the Shah to his throne. The result was that on an intelligence level Britain still had closer relations with the Shah than the Americans or anyone else. This proved invaluable in March 1962, when the Shah visited the USA and the subject of military assistance was discussed. Oldfield not only saw the Shah on that occasion, but helped to persuade him to accept American aid. Oldfield suggested to the Americans various topics they could usefully discuss with the Shah. There was a quite remarkable understanding between these two dissimilar men: it was as though Over Haddon and Teheran had suddenly adopted one another. The Shah felt he could talk to Oldfield with complete frankness and confidence. He was able to complain to Oldfield, as he would probably not have been able to do with anyone else among the British, that the British Foreign Office was populated by 'White Arabs'. The Shah stressed over and over again that he felt some of these officials were actually thwarting his efforts to get Iran accepted as a European nation. Oldfield was one of the first to realize that what the Shah hoped to do was to model Iran on Japan and to create a Western-orientated society out of a traditionally Muslim peasantry. The problem was that the Shah's authoritarianism showed itself in his impatient attitude to what he called 'Western Europe's obsession with democracy and the non-productive doctrine of consensus', something he regarded as being self-destructive in the long run.

Oldfield had a high regard for the Shah, even though he did not agree with all his authoritarian ways, which he feared might produce a counter-revolution. He was always disappointed when his view that the Shah was the West's stoutest friend in the Middle East with the exception of Israel was disregarded by some in the Foreign Office.

No doubt, too, he regretted that in stressing the supreme importance of Penkovsky the defector himself had been put seriously at risk when in the months immediately preceding the Cuban crisis the Americans had pressed for more information from him. This may well have been a factor in Penkovsky's arrest later in 1962 and his subsequent sentencing to death by a Soviet court in 1963. Oldfield always felt that in comparison with the lenience the authorities had shown to Philby, Blunt, Maclean, Burgess and many others in the Establishment the cynicism shown towards Penkovsky as long as he could be exploited was in some respects unforgivable.

Even when Philby defected to Russia in January 1963, he had his apologists in the intelligence world. There seems to be no doubt that Philby had been promised immunity from prosecution if he would cooperate with the authorities. He had made a confession of sorts, though few believe that it was anything more than a small part of the whole truth. The excuse was even submitted by some that Philby had been forced to defect to Russia at gun-point and had been forcibly removed by ship to the USSR. Not unnaturally the critics of the intelligence services suggested that if this was the case, then Philby must have been betrayed to the Russians by someone in MI 5 or MI 6.

Once Philby was reluctantly unmasked, it followed that inquiries had to be made into his pro-Soviet friends inside the Establishment. Blunt had been suspected ever since the defection of Burgess and Maclean in 1951 when Goronwy Rees had reported that Burgess had declared in 1937 he was working for the Comintern, with Blunt as one of his sources. The man who had slapped down Rees' statement and backed up Blunt's denials was Guy Liddell of MI 5. The authorities, not wishing for any publicity for their own shortcomings in failing to unmask Blunt long ago, decided that the best plan was once again to waive any prosecution, but to secure his confession and cooperation. Anthony Blunt was in fact interrogated by MI 5 in Oldfield's London flat in 1964, while Oldfield was still overseas.

These matters did not directly concern Oldfield in his relations with the Americans, but it was inevitable that the subject could not be avoided. The crucial point in such discussions was that it was actually from the Americans and the Israelis that the evidence against both Philby and Blunt was finally clinched. Here James Angleton played a useful and indeed vital role.

Towards the end of Oldfield's time in Washington Sir Dick White asked Oldfield and two other high officers in the SIS to submit their own nominations for a new deputy to 'C'. Oldfield replied with a three-page letter recommending his own claims for the post. Such was the confidence he had gained in Washington. The other two officers also urged the appointment of Oldfield. Thus he became number two in the chain of command. He was eventually succeeded in Washington by Mr Christopher Philpotts, a former naval officer who had joined the Foreign Office in 1943.

Back in Britain Oldfield started to pick up the threads of his life both in Derbyshire and London, delightedly renewing old acquaintanceships. His flat in Chandos Court, Caxton Street, Westminster, the one in which Blunt had been interrogated, had a large library in one room which was his especial delight. One estimate was that he had 'thousands of books in this room'. Certainly his collection was a large one and his catholic tastes ranged from classical to modern.

It was about this time that Oldfield started to take a keen interest in the case of Dr Otto John, the former head of the West German Federal Internal Security Office, who had been abducted to East Germany by agents of the KGB. This coup by the Russians was partly an attempt to cover up the mass arrests of agents of General Gehlen, head of the external section of the West German Secret Service. The

Gehlen Organization had been cunningly infiltrated by a Soviet agent named Felfe, and the plan was to draw attention away from Felfe, thereby ensuring that he could carry on undetected for another seven years, and to point the finger of suspicion at Dr John. The Soviet ploy aimed to suggest that he had all the time been an agent of the USSR and had willingly gone over to the Russians.

In 1955 Dr John escaped to West Germany, but was most unfairly tried and sentenced to four years' imprisonment by the West German authorities in 1956. He was released in 1958 after the remainder of his sentence had been suspended. Oldfield had always felt that Sefton Delmer, the former *Daily Express* correspondent in Berlin, had been shabbily treated and unrewarded for the sterling work he did during the war with his black propaganda team at Woburn Abbey. Richard Crossmann, the left-wing intellectual who had been helping direct psychological warfare in World War Two, had allowed his intellectually arrogant prejudices to deny any credit to Delmer, whom he disliked because he worked for a Beaverbrook newspaper. When Oldfield referred to this in a conversation with Delmer, the latter replied: 'You think I've been badly treated. You should meet Otto John. There is the most appalling miscarriage of justice I've ever come across in a so-called democracy. You must meet him.'

So Delmer introduced Oldfield to Dr John and the two men became great friends. They shared many interests in the intelligence world, both past and present, and music became a bond between them. 'Had the Western Allies exerted the same degree of control over the Gehlen Organization as they did over me and my office, Felfe could never have infiltrated it and the resulting well-nigh immeasurable damage would have been averted,' declared Dr John. 'The true background to my abduction only emerged gradually ... British journalists in London questioned me about my relationship with Kim Philby ... They discovered that at the time when I had been in Lisbon during the war, probing the possibilities of negotiating with the British government on behalf of the German Resistance, Philby had occupied the "Iberian desk",

142

in other words had been the senior SIS official dealing with Spain and Portugal.'[5]

Thus it dawned upon Dr John that, as he recollected the questions put to him by the Russians about Philby, they were anxious to find out whether at any time their man inside the SIS had been deceiving them. John was, of course, able to show that Philby had described one of his own reports about the anti-Hitler Resistance as 'unreliable' and had frustrated him when he defected to the British. Clearly, his testimony had removed any doubts the Russians might have had about Philby.

This alone was enough to cause Oldfield to take a keen interest in Dr John's case. But it also enabled him to see how many chances were lost of finishing off World War Two much earlier by neglect of the aid proffered by the German Resistance. He had seen how in the Middle East the use of Germans as double-agents had been enormously effective. Now he realized how this operation had been damagingly neglected in Western Europe. Dr John says: 'I told the Russians the truth: all our peace feelers had foundered on the obstinate determination of the British to maintain their treaty obligations towards the Russians. In all my interrogations with Michailov in which he asked for names and contacts in the British Secret Service I never mentioned Philby because I never suspected he was my anonymous adversary. Michailov finally convinced himself that the Soviet was not being cheated by a double-crosser in the shape of Philby and that they could rely on him. In this sense Philby – I am now certain – was rehabilitated by me with the Russians without my knowing anything about it.'[6]

In 1965 Mr Phillip Whitehead was making a film about Otto John. 'I did not know this at the time, but Maurice had been Dr John's British contact. The rough cast of the film included shots of two British agents who had been active in West Germany after the war. They were included in a sequence which implied (but did not state) that John had remained a British 'plant' when he went back to Germany in the late 1940s [he had actually defected to London in 1944]. Colonel Sammy Lohan, who operated the 'D' Notice system of bans on publication of anything that threatened national security, objected to the inclusion of this film sequence. "If that is seen, they are dead men." At that time I was sceptical. A few weeks later I was at the local point-to-point at Flagg in Derbyshire. These races take place on a Tuesday. There was a big crowd. Suddenly Maurice appeared at my elbow, out of nowhere. "Don't put people at risk just for a TV programme," he said. "I'll tell you the best explanation of what happened to John." That was all. The crowd surged as the race began and Maurice vanished as quietly as he had appeared. He kept his part of the bargain and I kept mine. The pictures were taken out. Maurice offered a subtle view of Otto John's motivation and kept in touch with John until he died.'[7]

Dr John, who spent some time in London in the late 1960s, struck up a close friendship with Maurice Oldfield. 'My wife and I got to like him very much. He became a very true and beloved friend. He took a great interest in music and most of the discussions between my wife and him were concerned with music.'[8]

9

The Difficult Years

From an intelligence viewpoint the late 1960s and early 1970s were fraught with difficulties for the SIS. There was turmoil at home and, rather more disturbingly, some disagreements between the SIS and the Foreign and Commonwealth Office. That in itself made these years difficult for any SIS officer of senior rank, but there were added problems of unhappy relations with the political Establishment, largely created indirectly by rifts within the hierarchy of MI 5.

Both Latin America and the Caribbean still occupied much of Oldfield's time and, following up on his sojourn in the USA, he cooperated closely with the CIA in various fields. A State Department telegram, No. 1190, of 29 April 1965, refers to activities in the Dominican Republic during the coup, and specifically mentions the 'fearless British vice-consul, Paul Rudd, in downtown Santo Domingo and his report on rebel tanks, etc.'

There was, in fact, much closer cooperation between Americans and British in the intelligence world concerning Latin America and Africa generally in the late 1960s than there had ever been before. Covert assistance had been given by the Americans at the request of the British to the anti-Jagan forces in what was then still British Guiana.[1] Joint consultation on African problems had been thrashed out in White House talks back in 1964, and by the following year J. Wayne Fredericks, Deputy Assistant Secretary for African Affairs in the State Department, had noted that 'Israeli aid to East Africa pleases the United Kingdom as an alternative to communist involvement.'[2]

Such close exchange of intelligence between the USA and Britain undoubtedly saved a lot of money, cut out duplication of services and in the long run was enormously beneficial. The British had helped the Americans considerably in information from Mexico where the SIS station was known as 'the Harem' because of the four blonde girls who worked in the office. This information was as varied as a tip-off of a plot to plant a bomb in Pope Paul's plane to details of left-wing exiles in Mexico who kept up links with Cuba and Russia. Later, to avoid overlapping of intelligence-gathering and to come to a friendly arrangement with the CIA Oldfield agreed to let the Americans have rather more of the actual work of intelligence collecting in Mexico.

One of the most agonizing decisions Oldfield had to take was during his term of office as deputy to 'C'. An MI 6 agent overseas had been arrested by the KGB. The man was not only an important agent, but in possession of vital information, disclosure of which could have caused the deaths of countless other people. There was more than a possibility that, if all else failed, the KGB might use torture to force him to talk. By an almost miraculous chance, the details of which cannot be revealed, there was the possibility of smuggling into the agent's cell a pill which would bring swift death and so save him from talking under the threat of torture. There was not much time to be lost in deliberating if the pill was to be smuggled in soon enough, so, with great reluctance, knowing that in effect he was sanctioning and encouraging suicide, Oldfield agreed to this subterfuge on the grounds that other lives would be saved as a result.

In the early days of the first Wilson government Oldfield was once confronted in his club by the late Richard Crossman, MP. Crossman was perhaps more distinguished for his compulsive tactlessness than for his undoubted academic achievements. On this occasion knowing, or sensing, that Oldfield had something to do with the world of intelligence, he blurted out: 'I know all about you MI 6 people. You employ a lot of right-wing MPs.'

'Ah, yes, perhaps,' replied Oldfield blandly, 'But you don't know how many left-wing MPs we may employ.'

Such relations as there were with the first Wilson government were on the whole extremely good. Oldfield could generally get along with politicians of all parties when dealing with the actual mechanics of intelligence. In fact, he probably got along much better with the politicians than with some of the civil servants, especially with a minority in the Foreign Office. Lord Wilson, as he now is, has more than once testified that while he could find little good to say about MI 5, he had nothing but praise for MI 6. On the other hand George Wigg (the late Lord Wigg) who, as Paymaster-General, had taken on the liaison link between the Prime Minister (Wilson) and the Intelligence and Security Services, gave the impression of taking an almost totally different view. Long after he had retired from this work, Lord Wigg told me in 1977 that 'as far as I am concerned MI 5 are the real professionals and MI 6 a bunch of amateurs.'[3] For a moment I thought he had confused the two services and that he had got his numbers wrong. I checked whether he really meant what he had previously said. To my surprise he confirmed this. I think there were two reasons for Wigg's prejudice against MI 6. First, he recalled that when Herbert Morrison had been Foreign Secretary at the time of the disappearance of Burgess and Maclean in 1951, he was kept in ignorance of the testimony of the Soviet defector, Krivitsky, which clearly pointed at Maclean. Wigg himself said that Morrison, when he left office, 'still persisted in the view that Foreign Office *ésprit de corps* was in part responsible for the affair [the failure to apprehend Burgess and Maclean before they defected]. *Esprit de corps*, apparently, had kept Morrison ignorant of information implicating Maclean which had been given to the Foreign Office by Stalin's former agent, Walter Krivitsky, in 1940; it had also kept him ignorant of the Volkov revelations, made through the British Embassy in Turkey.'[4]

Wigg, rather unfairly, equated the Foreign Office with the SIS. His second reason for being critical of MI 6 was that he felt that 'the success of UDI in Rhodesia in the sixties was due in part to MI 6 misreading the situation there. Their intelligence was so bad for so long that, when I was Paymaster-General, I had to organize a private team to get the right answers.'[5]

In the end, or so Lord Wigg claimed in his talk with me, the correct intelligence was obtained 'effectively and cheaply from two men, one a Tory MP, the late Captain Henry Kerby, and the other from a highly reliable, right-wing White Russian.'[6] This was a most improbable team to be employed by a Labour government, but at least it produced the right answers. For the record, I was personally acquainted with both Captain Kerby and the White Russian in question.

However, despite Wigg's prejudice against MI 6 (and no one who knew him would question his deep patriotism), I feel he did not altogether make the right deductions. In the beginning he had been an astute, efficient political student of the whole system of intelligence and counter-intelligence. As time passed he began to lose his grip on things, and undoubtedly he became worried over MI 5's concern about security at No. 10 Downing Street. Possibly in the Macmillan era intelligence from Africa generally had not been particularly good. Once the Commonwealth Office and the Colonial Office became merged with the Foreign Office it had certainly been less easy to improve it. But there is considerable evidence on the American side (which one can take as being dispassionate) that British intelligence on Africa was not merely good, but well directed in the late sixties. Released CIA classified papers confirm this statement.

Oldfield was never one to rely solely on reports from his own agents. He was always anxious to check such reports by paying attention to independent and disinterested witnesses in whatever part of the globe was concerned. The Right

Reverend Kenneth Skelton, former Bishop of Lichfield, testifies that 'when I was Bishop of Matabeleland in the 1960s, especially after UDI in 1965, I was able to feed various bits of information to Maurice via his sister in Over Haddon, and it was this which really began our friendship.'[7]

George Wigg's task was not helped by the fact that there had been two such totally different heads of the Foreign Office under Wilson as George Brown and Michael Stewart. The former was the man the Foreign Office loved to hate, the latter the man they gratefully accepted as one they could mould. The ebullient George Brown, one of the most forthright rooters-out of crypto-communists, had been almost the first senior Labour politician to do something about checking the infiltration of the party by the extreme Left in all its forms from crypto-communism to Militant Tendency. In the early days of the Macmillan government he felt he ought to be able to discuss this problem with MI 5. His request was rebuffed by none less than Macmillan himself, who, presumably, did not wish to be labelled as a collaborator of witch-hunters. There can, of course, be no doubt that Macmillan was absolutely right in making this decision.

When he became Foreign Secretary Brown again wanted to involve himself personally in the affairs of MI 6. He was promptly informed that this was not a prerogative of any Foreign Secretary, but he declined to take no for an answer and insisted on visiting Century House. As one MI 6 man puts it: 'George Brown had convinced himself that we were all caricature public school figures who couldn't get any job except in the Secret Service. We were Woosterish clubmen in his eyes and incapable of telling a communist from a Benedictine monk. Alas, if only he had known we were probably his loyalest allies, and some in the Foreign Office his biggest enemies. George had the right ideas about cleaning up that stinking Foreign Office, but the wrong ideas about us.'

No doubt Oldfield would instinctively feel he had to tread very carefully with George Brown. An unfortunate lack of communication meant that though Brown then represented a

Derbyshire constituency, and through this link they might have had much to talk about, he found Oldfield offputtingly donnish and severe. This was one of those most extraordinary examples of equals finding themselves unequal and a powerful factor in delaying Oldfield's promotion.

There was, however, one other minor factor. In 1968 Kim Philby's autobiography, *My Silent War*, was published in the USA, and his references to Oldfield made it quite clear that the latter was high up in MI 6. When Sir Dick White retired from the office of 'C', all overseas newspapers and magazines were naturally watching closely whether Oldfield would be appointed. It was then that the decision was taken, partly due to Foreign Office influence, that one of their own favoured people should become the new chief of MI 6. Thus it was that Sir John Rennie was chosen.

Certainly Sir John's appointment was intended to bring MI 6 more under the control of the Foreign Office. There was some suspicion that this was partly due to disagreements caused by the Nigerian-Biafran war in which the Foreign Office, then headed by Michael Stewart, showed a marked bias towards Nigeria. Rennie was originally a painter who had found early recognition of his talents in the Royal Academy and the Paris Salon. His first post on leaving Oxford was with the US advertising agency of Kenyon and Eckhart, of New York. On the outbreak of war in 1939 he was recruited into the British Government's information services in the USA, working first in Baltimore and then in New York. During this period he taught himself something of the up-and-coming subject of electronics, which much later he listed as one of his hobbies in *Who's Who.* Returning to London after a spell in the British Embassy in Washington, he took up a post in the Information Policy Department of the Foreign Office before moving to Warsaw in 1951. Two years later he was made head of the Information Research Department of the Foreign Office.

This department had been set up in 1949 on the suggestion of Mr Christopher Mayhew, then a junior Foreign Office minister to Ernest Bevin, and was designed to provide factual accounts of world-wide communist infiltration and subversion. The material disseminated, while being totally anonymous and not bearing any Foreign Office imprint, was not propagandist in style. IRD worked on a basis of mutual trust between the department and the recipients of its service. Much of its raw material came from Soviet bloc sources and their government-controlled press which IRD brought to the attention of the non-communist world. The department was closed in 1977, but this was kept secret until January 1978, when inspired stories announced its end with malicious glee, suggesting quite wrongly that IRD 'covertly planted material in Britain' and that 'anti-Stalinist material was infiltrated into trade union literature'. There was also the snide comment that Guy Burgess had worked in IRD.[8] Burgess was sacked after a month or two in the Department, while IRD lasted for nearly thirty years. During this period the essentially factual information which IRD purveyed was probably respected more than any other source of intelligence on the communist world produced by any other Western nation.

After five years at the head of IRD Rennie was posted first to Buenos Aires, then Washington. In October 1966 he was promoted to Deputy Under-Secretary with responsibilities for Defence matters, involving the chairmanship of a number of Cabinet committees. He became a vital link between the Foreign Office and the Ministry of Defence. The offer of the post of 'C' in 1968 probably came as just as big a surprise to Rennie as to many members of MI 6. In the obituary of Sir John Rennie in *The Times* it has been stated without any qualification that 'the top post in the Secret Intelligence Service became vacant. No suitable candidate was at that time available from within the Service.'[9]

This was very far from true. Oldfield had been a very obvious candidate for the post, not merely because he was Sir Dick White's deputy, but on account of his lengthy experience in both intelligence and counter-intelligence and especially for his sterling work in Washington. Rennie may have been an excellent Foreign Office servant, but he lacked many of the essential qualifications for the post of 'C'. His experience of intelligence was limited in that it was largely in the field of analysis, he was himself somewhat of a withdrawn character and did not easily commend himself to his new staff, and it was soon apparent that he was not particularly happy in his post. As somebody once commented on Rennie: 'Some slick politicians or FO type must have said, "ah, yes, Rennie, his hobby is electronics. Just the man for chief of the SIS in this technological age, what?" ' But, as he soon found out, electronics do not qualify one for making decisions. And in the field of decision-making Rennie was disastrously slow to act, always looking over his shoulder and far too apt to seek unworkable compromises.

One might have expected a Labour government to look upon Maurice Oldfield as an ideal 'new broom' for the SIS, a grammar school boy rather than from the public schools, a member of the Athenaeum rather than White's, a real professional rather than an officer in the Services. Yet just as George Brown had found Oldfield severe and donnish, so Michael Stewart also rejected him. The second Labour government of the Wilson era had allowed itself to be drawn markedly under Foreign Office permanent staff influence. Possibly, if George Brown had remained Foreign Secretary and had got to know Oldfield rather better, the story would have been very different. But the Foreign Office as a whole was intent on avoiding another strong man at the helm, and they took full advantage of Michael Stewart's tenure of office in strengthening their grip on the politicians and ensuring that their own ideas were put into action.

In this period Oldfield unostentatiously, but conscientiously, played a part in the life of St Matthew's Church, Westminster. Prebendary Gerard Irvine, the present vicar, came to the church in the late sixties: 'it was mainly a working-class congregation and Oldfield stood out as someone quite different, though he got along with his fellow parishioners quite marvellously. He made friends, helped people to get jobs and was entirely natural with them. He was a regular worshipper and occasionally he went on retreats, but it was the manner in which he was always

152

willing to help and advise any member of the congregation which was so very typical of his practical Christianity.

'He not only went out of his way to find work for some of the younger members of the congregation, but he generously paid for a number of the poorer members of the parish to go on pilgrimages to the Shrine of Our Lady at Walsingham. He was also a member of the Parochial Church Council. He did not speak much at these meetings, but when he did, it was very much to the point. I remember one Parochial Church Council conference at Woking when he was the life and soul of the party.'[10]

Though normally Oldfield always spent Christmas with his family up in Derbyshire, his work sometimes included duty in London at this time of the year. On these occasions he spent a few Christmases with Prebendary Irvine and his wife.

Oldfield always sat at the back of the church for security reasons. Later on, in the seventies, he was accompanied by plain clothes detectives because of various threats to his life by the IRA and other terrorist organizations. Another occasional worshipper at St Matthew's was the late Lord Bradwell, better known as Tom Driberg, MP. Sometimes Oldfield and Driberg met and talked at the vicarage, occasions upon which the vicar was probably more worried than Oldfield. For while Driberg was a devout High Church Anglican, and an informant for MI5, he was also a promiscuous homosexual, a former member of the Communist Party and a friend of Guy Burgess as well as a suspected informant to the KGB. Oldfield made a point of never being alone with Driberg and always having a witness to their conversation. 'It was never an easy situation for me,' he told a colleague, 'and it was odd that of all churches open to him Driberg should choose St Matthew's so frequently. It was even more difficult because, professionally speaking, I should like to have questioned him relentlessly. Yet, here we were on church premises, and how could I be uncharitable in the light of his own quite remarkable devotion to the Church. I still think he owed more to Conrad Noel than the doctrines of communism.'[11]

In all this time Oldfield did not hesitate to give his addresses and telephone numbers to *Who's Who*. In the 1970 edition his address at Chandos Court, Caxton Street, SW 1, was given together with the telephone numbers both for London and Over Haddon. The same applied when he moved to Marsham Court, Great Marsham Street, where he had a flat above Locket's Restaurant, which has always been popular with MPs owing not only to its proximity to the Houses of Parliament, but because it is even supplied with a division bell. Oldfield would sometimes have meals sent up to his flat from the restaurant, though ocasionally he would dine in Locket's. One of his companions on such occasions would be Sir Max Aitken, Lord Beaverbrook's son.

The flat in Marsham Court was somewhat larger than that at Chandos Court. It was very much a bachelor's flat and its furnishing was as modest as the man himself. Oldfield was not one to place great value on personal possessions, or the acquisition of antiques. His furniture was generally utilitarian and precedence was always given to his collection of books and (much later, after he became 'C') to the Jak cartoons featuring him in the *Evening Standard*, which he avidly collected. These were framed and displayed on the walls. One photograph had pride of place – that of his father carrying a milk-pail. There were also a few pictures of Malayan scenes.

For some time in the sixties concern existed in American and British intelligence circles that the situation in Libya was rapidly developing into a threat to the Western world. The CIA had already discovered that the Egyptians were secretly financing Malcolm 'X', while as early as March 1964 a warning had been given to the State Department that the Libyan situation was extremely dangerous and that President Nasser aimed to overthrow the Libyan monarchy and annexe the country to Egypt, thus bringing in its oil revenues to solve Egypt's economic problems. But ultimately it was Colonel Muamar Gaddafi who seized power from the aged King Idris of Libya, having modelled his political philosophy on that of President Nasser.

Under the Senoussi rule relations between Britain and

Libya had been extremely good, dating back to the era of British military government of that country when the Italians and Germans were finally expelled from the area. It made sense to win back Libya to the Western side, especially as every testimony from intelligence sources in Egypt showed up Nasser for the scheming, unscrupulous scoundrel that he was and not the master statesman that some of his bemused admirers in the Foreign Office and in political circles thought.

Not unnaturally some thought there was scope for a clandestine operation which would put a member of the Senoussi family back on the throne of Libya. This was very much a view of some in MI 6 and others outside it who had had experience of independent, commando-style operations in the Yemen and elsewhere. Unfortunately at this stage there was unsufficient chance of cooperation with the Americans who had taken far too literally the idea that any fanatical Moslem must be anti-Marxist. This was, of course, a total misreading of any fanatical sect which will inevitably support anyone, however evil, as long as they agree to be allies.

In the Rennie era at Century House a somewhat hypocritical policy was adopted which, like all such policies, was doomed to failure. The plan was to encourage independent mercenaries to do some of the dirty work which MI 6 was not prepared to do, and then, of course, if such assignments failed, to deny all knowledge of the matter. Thus an independent plan was submitted by a Libyan loyal to the Senoussi to Colonel David Stirling, one of the most spectacular and outstanding leaders of the wartime SAS. The proposal was that a team of British volunteers should be landed on a Libyan beach, driven to a prison where some hundred or more political prisoners were held, rescue them and pave the way to a restoration of the monarchy. One recommendation for the scheme was that most of the personnel would be former French SAS men, or mercenaries of other nations.

Undoubtedly the project had a chance to succeed, but probably only if there could have been Anglo-American agreement to it. All such clandestine schemes require arms and in this instance the arms had to be obtained from foreign sources. They were ordered from a firm known as Aramisco in Vienna. The purchase included machine guns, hand grenades, anti-tank grenade launchers, a quantity of ammunition, shells, blasting fuse, plastic explosive plus detonators and a blasting machine and electric detonators and incendiary grenades. The transit agents for Aramisco in Vienna were Omnipol, Prague, and a letter dated 10 May 1971 from a company in Yugoslavia handling the shipment stated that these arms were purchased in January of that year by one of the former long range desert free lance operators (code-named CHARLES II) from the Czech state-owned arms combine Omnipol in Prague. It was further confirmed that the arms were flown to Yugoslavia from Prague and stored under Yugoslav Government Transit Permission No. 3351 2/88765/4.1871.[12]

To obtain arms from a Soviet satellite source and then route them via Yugoslavia for collection was taking a great risk from a security viewpoint, but this hazard was increased by the fact that the arms were to be dispatched from Yugoslavia via Duala in the Cameroons to Chad, which had a common frontier with Libya. Unfortunately Colonel Stirling, who ought to have masterminded the project, was ill at the time and the job went to a former SIS man. The Colonel, with his experience in the Long Range Desert Group, would surely have found ways to avert such obvious dangers.

Belatedly the SIS warned that the operation should be called off, well aware that from a security angle it was well nigh doomed. But the warning came too late. One of the vessels embarking on the attempt was arrested by the Italians in Trieste, while two other craft were wrecked off the North African coast. This unfortunate chapter of accidents in which MI 6 had but a watching brief is perhaps a permanent reminder of the need for more ambitious, professionally controlled planning for any such operations in future. The Mossad is perhaps the only secret service in the world which could have brought off such a coup on its own initiative. But with Anglo-American cooperation a restoration of the Senoussi to the Libyan throne might have succeeded.

On one occasion when he was deputy to 'C' Oldfield was somewhat perturbed by a message which came over on telex hinting at some form of dubious tricks by an agent during the Bangladesh crisis, ending with the comment 'the sods are at it again'. Feeling that this sort of language, and especially any suggestion of trickery, was hardly the kind of thing he wanted the female staff at Century House to read, he sent a reprimand through his personal assistant. Ten minutes later back came a laconic reply to the effect that the sentiments of any female staff in London should hardly be influenced one way or another, as there was no SIS station at the place the message was being sent from and the actual message was sent by one female on behalf of others. 'For once,' said Maurice, chuckling over the story afterwards, 'I was unable to answer back.'

His sense of humour could be both self-indulgent and puckish. Mr Jeffery Ede, of the Public Record Office, remembers a party which he gave in the garden of the Chancery Lane offices of the PRO when he introduced Maurice 'to my medievalist colleague, R.F. Hunnisett. The latter asked Maurice what he did and got the disarmingly frank reply that he was the head of MI 5! This was before he became head of MI 6.'[13]

But there were a number of frustrations at Century House during the Rennie regime. When Edward Heath became Prime Minister there was pressure on the SIS through some in the Foreign Office for MI 6 to keep what was technically called 'a watching brief' in Northern Ireland. Oldfield was very doubtful from the beginning about the wisdom of this, feeling sure (and he was right) that a watching brief would soon be turned into something much more active. He took the view, quite correctly according to precedent, that the SIS traditionally only operated in foreign territory and that Northern Ireland was part of the United Kingdom where the operatives should be MI 5 and not MI 6. But the Prime Minister did not agree with this view and Sir John Rennie acquiesced with the call for MI 6 to intervene in Ulster.

Of course, inside the Republic of Ireland MI 6 had been active to a limited extent for some years, though even in this sphere Oldfield was none too happy about some of these activities. He felt that there had been crass stupidity and carelessness in the choice of some intelligence agents in this field. He feared that one day MI 6 could be held up to ridicule because of this tendency – 'the idea that you can trap the IRA with a criminal buffoon is one of the wilder fantasies this side of the Irish Sea,' was how he put it. Much later these fears were to be fully justified.

Rennie had agreed to the appointment of an SIS chief of station in Northern Ireland early in 1971. The real purpose behind the SIS setting themselves up in Ulster was not so much to aid MI 6 as a feeling by some in the Foreign Office that this was a field in which they could usefully operate. There were various views as to exactly what that usefulness could be, but behind this thinking was the idea, admittedly vague, sometimes even incoherent, that perhaps the Foreign Office, acting in concert with the Republic of Ireland, could solve Ulster's problems rather better than the politicians, the army or the police. Some inside the Foreign Office went further than this and visualized that ultimately there could be an Anglo-American-Irish approach to the Ulster question, resulting in a United Ireland which would become a full member of NATO. An ambitious and airy-fairy dream by any standards, but one which needed to be kept quiet because inevitably it would involve granting independence against the wishes of a majority of the population.

However, the tendency to encourage SIS activity in Northern Ireland also dated back to the previous Wilson government, as Wilson, mistrusting MI 5, liked to have his own lines open to Ulster via MI 6. So for quite a long time there had been an MI 6 man seconded to the Northern Ireland Office to look after and coordinate intelligence. But from 1970 onwards more SIS personnel were brought into the province. According to the *Irish Times*, 'MI 6 officers have usually come to the North as civil servants, though some have also been known to pose as insurance officials, post office personnel and journalists, among other disguises.'[14] This same report added that 'MI 6 officers sometimes operate under diplomatic cover from the British Embassy in Dublin, although they have appeared in other guises. Their main concern is to monitor Provisional IRA activities and to report on the Irish Government's political and security policies, although the size of the USSR's Dublin Embassy also occupies their attention.'

Thus from the early seventies there had been a procession of SIS men to Belfast, nearly all of them not only having the status of diplomats, but being regarded as sound FCO types. Curiously, few of these had had much European experience; most were from the Far East or Moslem countries, and much the same applied to MI 6 men inside the Republic of Ireland. Yet another reason for the SIS presence in Ulster was said to be the need to monitor Soviet and other foreign terrorist organizations' interests in the province. But, as Oldfield pointed out, this was very much a job for MI 5. What actually happened was that relations between MI 5 and MI 6 deteriorated markedly inside Northern Ireland and resulted in the early seventies in some unforgivable mix-ups. In some instances these became the cause of killings rather than their prevention.

Throughout 1970 and the earlier part of 1971 there had been a steady flow of intelligence from overseas of Soviet attempts to step up subversive tactics in Britain. During 1970 Scotland Yard prepared a warning for all British Members of Parliament about a widespread KGB plot to compromise and blackmail them, more especially those with left-wing views. Oldfield felt very strongly that this warning should have been passed on to families of British Servicemen with NATO troops in Germany. Apparently no action had been taken in this direction, but Oldfield became worried when intelligence came back to him that the East Germans had obtained a remarkably accurate 'order of battle' for British troops stationed along the East German border. As a result of an alert going out from the SIS in London an East German secret agent, one Rolf Dreesen, was arrested after having delivered detailed information on British troop movements along the East-West German border over the previous six years. He had been running three hotels in the Harz mountains where holiday guests included British Service families from the Rhine Army.

It was a long time before the SIS could bring pressure to bear on government action against the increase in Soviet espionage and subversion in Britain. But eventually, when Heath came to power and Sir Alec Douglas Home was at the Foreign Office, Rennie, backed by Oldfield and Sir Denis Greenhill, (now Lord Greenhill of Harrow) at the Foreign Office, a positive move was belatedly made. One hundred and five Russian diplomats and officials working in London were ordered to return home.

Chief Of The SIS

Oldfield's ultimate appointment as 'C' could not have occurred in more inauspicious circumstances. What precipitated the announcement in February 1973 that Sir John Rennie would be retiring before his sixtieth birthday – an unprecedented story to appear in the press – was the fact that the Hamburg magazine, *Stern*, had disclosed his identity in reporting that his son and daughter-in-law had been sent for trial at the Old Bailey, accused of possessing Chinese heroin. Until then British newspaper reports of the hearings of this case had not revealed the names of the defendants because the identity of the father was covered by a D-Notice.

Thus it was that when Oldfield became chief of MI 6, this news was revealed in the home as well as the overseas press. To some extent the delay in giving him the job was as much to blame as anything else for all this publicity. For years he had so clearly been the man who should have had the post and of course his identity had been blown by Philby. The *New York Times* had hinted at Oldfield as the probable new head of MI 6 in February 1973, as soon as it was known that Rennie was to retire.

When Oldfield was actually appointed to the post his name was covered by a D-notice. The journalist and author

Chapman Pincher got round this by drawing attention to the remarkable similarities between the nameless chief and the then Prime Minister, Edward Heath. Both were bachelors of the same age who had reached the top from humble origins. Both had won scholarships to universities and served in the army in World War Two, reaching the rank of lieutenant-colonel. He added that both were 'inclined to over-weight and, incredibly, both were organists.' No name was mentioned, but the meaning was clear to the initiated.[1]

It was *Stern* once again which ultimately published the real identity of the new 'C', closely followed by the American press. Oldfield was always convinced that the story was planted on *Stern* by someone in Britain who was anxious to reveal the truth. But there is little doubt that one way or another the story was bound to be published within weeks of his appointment. When I was researching my history of the Chinese Secret Service, one of my Chinese informants told me 'for a long time we have been watching Oldfield's career with interest. We know he has been a specialist on South-East Asia and we have been noting every move he has made since the late fifties.'[2]

In August 1973, the London *Evening Standard* actually published a full-page photograph of Oldfield, naming him as head of MI 6. On 6 August Mr Marcus Lipton, Labour MP for Brixton, put down a question to the Prime Minister asking him to withdraw the D-notice which prevented British newspapers from disclosing the identities of Secret Service heads. Mr Lipton said: 'This sort of mumbo jumbo is a waste of time because every foreign embassy in London knows who the head of the Secret Service is from the moment he is appointed. So what is the point of stifling the press? I certainly see no point in issuing a D-notice after his name has been published. We know who the head of the security service is in other countries, so why should we be the only country in the world to maintain this façade of keeping his name secret?'[3]

This statement was made at the very moment that the Foreign Office was insisting that 'Mr Oldfield is employed on extra-departmental duties' – surely a phrase worthy of the TV programme *Yes, Minister.*

There is no denying that Oldfield was Edward Heath's personal choice, and that in those first months of their association the two men got on together extremely well. Doubtless their mutual interest in music was a great help in establishing a rapport. But perhaps the Prime Minister's principal interest in the SIS at that juncture was whether they could help him with economic and political intelligence relating to Britain's membership of the European Economic Community which had come into effect in January 1973. The need for this was something which Oldfield had fully appreciated and even anticipated in the period in which he was deputy to 'C'. This was very much a new field of inquiry for the SIS and Oldfield warned that it might well take years rather than months to get full value from such intelligence-gathering.

While serving in the Far East Oldfield had been enormously impressed by the way in which the Japanese Intelligence Services had given intelligence-gathering a new meaning. What they had achieved since World War Two was to concentrate not merely on obtaining intelligence which would make them a more prosperous nation, but also improve the quality of their life. By keeping pace with all such developments in other parts of the world and then soaring ahead of other nations by exploiting their intelligence-gathering more effectively, the Japanese had made themselves a world power. As Oldfield occasionally told colleagues who were often lamentably unimpressed by his theories on this subject, 'whereas we only have one "think tank", and that largely made up of part-timers, the Japanese have twenty or thirty. That is why they succeed.'

'Somewhat soulless and lacking in mystery – at least compared with those rambling old offices in Broadway' was how the new 'C' smilingly commented on the new MI 6 headquarters in the twenty-storey monolith which was Century House, just across the Thames from Westminster Bridge. Its official title was Government Communications Bureau, and in 'C's' office hung a framed copy of George Washington's instructions to General Elias Dayton, made on

26 July 1777: 'The necessity of procuring good intelligence is apparent and need not be further urged. All that remains for me to add is that you keep the whole matter as secret as possible. For upon Secrecy, success depends in most enterprises of the kind, and for want of it, they are generally defeated, however well planned and promising a favourable issue.'

There was considerable satisfaction in the SIS at Oldfield's appointment. Though sometimes giving the impression of being shy and enigmatic when in his office, he was extremely popular with his staff who had feared that he might once again have been overlooked when it came to choosing a successor to Sir John Rennie. It had been said that his main strength was as a counter-intelligence officer rather than an active procurer of information. This is rather a distorted assessment of the man. True, he made his name as a counter-intelligence officer, but it would be nearer the mark to say that he used those talents in the pursuit of information and, more especially, the analysis of its worth. If Sir Stewart Menzies had had similar qualities, he might have made a more effective chief, aware of the dangers of his ranks being infiltrated.

Under Oldfield MI 6 gradually became rather better organized and more selective in its field operations and the type of intelligence it sought. He was a glutton for work and, as 'C', he lived on his nerves just as much as he had in the past, frequently chain-smoking as he did so. If he had a fault, it was perhaps that he took on a great deal of additional work himself that he should have delegated to others. This was not so much that he found it difficult to delegate, or that he mistrusted people, but that he was ultra-conscientious and in his own way found it easier to tackle things himself than pass them on to others. Undeniably, too, his mind reacted much more quickly than those of some of his colleagues, thus making it seem to himself that he could get a particular job done on his own much more quickly. He was fully conscious of the limitations of some of his subordinates and, though privately critical of them, preferred not to have confrontations.

His tendency to take on extra work himself rather than to

delegate it led to his travelling around more than was usual for a chief of the Service. When close colleagues commented on this, he would smile quietly and say 'It keeps me in touch. I learn a lot more than I should otherwise.'

Not that he would ever reveal what else he learned. When there was a need for discretion, or if awkward questions were being asked, whether in conversation with one other person, or at a party or reception, the new 'C' was extremely adroit at being discreet without causing any embarrassing silences or moments. His tactics would be immediately to launch out with a number of stories. 'He was very good at putting people off the scent,' said a colleague. 'And he had an enormous fund of stories. It was not always easy to remember them because I have always believed that, certainly when on duty as it were, Maurice's aim was to talk in such a way that nobody would remember exactly what he had said.

'I do remember, however, that once at a party a rather probing ambassador of another nation was commenting on how Maurice managed to travel around. It could have been rather a tricky situation as the ambassador was obviously fishing for information, maybe anxious to see if he could conjure some gem of intelligence out of Maurice. "What sort of things do you find out on your travels?" was the ambassador's question, half banteringly, but partly serious.

' "Well, last week," replied Maurice, "I had quite an interesting experience in one foreign capital. It was a Saturday night and I wanted to attend Holy Communion next day, so I mentioned the fact to our ambassador, adding that presumably the embassy chapel would be open. I was somewhat surprised when he said that the chapel had been closed down for some years.

' "Well, where is the nearest Anglican church?" inquired Maurice. To which the British ambassador in question replied that it was some forty miles away. Maurice indicated that he would like to go to it. The ambassador, obviously put out at this request, tried to persuade his guest to forget all about Holy Communion: surely it could wait for another week in the circumstances? But Maurice was adamant.

'And so, at five-thirty the next morning, the ambassador and Maurice were respectively woken up with cups of tea, then they piled into a car and drove off to the distant church. When they got there Maurice said to the ambassador: "Won't you come in, too?" "Thanks, but I'd prefer to wait in the car," was the somewhat stiff response. Maurice thought the situation was very amusing, but I dare say the ambassador took a very different view.

'Anyhow, the point is that this is the kind of story Maurice would tell when he wanted to draw somebody off the scent. Note that he pointedly told the story about one ambassador to another. An oblique but polite warning? Perhaps. Having told his story, Maurice would pass on to someone else at the party.'

At the time of Oldfield's appointment as head of MI 6 there were muted criticisms in some quarters that the SIS had to get permission from the Foreign Office for almost everything they tackled. It was never quite as bad as that, though under Sir John Rennie the situation had tended to get that way. Oldfield knew exactly when to refer, and when not to refer, when to accept a Foreign Office decision and when to argue his own case and plead for a reversal of that decision. In the early days of his new office Oldfield regularly saw Sir Thomas Brimelow, then Permanent Under Secretary at the FCO. Later he had to make a similar relationship with Sir Michael Palliser. But there was a mutual respect between Permanent Under Secretaries and Oldfield in that each treated the other as a professional. Sir Thomas Brimelow (now Lord Brimelow) and Oldfield were both committee members of the Athenaeum Club. Maurice was affectionately known behind his back as 'Moulders' at the Foreign Office.

Some of his critics both inside and outside the Secret Service asserted – quite unfairly as far as one can judge – that Oldfield was not ruthless enough, that he tended to discourage covert projects of what were known as the 'special operations' type. His wide experience both in the field of counter-intelligence and intelligence-gathering and especially in the United States had convinced him that many dubious field operations could boomerang against the Service which planned them. He was always adamant that it was vitally important for any Intelligence chief to ensure that those under him did not at any time confuse the collection of intelligence with any operations which involved sabotage or assassination. No intelligence service could possibly hope to be respected if it descended to these levels except, of course, in wartime, and he stressed that this rule should apply as much to the intelligence services of the democracies as to those of communist and totalitarian states.

'Once you start on that path, there is no end to it,' he would explain. 'You start something that never goes away. I am not saying that a special operation is not sometimes necessary and that lives may be lost as a result – the rescue of a colleague might justify it, or even the rescue of a defector. But even then there are risks. But the real tragedy is when special operations as they are called become a way of life, and then they escalate and are often staged when it is quite unnecessary. Surely the Watergate scandals taught us that.'

It was his fears about the misuse of special operations by the SIS in Northern Ireland which caused Oldfield to oppose the extension of MI 6 activities in Ulster, leading to the first major disagreement with Downing Street, reiterating that this was work which MI 5 should do. Behind these fears lay some hard-headed commonsense reasoning. Though he did not openly express such an opinion, Oldfield was privately convinced that one of the great strengths of the SIS was its relative freedom from political control. More recently he had been well aware of the dangers of a much greater degree of Foreign Office control, but his real fear was that any excesses in the field of special operations and the publicizing of blunders accruing from these could lead to tighter political control of the Service, as well as giving it a bad image in the media. Those results, he was convinced, would lead to a lowering of morale inside the Service and a decline in efficiency. What was happening across the Atlantic Ocean regarding the washing of the CIA's dirty linen in public only strengthened that belief.

That Oldfield was absolutely right in his assessment of

these dangers was proved shortly after he became 'C'. Two brothers, Kenneth and Keith Littlejohn, raided the Allied Irish Bank's premises in Grafton Street, Dublin. They left fingerprints and an incriminating address in the back of their getaway car. Arrested in England, proceedings for their extradition to Ireland were held in secret, with the Attorney General referring to 'matters which might imperil national security'. The brothers' appeal against extradition was also held in secret. Meanwhile the Littlejohns had created a furore both in Ireland and the United Kingdom by alleging that they had been employed by MI 6 to rob banks and carry out assassinations in the Irish Republic.

Oldfield had never given any of his agents a 'licence to kill' and killing, except in self-defence, had been officially barred in the Secret Service for some years. It is true that the adverb 'officially' might cover up some actions about which the SIS hierarchy would pretend to know nothing, but on the whole the ruling had been kept. Oldfield was rightly furious at the damage which the Littlejohn brothers' allegations might do to the Service, and he acted instantly. By nature he was opposed to anything like the gangster tactics which had been attributed to the Service, and he lost no time in calling the staff into the canteen at the top of Century House and denying the allegations. In addition he gave his solemn personal assurance that there was no truth in the stories.

Maybe not, but there was an unfortunate link between the brothers and the Secret Service. Though the Littlejohns had not been given guns and explosives as they claimed, nor ordered to carry out the tasks they alleged, they had been interviewed by an MI 6 man after volunteering to help against the IRA. Eventually even the Ministry of Defence had to admit that Kenneth Littlejohn had been 'put in touch with the appropriate authorities' and had been told that, if he had information about the IRA, the British Government 'was prepared to receive it'.

Littlejohn had insisted that the bank raid was authorized by his MI 6 controller known by the code name of 'OLIVER' and that it had been carried out in an attempt to discredit the IRA.

While it was always Oldfield's aim to make sure that a

permanent precedent was not set up by the opening of the MI 6 station in Northern Ireland, he decided that much greater care should be taken in the selection of personnel sent there in future. Up to 1973 the value of the MI 6 station could be questioned, though this was due as much to political ineptness in the direction of Ulster's affairs as to failure on the part of the SIS. The appointment of William Whitelaw as Secretary of State for Northern Ireland had not helped what little progress the SIS had been making not merely in the north, but in the Republic, too. For Whitelaw had turned himself into a kind of supremo on both security and intelligence in Ulster – not at all the role for a politician who hopes to succeed – and he had opened up contacts with the IRA.

From then on there was appeasement on the political side and, not unnaturally, a drying-up of intelligence for the SIS. The IRA, as was only to be expected, took Whitelaw for a long and bumpy ride when he accepted their cease-fire proposal. Just as Oldfield was ensuring that his men in Ulster were not just professionals, but skilled in the interpretation of political intelligence, the flow of information which MI 6 had been getting from Catholics and IRA alike more or less dried up. Temporarily, too, there was less cooperation with G-2, the Irish Republican Intelligence Service. Everyone was waiting to see what Whitelaw did next and wary of being compromised by speaking out of turn. Not surprisingly, by February 1973 there was once again widespread violence in the province and Whitelaw had succeeded in alienating the Protestants as well.

All this was bad enough, but when the affair of the Littlejohn brothers embarrassed the British Secret Service, Oldfield had much more to worry about. As deputy to Rennie he had occasionally expressed doubts as to the lack of control which 'C' had over the innumerable sub-agents, or 'cut-out' men, employed by SIS officers. He felt that the care and trouble taken in vetting, screening and double-checking new SIS entrants could be wasted if they, in turn, were to be allowed too much freedom in setting up sub-agents without similar close screening being carried out.

But now, with the Littlejohn case throwing a most undesirable spotlight on the Secret Service, Oldfield decided that some swift check on the employment of sub-agents and 'cut-out' men was necessary. It was a view which the Foreign Office shared. What he learned from this inquiry was far from reassuring: too many people had been casually recruited as part-time, or potential informants to the SIS – often the very type who would be the first to betray MI 6's vital rule that, when one was discovered by the opposition, one kept quiet. One such was Howard Marks, an ex-grammar school boy who had won a scholarship to Balliol College, Oxford.

One of Marks' Oxford friends had been Norman Hamilton McMillan, who had joined the FCO in 1968 and later been appointed Second Secretary in Vienna. When it became known that Marks had struck up an acquaintanceship in Amsterdam with James McCann, a gun-runner and arms smuggler for the PIRA, McMillan was sent out to establish contact with his old friend. This was in December 1972, at a time when MI 6 were anxious to obtain the maximum intelligence on the PIRA's arms-running links with the continent. Another subject in which the SIS was also interested was that of drug-smuggling as so often this was associated with clandestine traffic in arms. The outcome was that Marks was asked to report back on all McCann's activities and contacts whether in the field of arms or drugs. He agreed to do this.

There was some evidence that Marks had subsequently provided MI 6 with intelligence on the smuggling of both arms and drugs into Ireland, mainly through sources in Holland. But, when making inquiries into the use of sub-agents after the unwelcome publicity caused by the Littlejohn case, Oldfield was horrified to discover that there had been a tendency to use informants indiscriminately and without fully weighing up the risks involved. There was the case of a female SIS operative who had employed three of her lovers as informants, one of whom was a member of the Italian Communist Party. What was really frightening was that each of them had been told where their information was going and none of them had been vetted. Fortunately no real damage had been done. 'He handled the lady in question with superb aplomb,' says one of his colleagues. 'He just made a quick trip to the continent, chatted to her over several drinks, wagged a finger more humorously than angrily and managed to spare her from any disciplinary action while snuffing out the sources of potential trouble.'

But with Howard Marks it was different. It did not take long to discover that psychologically he was totally unfitted for the role the SIS had given him. In other words he was the type of informant who could not resist the temptation to work for both sides. A check revealed that his relationship with McCann often worked as much in McCann's favour as that of MI 6. An order went out to keep Marks at a distance. In August 1973, Marks was ordered to return to London from Amsterdam and told to make any future contact only through a third party.

But the attempt to disentangle MI 6 from Marks was not successful in the long run. On 16 November 1973 he was detained by the Dutch police and later returned to Britain voluntarily, to be charged with a drug offence. This was to prove just as serious an embarrassment to the SIS as the affair of the Littlejohn brothers, though this was a political time bomb which did not explode until long after Oldfield had left the Service. In March 1974, the Littlejohn brothers broke out of Mountjoy Prison in Dublin and made further statements about their alleged service for MI 6. The following month Marks mysteriously disappeared from his Oxford apartment, later claiming that he had been kidnapped.

For seven years Marks was on the run, travelling on forged passports supplied by his associates. In May 1980 he was once again arrested by customs officers who found him in the Swan Hotel, Lavenham, Suffolk. Charged with both drugs and passport offences, at his trial at the Old Bailey he insisted that he had been recruited by MI 6 and that McMillan had told him 'it would be a good idea' to use the Amsterdam boutique, Annabelinda, which he had set up with his girlfriend as a branch of a similar boutique in

Oxford, as a 'front' for obtaining information on McCann and the PIRA gun-running operations in Holland. Lord Hutchinson, QC, representing Marks, said he was 'in reality a spy who had been left out in the cold by British Intelligence. He had been told: "You are on your own, old boy!" That was the way of the Secret Service.'[4]

Marks claimed in court that his information had led to McCann's arrest in Vancouver where he prevented an extradition attempt, but there is no confirmation of this claim. The trial ended with Marks being acquitted on a drugs charge, but found guilty of making false passport applications.

Oldfield was not helped in his dealings with the British government on Northern Ireland because there was no proper coordination of intelligence in that province. In theory the presence of an MI 6 station should have ensured this. But there was nobody to guarantee that the intelligence gleaned by the SIS, the army and the police respectively was comprehensively analysed and interpreted. Those intelligence operations conducted by the army had been neither imaginative, nor particularly successful. Only when the SAS sent a squadron to Ulster in 1974 did any real improvement occur.

Collaboration between the Foreign Office and the SIS regarding Northern Ireland was greatly strengthened after Oldfield became 'C'. This provided a London-Dublin-Belfast link which possibly gave the Foreign Office a better overall view of the situation in Northern Ireland than that of the Northern Ireland Office in Belfast. On the other hand what was happening was what Oldfield had always feared: some of those in the IRA and Republican-minded ranks who had kept in unofficial touch with British representatives were not prepared to do so since the SIS set up a station in Belfast. This may not seem to make sense in the light of the attempts made on the political side to establish contacts with the IRA and its various factions, but then the complexity of the Ulster question rarely does make sense. As one PIRA activist put it: 'In the past we had an informal understanding with some of the Brits. We knew who to trust and who to talk with, and they felt much the same about us. We trusted one another and sometimes it worked. But with Willie Whitelaw having put his clumsy foot in it more than once, and with the Secret Service muscling in, nobody could tell any more what sort of traps they were preparing for us.'

Despite all these hindrances and irritations, MI 6 did score some quiet successes in both north and south, some of which led to a closer understanding between the police forces of Ulster and the Republic. To judge from the comprehensiveness of certain of the Service's intelligence reports on the area, MI 6 had established agents and informants inside the Garda (Irish Republican Police), the Irish Army and some Republic government departments.

Edward Heath gave the impression in some quarters of being unduly nervous about what the SIS might, or might not be doing during his term as Prime Minister. Maybe the Prime Minister was getting some private intelligence which clashed with what he was told by the SIS. Possibly he was a victim of Soviet disinformation. In the latter half of 1970 stories had been put out in various parts of the world that the Russians were planning to achieve dominance in the Indian Ocean. One claimed that they intended to set up a base on the island of Socotra, another that they were seeking a base in Mauritius and special facilities in Singapore. Much time was spent in knocking these fabrications down. In fact almost every one of the rumours was planted by the KGB. But to lend credence to them Russian ships steamed past Singapore while the Commonwealth Prime Ministers' conference was in session there. The other Russian ships arrived off Diego Garcia, an uninhabited British possession in the Indian Ocean. These moves were not made accidentally; they were quite deliberate. A major topic at the Singapore conference was whether Britain should sell arms to South Africa. By showing the Russian flag in the Indian Ocean at this time Russia was in effect bolstering Heath's case for wanting to sell arms to South Africa, despite the bitterness this proposal had aroused among some Commonwealth countries. The Soviet Union hoped Britain would sell arms to South Africa and – as they believed – thus ruin any future relationships with Black Africa.

The SIS insisted that the reports of bases being established in such places as Socotra and some uninhabited islands in the Indian Ocean were erroneous. Until 1967 Socotra had been under British protection, but was then handed over to the Democratic Republic of Yemen. Two years later similar rumours were being bandied around and Oldfield was personally asked to make absolutely sure there were no Russians on the island. 'Nothing but frankincense and myrrh and some date palms on Socotra,' Oldfield duly reported back. 'It made a day out for one of our chaps.' The latter remark was an amused aside to one of his colleagues, not to the Prime Minister.

It was on such occasions as this when Oldfield was able to restore a sense of proportion with a modest joke that he endeared himself to his staff. Though some took the view that he spent too much time agonizing over moral issues and whether or not he was doing the right thing, morale among the rank and file visibly improved during his period of office. It is true that, to the impatience of some of the Young Turks in the Service, he spent a good deal of time weighing up what he believed were important moral issues because he took the standpoint that failure to do so could mean the democratic ideal could not survive.

Eventually Oldfield was able to clear up some of the muddles in Northern Ireland which had been perpetrated in the Rennie era. Late in 1973 and in the early part of 1974 the Special Branch, Military Intelligence and MI 6 were joined by a stronger MI 5 presence in Ulster. Oldfield welcomed the replacing of some of MI 6 by MI 5, as he thought this made sound constitutional sense as well as preventing a lot of mistakes. So at Stormont Castle the MI 6 officer was relieved by Dennis Payne of MI 5, and the intelligence controller at Lisburn, Craig Smellie of MI 6, was replaced by Ian Cameron of MI 5. Unfortunately, though these moves made sense and initially all went smoothly, much later MI 5 also committed blunders in Ulster.

Oldfield had always got on very well with the Israelis and had a high opinion of their intelligence and security services. He regarded both the Mossad and Shin Beth, the Israeli counter-espionage organization, as being among the élite of the world's secret services. Liaison between MI 6 and the Mossad had been excellent and there had been a fair exchange of intelligence between them up to the period when Rennie was made 'C'. The Mossad had more than once tipped off MI 6 about Palestinian and Libyan aid and shipments to the IRA. But Oldfield was somewhat perturbed when he learned that shortly after he took office as 'C' Mossad-British relations were at 'stand-off', as one astute Israeli observer phrased it. His confidence in the Israeli Intelligence Service left him in no doubt on this score, putting the blame quite firmly on political stances by the Heath government.

There have been suggestions that British Intelligence slipped up in failing to predict the impending attack on Israel by the allied Arab countries in what came to be known as the Yom Kippur War. Nothing could be further from the truth. The intelligence was there all the time: it was the political analysts outside MI 6 who neglected to interpret it correctly. Much the same applies to the Americans and the Israelis, though for different reasons. The Americans afterwards complained that NSA reports of 'Egyptian-Syrian war preparations were so voluminous – hundreds of reports each week – that few analysts had time to digest more than a small portion.' The Israelis on the other hand took the quite logical view that, after their defeat in the 1967 war, the Arab countries would be unlikely to launch another attack on Israel unless they had established real military superiority over them. This the Arabs had not done. The Israelis' mistake was that they had forgotten two vital factors: first the Arabs' need to fight a war if only to try to bring in the Western powers as mediators sympathetic to their aspirations, and, secondly, that the Yom Kippur period was an ideal time to launch a surprise attack.

Information from Israeli sources states that when the war broke out in the autumn of 1973, 'we had assessed that cooperation had not been expected from Britain, and, consequently, there were no scores to settle. It wasn't MI 6's fault, but the politicians. Thus when the chips were down, it was Germany, not Britain, who helped most, if only indirectly. Both the United States and Israel had expected that at the very least Britain would cooperate in allowing landing and trans-shipment rights, although, of course, the USA might have placed higher expectations on British assistance. But we understood exactly how Maurice Oldfield, who was on our side, was unable to help as he might have wished.'

Oldfield's personal view was that as relations with the Israeli Intelligence Services were not as good as they might have been, this was a supremely opportune moment to make amends and so restore the special relationship. From that moment on he was opposed to the Heath Government's policy on the Yom Kippur War. It could be argued that a Secret Service chief had no right to be involved in political arguments, but in this particular instance Oldfield had the interests of his own Service to uphold. These interests not only lay in some cooperation with the Israelis, but in the question of SIS's interpretation of the so-called 'oil weapon'.

Oldfield was and always had been 'oil-minded' in his quest for intelligence. This dated back to the time of Mossadegh. But he also reasoned that some of the Western powers had foolishly allowed themselves to be bemused by the 'oil weapon', that when oil was mentioned, they invariably thought of the Middle East and not of all the other sources throughout the world. The whole question of oil supplies had been turned into political blackmail by the OPEC members, yet in truth when OPEC members imposed a ban on supplies to the USA because of the latter's support of Israel in the Yom Kippur War, imports to America were down by only slightly over five per cent.

The Arabists among British civil servants once again helped to influence foreign policy and they, of course, were aided by the fainthearts who always preferred a neutral stance when a small war broke out. On 15 October *The Times* was reporting that 'Britain yesterday was sticking to her embargo on arms deliveries to either side in the conflict, despite protests by British Jews that this policy in practice discriminates against Israel.' Yet at the same time no attempt was being made to prevent the shipment of Scorpion light tanks from Britain to Dubai, one of the member states of the United Arab Emirate.

Egypt had without warning launched war on Israel. Yet the Security Council of the League of Nations had called for an immediate cease-fire 'without apportionment of blame'. While converted Israeli jumbo jets had begun picking up supplies of American rockets and munitions from a US naval airbase in Norfolk, Virginia, Britain had put a stop on the export of all arms to those countries engaged in the Middle East war. Intelligence reports poured in showing how unfair this embargo was and telling of continuing Soviet arms shipments to Egypt, but the British Government declined to change course, upsetting both Anglo-Israeli and Anglo-American relations.

On 16 October the British Government was criticized in the House of Lords for refusing to lift the embargo on arms to the Middle East so that supplies of spare parts for tanks could go to Israel. Lord Janner asked 'how we dared to refuse to supply the Israelis with the necessary parts to enable them to use the tanks that we had sold to them.' It was pointed out by Lord Shinwell that Israel had actually paid for some of these spare parts.[5]

Meanwhile French Mirage jets were being supplied by France to Libya, despite the fact that another EEC country, Germany, was asking the United States to stop supplying arms to Israel via German ports. Inconsistently Germany had actually given some unofficial aid to Israel. Privately, Oldfield was convinced that Heath was simply going tamely along with the EEC viewpoint and not attempting to give a lead. He was even more despondent when he learned that United States satellite intelligence had detected a heavy Soviet airlift to the Middle East, with cargo aircraft being diverted to pick up troops. This confirmed his worst fears.

There was another bombshell in early November when it became clear that the British Government would not allow the United States the use of the main RAF airbase in Cyrpus during the Middle East fighting. While American officials were not inclined to make an official complaint, they made it abundantly clear that this was 'another action in a pattern of ... consistently unhelpful behaviour by the British Government during the crisis. "Rolling barrels in our way." '[6]

Prior to this the RAF base at Akrotiri in Cyprus had been used for refuelling the secret Mach 3 SR reconnaisance aircraft, flights of which were not officially acknowledged. These planes' photography over the Sinai Desert had been vital to the United States. The British embargo on spare parts for Israel was also resented in the USA; Oldfield had to answer for his government's failure to the CIA as well as to the Israelis. It was swiftly realized in Washington that once the Soviet Union started to send in supplies to Israel's enemies, the arms embargo to both sides became a nonsense and there was a distinct possibility that Israel's survival was threatened by its too rapid consumption of ammunition. It was then that the USA changed its attitude, whereas Britain did not. Prior to this America had hoped that Russia would at least restrict its supplies to Egypt. Yet Britain would not even allow American planes delivering material to Israel to have landing rights in Britain.

'It will take a long time for us to mend our fences with the Mossad,' was Oldfield's comment.

Whether this disagreement on policy delayed the conferment of the usual knighthood on the head of the SIS is a matter for conjecture. But failure to confer such a title was duly noted in the media. In 1974 the *Daily Mail* reported that 'the biggest secret currently involving Mr Oldfield is the mystery of why he has not been knighted. He was appointed by Edward Heath eleven months ago, but had been notably absent from subsequent New Year's and Birthday honours lists. Unkind observers of the security scene are saying it is because he is a member of the wrong club, the Athenaeum. His predecessors, Sir John and Sir Dick, were respectively members of Brooks and the Garrick.'[7]

It was not until January 1975 that Oldfield was made a

Knight Commander of the Order of St Michael and St George, by which time the Heath government had been succeeded by the third Wilson administration. Oldfield's father had been present at his son's first visit to Buckingham Palace in 1956, and his mother had lived to see him get his knighthood on the same day as Charlie Chaplin got his. On this occasion two of his sisters accompanied him to the Palace.

Relations with the Mossad were gradually improved from mid-1974 onwards. It should perhaps be stressed that if Oldfield was upset by some aspects of Edward Heath's foreign policies, he made no secret of the fact that with Julian Amery, then a Minister of State at the Foreign Office, he established an excellent working relationship: 'by far the most well informed and intelligently-minded minister with whom I have ever had to deal,' was his private opinion.

Mr Amery had been liaison officer to the Albanian Resistance in 1944, so he understood quite a bit about the twilight world of espionage and resistance movements. Because of this Albanian link Oldfield always regarded him as 'a friend of the "friends" '. 'I did not really know him until he became head of his Service,' says Mr Amery. 'I saw him regularly of course when I was Minister of State at the Foreign Office and we consulted each other both before and after that period. He was a great collector of anecdotes. His ability to produce these easily suggests a memory that must have been very useful in his professional capacity. If there was a weakness, I think it lay in a reluctance to thrust his views on others, a product partly of a strong sense of security, but also of an innate modesty and perhaps under-estimate of his own importance.'[8]

When the Wilson government was established once again in 1974 and James Callaghan was appointed Foreign Secretary, the latter was carefully briefed by Oldfield on the damage which had been done to relations with Israel through the influence of the Arabists in the FCO. Callaghan soon made it clear that, despite the oil embargo by the Arab producers, brought about by the Israeli forces establishing themselves on the banks of Suez, Britain's friendly relations

179

with Israel must not merely be maintained, but strengthened. The previous government's quite unjustified policy of bending towards the Arabs must be changed. Changed to some extent it was, though there was a strong lobby inside the FCO which maintained that the chief priority should be the avoidance of another oil embargo. Oldfield's answer to such political cowardice was that attention should always be paid to alternative oil-producing nations. For this reason he was keen to strengthen his intelligence-gathering in countries such as Mexico and elsewhere that oil could be found.

Nor did he merely keep an eye on the more obvious oil-producing areas outside the Arab world. He was always keen to get early intelligence of plans for oil prospecting in previously unexploited territories. His experience in the Far East had shown him that the New China News Agency in Hong Kong (generally regarded as an unoffical branch of Chinese intelligence) and the Bank of China kept a close watch on the movements of stocks and shares relating to the oil markets of the world. Who was going to develop what was the main question. After that it was how does this affect us? For these two reasons he was on various occasions interested in reports on places as remote as the Spratley Islands in the South China Sea and alleged oil prospects in the Antarctic.

At about this time Oldfield became involved in inter-departmental and inter-Service wrangles concerning MI 5 as well as MI 6. There were members of both services who were openly criticizing what they regarded as lamentable lapses in security, and in keeping watch on potential suspects. While some of these criticisms were justified, others bordered on the paranoid with potential traitors being imagined on almost every level of the Services. As a result a great deal of time was lost pursuing false trails.

One of the impediments to actually catching a traitor in one's own ranks is that, unless one can actually find him in the act of passing secret documents to a foreign agent, or being able to prove that such documents were passed, it is extremely difficult to bring charges which would stand up in a court of law. This applied for a long while in the cases of both Blunt and Philby. It is, of course, a case of 'heads I win, tails you lose', because either way the media and the public will criticize the Services. If someone is charged, successfully prosecuted and jailed, then the laxity which permitted the mole to operate is deplored. If the matter is suppressed, the man concerned dismissed but given immunity from prosecution, then, should these facts ever be revealed, the Services are damned for covering up.

Sometimes the situation calls for publicity and a trial: possible deterrents to treachery. But regardless of what the public may think, sometimes the best policy is 'least said, soonest mended'. If no action is taken, enemies are left guessing, unable to make capital.

Oldfield instinctively had built-in defences against clamours for arrests and instant action. This should not be regarded as a weakness. Nor should it be taken as in any way condoning treachery. It was simply a question of finding the professional answer to such problems. As a result of the interrogation of Anthony Blunt, one Soviet sympathizer who had been a member of MI 6 in various countries since World War Two days was unmasked by Oldfield. In this case Oldfield himself tackled the agent who responded by making a statement but again insisting, with much justification, that no charge could be brought against him. He was allowed to resign from the Service.

The agent in question bore no malice against Oldfield. Not only did he attend the memorial service for his chief, but he paid a tribute in a letter to me that Oldfield was 'a devout, kindly person'. Maybe he had regrets.

On the subject of the tangled webs in which a secret service can get caught up from time to time (not least when double agents are used), Oldfield put into forthright English vernacular an old Russian moujik's advice. The Oldfield version of this was: 'If you find someone has put you in the shit, always remember that that person is not necessarily your enemy. And if somebody gets you out of the shit, remember he may not be your friend. If, however, you get out of the shit, don't talk about it.'

Prior to the controversies in intelligence circles in the mid-seventies, when Rennie retired from the office of 'C' and Sir Martin Furnival Jones retired from being head of MI 5, it was proposed that Oldfield should be appointed Director-General of MI 5. The argument went that Oldfield was outside the Service, which had been riddled with suspected traitors, that he had also been a counter-intelligence officer in Military Intelligence, and therefore would be an admirable, disinterested new chief. There was, however, considerable resistance to this idea inside MI 6, most of whose senior officers were appalled at the prospect of losing a man of Oldfield's experience and capabilities.

Ultimately Sir Michael Hanley was made the new head of MI 5, and Oldfield stayed on with MI 6.

11

A 1977 Threat To The Falklands Averted

When Wilson returned to power after Heath's election defeat in 1974, Oldfield soon established good relations with the new Foreign Secretary, James Callaghan.

Relations between Wilson and Oldfield, however, could be ambiguous. On the one hand the Prime Minister still had a high regard for MI 6. One former member of MI 6 told me: 'I can only say that Harold Wilson told me, quite spontaneously, in January 1977, that he had the highest opinion of MI 6, whereas of MI 5 he would utter no good word. Indeed, he accused MI 5 of conspiring against him and trying to bring down his government. MI 6 at the time of which he was speaking was under Oldfield.'

Yet in the latter part of Wilson's last premiership he seemed to avoid Oldfield. Once he crossed the street to do so. Oldfield himself professed to be puzzled by the incident. If he surmised the reason for it, he kept it to himself. The fact is that admiration for MI 6 did not stop Wilson developing fears about nefarious operations against him by ill-wishers, British and foreign. However much he professed to admire MI 6, he still proferred to make his own personal inquiries on matters concerning either service.

Nor, in fairness to Wilson, should this be considered in

any way wrong. There are precedents for such inquiries among such diverse premiers as Lloyd George, Baldwin and Churchill. Wilson had every justification for doubting the reliability of MI 5 over a number of years. The real complaint is that these inquiries came to be publicized and thus aggravated the situation. It soon became known that when the Prime Minister thought there might be attempts by the CIA to infiltrate the Cabinet Office, he asked his publisher, Lord Weidenfeld, to take a confidential letter to a mutual friend, Senator Hubert Humphrey, who had been vice-president of the USA in an earlier administration. Humphrey passed on the letter to George Bush of the CIA.

The query put in this letter was whether two named men whose activities seemed suspicious to Wilson had ever worked for the CIA. The answer from the CIA was that they had not. None of these manoeuvres helped either the SIS or MI 5, and the publicity which ensued did no good to either service, or to the current Lord Wilson of Rievaulx. To complicate matters the vendetta against certain highly placed former officers of MI 5 had been taken up by a member of MI 6, who had become involved in the investigation of a certain MI 5 officer. Nothing had been positively proved against him and the Fluency Committee which had considered the case had proposed no further action. Attempts were made to persuade Oldfield to intervene, something which he rightly declined to do, as this was not his direct concern.

How did MI 6, or rather a member of this service, become involved in the investigation of MI 5? Some years previously, long before Oldfield became head of MI 6, a high officer of MI 5 was being investigated and kept under surveillance. It was realized that all the professional 'watchers' of MI 5 would be known to him, so outsiders needed to be sought. Why they did not recruit from the Special Branch is not clear: this would have been the obvious move. But, according to unofficial reports, six 'watchers' were engaged, at least one of whom was from MI 6. It was this 'watcher' who considered that the investigation of the man from MI 5 had not been satisfactorily followed up.

Oldfield was intensely annoyed at MI 6's involvement. It was not that he wanted to obstruct inquiries, as some alleged, but that MI 6 should not have been involved in the first place and that it detracted from their own vital work. For the record, it should be noted that 'C' was adamant that, when a positive vetting of MI 6 personnel was called for, he should be vetted, too. 'As a bachelor,' he stressed, 'I am particularly vulnerable.'

Not all business was without its amusing side even at Century House. In a letter to an old friend, dated 24 February 1975, Oldfield wrote: 'I have just entertained the Private Office with Pope Gregory's injunction about washerwomen. Is there any room for P/As – they can be decorative? (*pace* F——).' Here Oldfield seems to be comparing the washerwomen who accompanied the Crusaders with the modern P/A. Exactly what this papal injunction was is not clear, but it would seem to refer to Pope Gregory X (Teldaldo Visconti, Archbishop of Liege) and the early 1270s. Gregory issued a number of instructions about Christian behaviour in the Crusades.

Rather more amusing was the fact that somebody suddenly became concerned that the SIS might have a menacing skeleton in its archives in the shape of a ghost of the late Ramsay Macdonald, Prime Minister of Britain as head of both Labour and national coalition governments. During the years between the wars rumour had it that Macdonald had been threatened with blackmail by a Frenchwoman with whom he had compromised himself. Oldfield was asked to find out whether the Secret Service had paid off the woman to silence her. He went over to Paris and made some inquiries. To his huge delight he discovered that it was not the SIS who had paid out £10,000 to settle the case, but the Foreign Office. 'I'm rather relieved to know we weren't mixed up in such irrelevant business on tax-payers' money,' he chuckled.

Maybe this remark reflected Oldfield's own concern about not exploiting the tax-payer. Compared to some previous holders of his office, he had casually, if not contemptuously, dismissed many of the perks that went with it. 'He never drew the perks he was entitled to,' said one colleague. 'He could have had his flat paid for by the authorities, but he paid for his own. He was always considerate for his bodyguard. Even when this applied to a weekend off somewhere, he would say "my bodyguard has a date this weekend, so it makes things a bit awkward. You do understand, don't you?" He had much the same attitude towards money. He would leave quite a lot of money lying idle in his account and not attempt to reinvest it.'

Oldfield regarded Callaghan as 'a breath of fresh air' after the time-wasting tittle-tattle of the last days of the Wilson government. He also developed a sincere and friendly relationship with Callaghan's first Foreign Secretary, Anthony Crosland, an academic like himself and possibly one of the most promising ministers at the FCO since World War Two. It was Crosland who, quite effortlessly, defused the Icelandic fishing crisis and steadily set about finding a solution to the Rhodesian problem. Had Crosland lived, much might have been accomplished in the sphere of British foreign policies. Conscientious, relentless in driving himself ever forward in the cause of his country, absorbing intelligence as swiftly as did Oldfield himself, his premature death robbed Britain of an outstanding politician.

Anthony Crosland's widow, Mrs Susan Crosland, recalls meeting Oldfield some time after her husband's death. She took a note of their conversation immediately afterwards and it consisted of Oldfield's fondest recollection of a talk with her husband.

Oldfield referred to what he described as 'the loveliest moment I've ever had with a Foreign Secretary. I'd asked for an appointment to discuss a particular matter. An hour was allowed. We got through it in ten minutes.

'I got up to go, and Tony said, "Look, we've gained fifty minutes on the day. Let's cover the waterfront."

'We talked. I told him that one of the things we had been able to do was to save some people in South East Asia because our Australian friends in that Talmud were able to let us have some men to deploy.

'I got up and started to go and – it was January – wished

him a happy new year.

' "Thank you very much," he replied. "You know, I must congratulate you on your choice of words."

' "I'm delighted, Secretary of State, that you like my choice of words, but which of them appealed to you?"

' "I must confess to you, Maurice (we were on those sort of terms), I never expected any 'C' would be sitting in that chair and would describe the Australian Labour Party to me as a Talmud."

' "Oh, my God," I replied, "what have I done?"

' "Well, what did you mean?"

' "There are too many bloody lawyers in that government." '[1]

In this period Sir Maurice established what proved to be a mutually worthwhile relationship with Mrs Thatcher, then the recently elected leader of the Conservative Party. She was anxious to have some briefings on the various problems of the day touching on intelligence and security. An intermediary paved the way for such talks, which were welcomed as much by Oldfield as Mrs Thatcher. The Prime Minister, Callaghan, gave his approval and from then on the Conservative leader and Sir Maurice became firm friends.

By this time Oldfield had acquired considerable confidence in handling such delicate matters, even to the extent of creating something of a precedent for an SIS chief to give advice to a leader of the Opposition. Perhaps, however, the nature of this advice needs to be spelt out rather clearly. It was not a question of supplying the Opposition with the kind of detailed information which 'C' would normally give either to the Prime Minister or the Foreign Secretary. Oldfield's role was to provide some of the facts of life in the intelligence world to a newcomer who might easily become the next Prime Minister. It was a meticulously careful seminar, invaluable in its way, but no more and no less, and intended to preserve a politician from falling into pitholes. Oldfield's impression was that Mrs Thatcher was an astonishingly swift absorber of facts who was able very quickly to make up her own mind upon difficult issues.

Most people who have in any way been concerned with

intelligence-gathering will know that there has been a tendency among British chiefs of the Service and other senior officers to talk to their subordinates in whispers and vague hints, to avoid being positive. So often somebody will be given an assignment without being told exactly what it involves, sometimes without knowing the object of the exercise. Oldfield was not like that. Both in the Middle East in the war, where he really learned his craft, and in MI 6, unlike many of his colleagues, he would go out of his way to explain the whole situation to an agent. Nobody under Oldfield was left in any doubt as to what his mission was. When he did delegate, it was done with quiet assurance, conveying to the other man just what was required of him.

Oldfield also believed that MI 6 gave excellent value for the funds expended on it, and for this reason he fought hard for better financial terms for the Secret Service. Indeed he was right. For the best part of a century the British Secret Service has provided incomparably good, professional service on a shoestring. If anyone doubts this, ask the CIA. Or, for that matter, ask the KGB, for more than one defector from that Service has testified to the admiration of the Russians for the efficient manner in which our Intelligence and Security Services operate with such small manpower and modest funds.

It was reported in the New York *Herald Tribune* that Oldfield 'had displayed remarkable success in expanding his SIS budgets at a great rate'.[2] This assessment may have been based upon the fact that the secret vote had increased from £10 millions in 1967 to £17 millions in 1972, and up again to £22 millions under Oldfield in 1975. But, as has been mentioned before, any such figures are likely to be misleading. By the early 1980s such costs were ostensibly between £46 million and £40 million, whereas some skilled financial investigators would put it at nearer £250 millions.

In his own quiet way Oldfield was also a public relations officer for the SIS. He would probably have been horrified at any such description of himself, for while he would agree that secrecy had sometimes been carried to ridiculous lengths (like pretending the Secret Service did not exist), he strongly believed that the SIS should not be exposed to probing inquiries by Parliamentary committees in the same way that the CIA had been hampered by some Congressional inquiries. He kept in touch discreetly with a few journalists, which was in itself a departure for any head of the SIS. When a colleague once tried to warn him that there were risks in such contacts, Oldfield replied: 'There are only risks if one talks too much. In any case when the famous Admiral Hall was head of the NID, he brought off some of his greatest coups by exploiting his friendship with Marlowe, the editor of the *Daily Mail* in those days.' On one occasion Oldfield went to Hurstpierpoint College at the invitation of its chaplain, his young friend, the Reverend Gerald Buss, to talk to sixth-formers about MI 6. He even agreed to answer questions. Inevitably, he was asked whether there were James Bond types in the Service. 'Intelligence isn't like that at all,' he replied. 'Intelligence is about people and a study of people.' This was a theme he used constantly to reiterate in the office.

This emphasis on people and the study of people may seem rather cryptic, taken out of context. But Oldfield would sometimes enlarge on the theme. 'It is not simply a question of studying people on *the other side*, but studying one's own as well,' he would say. 'We have to learn about one another, not just about strangers.' He insisted that this particularly applied to the head of the Secret Service when he had to assess his agents and colleagues.

'Maurice and I disagreed on one thing,' one of his overseas agents, now retired, told me. 'He was all for moving people about from one area to another every three years or so. I argued that a particularly good man in his own area needed to be kept on and that this good man's informants might not want to talk to a new man.' Oldfield was, in fact, conscious of this criticism and agreed that there could be exceptions. But he gave various examples of where the reverse was true – where some potential new informants were lost to the SIS simply because they felt the man they had to contact was too well known as belonging to MI 6.

It was the defector and the enemy agent who could be

'turned' who really fascinated Oldfield. 'For preference I should like to be the first person to hear what such a man has to tell,' he said. 'That is rarely possible. Failing that, I always like to study the first available verbatim report of what he *first* said. *First*, not second, or third time. For it is what the defector says on this first occasion which is vital. What he says then needs to be carefully weighed against anything he may say later, because it is the later material which is often the least reliable. You see, later on such a man is under pressure to try to remember more, or to tell more. It is not so much that he will set out to deceive as that in trying to remember he will deceive himself. He begins to feel under some stress and he may well tend to tell you what he thinks you want to hear. Sometimes this is deliberate, but more often it is a subconscious reaction. So what evidence you get then may well be an erroneous recollection, sheer imagination or deliberate invention. That is when the defector sometimes falls victim to his own fears and suspicions.'

While Oldfield loathed 'dirty tricks' in the game of espionage, he was sufficiently realistic to know that trickery was often necessary. He was a master of the arts of deception and knew how and when to disinform. He tried to provide deeper cover for his agents and did much to push the Service further underground, making it smaller and more effective.

In 1975 terrorist attacks in London were stepped up, with the result that the aid of the SAS (Special Air Service Regiment) was increasingly sought. This culminated at the end of the year in the trapping of a PIRA 'active service unit' in a flat in Balcombe Street, but on 13 October of that year there was an attempt to kill Oldfield himself, a feat which would have rated among the PIRA's greatest successes. The head of the SIS would frequently dine in Locket's Restaurant on the ground floor of Marsham Court, where he lived. On this particular night two female passers-by noticed a black holdall wedged between the railings and the window-sill of the restaurant. Luckily, they had sufficient public spirit to go in and warn the night porter. Once he looked into the holdall he lost no time in informing the police. For inside it he found a thirty-pound bomb in a device which contained about twenty bolts, each of which were three inches long. The actual bomb was the largest which had been used in the current terrorist campaign in London and elsewhere, and it was only defused by explosives experts some three minutes before it was due to go off. MPs dining in the restaurant at the time were requested to leave. Immediately above the restaurant Sir Maurice was actually at home at the time, and had the bomb blown out Locket's ceiling, he could easily have been killed. Next day it was established that the bomb was made from commercial gelignite produced in the Irish Republic.

While it was at first thought that the prime target for this bombing was the various Members of Parliament dining at Locket's Restaurant, the position of the bomb right under Sir Maurice's flat strongly indicated that the PIRA were out to get him. Several weeks later when police launched a raid against a PIRA 'safe house' in another part of London they found a batch of newspaper clippings, all concerning Oldfield.

Though unaffected personally by this experience, Sir Maurice was irritated by the need for increased security wherever he went, as well as being somewhat embarrassed by having to lunch at his club under the scrutiny of security guards. A similar routine prevailed when he attended church. 'He was always accompanied by plain clothes police,' said the vicar, Prebendary Irvine. 'For a long time I couldn't understand why Sir Maurice sat at the back of the church. Eventually it was explained to me that he did this for security reasons. There were unpleasant moments from time to time. On one occasion a bomb was found in the organ loft. Notes were left in hymn books saying "The IRA will get you" and other sinister graffiti were perpetrated in the church itself.'[3]

A new organ was installed in St Matthew's Church in 1977, and six weeks afterwards, in May of that year, the church was burnt down. The cause of the fire was never positively established, though the new organ's electrical circuit was suspected. The vicar doubts this: he thinks it may well have been started deliberately.

Sir Maurice was one of the first to rally round and help after the fire. One aisle, relatively untouched by the fire, was restored as a temporary place of worship and an organ was loaned to the church. Brian Fretwell, who had been the organist, left about this time to study for entry to the church, and Oldfield promptly volunteered to take on his post on a strictly voluntary basis.

Mr Fred Bardwell remembers Sir Maurice taking his organ playing seriously, but with the occasional jest thrown in. He would sometimes experiment with unexpected items as voluntary music and he maintained that some of the music of Grieg and certainly Beethoven's Moonlight Sonata could be better appreciated on the organ than on any other instrument. On several occasions he entertained parisioners in his flat.

When Anthony Crosland's life was cut short by a sudden stroke in 1977, Oldfield was distinctly downcast. He felt that Foreign Secretaries were changing too frequently. During his period of office he had already served under Lord Home, James Callaghan and Crosland. Dr David Owen, who succeeded Crosland, soon came to rely on and greatly respect Oldfield's qualities. In fact Dr Owen was initially more enthusiastic about Oldfield than the latter was about learning to work with a new Foreign Secretary. The truth was that Sir Maurice realized he had got to start all over again, establishing a delicate relationship. Dr Owen had the great advantage for a Foreign Secretary of relative youthfulness. He wanted to know and to learn and he wished perhaps to cross frontiers that previous Foreign Secretaries had neglected. Probably Oldfield was kept more on his toes by Dr Owen than by any other Foreign Secretary of his time.

Dr Owen told me that when he became Foreign Secretary, 'you never acknowledged the existence of MI 6 in answering questions in the House of Commons. You never admitted that we had intelligence services. Strangely enough, I, who have always been in favour of open government, argued against it. It seemed to me that it was an absurd but rather

192

useful convention. You either reveal a bit and then you reveal a lot more, or you just reveal nothing publicly, because to do so could put at risk other people's lives, quite apart from damaging the effectiveness of our intelligence services.'[4]

On this question of open government in relation to both the intelligence and security services Mrs Thatcher, as Opposition leader, was brought into contact with Oldfield, with the Prime Minister's approval. This was one of those now regrettably rarer instances of how under the British parliamentary system, Government and Opposition can in the national interest actually work together. At this time there were considerable murmurings about traitors within the ranks of the Establishment and at least two authors, including myself, were hot on the trail of denouncing Sir Anthony Blunt, as he then was. Though there were some who took the view that silence was preferable, there were others who felt that in the long run it could be devastatingly damaging. For not only had Blunt been able to get away with his treachery, but he had *actually been knighted after he was strongly suspected of this crime.*

Thus various kites were being flown for suggested changes in the running of the intelligence and security services and for possible control of the latter through parliamentary committees. Some MPs were mindful of the Senate and Congressional Committees in the United States which not only freely probed into security matters, but actually interrogated defectors and intelligence services witnesses, their findings being published in the form of printed reports. In recent years, as a result of such reports, the American public were better informed on suspected villains inside the British security and intelligence services and among members of Parliament than were the British people. The laws of libel made it difficult for parts of these reports to be reproduced in the British press. This anomaly was undoubtedly a potent factor when the Conservative Government under Mrs Thatcher conceded that Blunt was a traitor and officially admitted the existence of MI 5 and MI 6. Yet as a general rule not only will the government of the day refuse to answer questions about the intelligence services, but the Table Office refuses in the first place so that often questions cannot get on to the Order Paper.

There was some speculation at the end of 1975 whether Sir Maurice would not resign from the Secret Service, partly because his cover had been blown and he was the target for attacks, but equally because he had been serving under great stress and his family might also be threatened. In some quarters, too, the idea had been mooted that this might be the right moment to introduce a super-intelligence chief, a co-ordinator, possibly attached to the Cabinet Office, who would have control of MI 5 as well as MI 6. It was from the beginning a non-runner. It might have worked in Soviet Russia, but it would be highly unlikely to be satisfactory in the United Kingdom. Dr Owen himself was against the idea of any overlordship of the intelligence and security services.

Another question which arose at this time was whether the Thirty Years Rule, concerning the release of official records, should apply to the Secret Service. Obviously, this was an attempt to open up intelligence records. Oldfield felt that it should not apply for the simple reason that it could still cost lives even after that lapse of time.

'I probably talked with or used Oldfield rather more than any other Foreign Secretary,' says Dr Owen. 'It was invaluable and I learned a lot. I found him excellent on Africa generally. Sometimes we would have arguments about missions. He would put up his plans for such missions and explain everything. Then I would ask questions. Sometimes I said "OK", sometimes I demurred. Sometimes he would come back and quietly argue his case, putting forward the reasons why he thought I should reconsider the matter.'[5]

This succinctly sums up exactly what should be the relationship between a Foreign Secretary and the head of the SIS. Each inevitably has somewhat different objectives. But surely the ideal is where these can be discussed together, thrashed out by argument and counter-argument, with one reservation: the head of MI 6 may on occasions know rather better than the Foreign Secretary whether or not a certain mission is essential. He has all the facts at his finger-tips. A patriotic and honest 'C' might then feel that he must act without telling. With some Foreign Secretaries this might be desirable. But here, I am sure, anyone so politically-minded in the non-party sense of the term as Sir Maurice would have agreed that this is the exception to the rule.

Perhaps Dr Owen summed up this whole situation best in a broadcast programme on the subject of intelligence in which he took part. 'I wouldn't draw up a set of Queensberry rules for them [the SIS]. But there would be limits to what I would expect to be done. Some of the things they don't tell you about, and it's probably wise that they don't tell. I don't want to be told the most intimate detail of their techniques, exactly what they're up to ... What I want to be told is if a particular episode had a political content in it, then I would have to authorize it ... I'm sure things go on that have never been told to Ministers ... I'm sure we don't know the whole answer ... I mean I did an exercise once when I first became Foreign Secretary. I wanted to see what was referred to me. And over a six-month period we went back through all the cases. And I checked out what ones they were referring up to me, and what ones they thought were non-political if you like. I found, I must confess, that they were scrupulous and that they had referred the right ones to me and they had been very good in sorting out what was technical detail and what was something which involved political content and required the authorization of the democratic political leadership.'[6]

In this latter period of Oldfield's term of office as 'C' he became something of an elder statesman himself, if only strictly as an adviser – not merely to the Prime Minister and Foreign Secretary, but to the Leader of the Opposition, for whom he soon came to have a high regard. Both James Callaghan and Dr Owen agreed that Mrs Thatcher should also be consulted on the question of whether the Thirty Years Rule for release of public papers should not apply to SIS documents. Thus, despite clamour for increasing open government and greater access to information, there was consensus between the two major parties on the need for safeguards on security grounds. Oldfield was able to show

how the release of such information *even after thirty years* could in some instances cause people's deaths. But many people inside and out of Parliament felt this should not be used as an excuse to prevent all SIS papers remaining classified after so long a period.

In the last few years as Director-General of MI 6 Oldfield had been greatly heartened by the technological progress made by the Secret Service. He had always enthusiastically welcomed all ideas for the development of new 'spook gadgets', as they were known in the trade, even if he expressed doubts on the lie-detector. Perhaps one of the major feats during his term of office was the successful application of the laser bug. This had been developed in the early seventies at the highly secret Joint Services Electronic Research Laboratory at Baldock in Hertfordshire. The laser was beamed at a window pane as far distant as a quarter of a mile and enabled those listening to hear all that was being said through voice vibrations on the window. But this was but one of a number of secret technical developments in the seventies.

In July 1977, a report appeared in the London *Daily Express* from Chapman Pincher stating that 'a war had broken out between the Secret Service and the Foreign Office following one of the worst intelligence failures for years,' adding that it 'could result in the quick retirement of Secret Service chief Sir Maurice Oldfield.'[7] He referred to the Left-wing coup in the Seychelles in the previous month when Albert René seized power while the Seychelles President, James Mancham, was attending a Commonwealth conference in London. The complaint was that MI 6 had failed to give either the President or the Foreign Office any warning of possible trouble, despite the fact that anti-Mancham men from the Seychelles had been training for just such a coup in Tanzania for some months previously.

Dr David Owen, who was Foreign Secretary at the time, has no recollection of any row concerning this affair and says that there was 'neither an offer of resignation, nor any suggestion that one should be made.' This, of course, should not be interpreted as indifference to what was undoubtedly an unfortunate lapse in intelligence-gathering, but the fault cannot entirely be laid at the doors of Century House. It had been clearly indicated by the very first Wilson Government that intelligence-gathering operations in independent Commonwealth territories should be drastically curtailed. When James Mancham became first President of an independent Seychelles group of islands, he wanted to set up his own intelligence service with the help of the British. Astonishingly, he was informed by the Foreign Office that any funds he required to finance this would have to come from the Ministry of Overseas Development. As the funding of such a service could hardly be justified as overseas aid in the interests of social welfare, his request was not unnaturally turned down. Nevertheless, Mancham was worried about the possibility of a coup being launched against him and he had said as much to a representative of MI 6. In this instance while an on-the-spot French intelligence officer told Mancham that trouble was afoot, MI 6's informant gave an assurance that all was well.

Two outstandingly successful intelligence successes against the KGB were, however, staged in this period, though details of these cannot be revealed. It is perhaps sufficient to indicate that they involved the winning over of at least two high level defectors who provided a wealth of information and who had been carefully observed and briefed for a few years. Another coup was discovering a massive espionage plan launched by the Iraqi Directorate of Military Intelligence at the instigation of the KGB. Under a secret Soviet-Iraqi arrangement on intelligence in 1973, officers from all branches of the Iraqi Intelligence Service were sent to the USSR for training each year. At the same time the Soviet advisers were attached to Brigadier al-Azzawi's Directorate of Military Intelligence by the Russian GRU (Military Intelligence). The object of this exercise was to use Iraqi diplomats all over Europe to obtain top-secret intelligence from NATO.

It is often wrongly assumed that because money for intelligence-gathering is so grudgingly granted to the Secret and Security Services, they must be less effective than those of other powers. There is also the view that now that Britain no longer has an empire, its Secret Service does not count for much. True, MI 5 has been greatly hindered in its work because that organization requires so many 'watchers' to keep an eye on the huge staffs employed in Britain not merely by the Soviet Union, but all its allies among the Eastern European countries. But the two great strengths of MI 6 are, first, its vast store of experience dating back the best part of a century, compared, say, with the CIA which has only been in existence since World War Two, and, second, the high quality of most of its operators. In quality and experience MI 6 more than makes up for its lack of numbers and funds. Small it may be, but, relatively, so is the Mossad, yet tiny Israel's intelligence service rates as among the best in the world. Possibly MI 6 employs not many more than five hundred personnel compared with nearly twenty thousand in the American intelligence services. But the British operator is much more of an all-rounder than his average American counterpart. Usually, he speaks more languages rather better, has a wider knowledge of more countries and – perhaps vitally important – he can tackle his own encoding, decoding, recruiting and form judgements of his informants' reports. In this respect the incident of the Seychelles was an unfortunate exception.

Nor is this a purely British view. One former CIA operator, Mr Frank Snepp, has paid this tribute to the MI 6 man: 'British intelligence operatives are generally better trained in tradecraft than Americans are. I knew several young fellows in British intelligence who knew a heck of a lot more about tradecraft than I did, or my colleagues did.'[8]

It is worth noting that Mr Snepp had been operating for the CIA in the Far East – in the very areas in which Oldfield had been patiently building up a new network in the late fifties. As a field officer in Vietnam in the seventies, he worked closely with MI 6 and must therefore be regarded as qualified to make such judgements.

In the mid-seventies Oldfield was particularly pleased that liaison with the French improved in many respects on the previous decade. This was partly due (according to French sources) to an appointment Oldfield made which pleased the SDECE (*Service de Documentation et de Contre-Espionage*). But the relationship was made much smoother by the new chief of the SDECE, Count Alexandre de Marenches. Both men shared certain views, notably the need to protect secret services from rogue elephants in their midst. De Marenches, an army colonel, a member of the French Jockey Club and a Knight of Malta, had been given this post to purge the service of some of its violently anti-American members and the *barbouzes*, men often mixed up in the type of violence associated with mercenaries and the drug traffic. Oldfield regarded the SDECE as being exceptionally well informed on the Arab countries and some of the Soviet satellite nations. There was also a useful exchange of intelligence on Latin American states.

It is unquestionable that British intelligence helped to defuse a dangerous situation during the Cuban missiles crisis. Almost certainly in the years to come intelligence services will play a vital role in helping to prevent wars. A fascinating question, however, is whether Oldfield, almost single-handed, crowned his career by helping to prevent a war in 1977 – no less than an invasion of the Falkland Islands by the Argentines. Did he achieve then what the politicians, diplomats and Secret Service failed to do in 1982?

Mr James Callaghan, who was Prime Minister at the time, claims to have told Sir Maurice in 1977 about a covert British fleet deployed in the South Atlantic, ostensibly with the aim of giving the chief of MI 6 the chance to inform the Argentine junta that Britain would not stand aside if any move was made against the Falklands. Furthermore Mr Callaghan has claimed that this action deterred the Argentines from invading the islands.[9]

Certainly the Cabinet acted with commendable promptitude on that occasion, and, despite some objections from the Defence Minister, the Prime Minister and the Foreign Secretary ordered two frigates and a submarine to be dispatched to the South Atlantic, as well as making plans for an exclusion zone of some twenty-five miles around the Falklands.

When the Lord Franks Committee made its report on the events leading up to the Falklands War of 1982, the assertion that Argentina was informed by the British Government of its decision to send a task force in 1977 was rejected in a negative way. The report's comment on this was 'The facts relating to the deployment of ships in the area in November 1977 are set out in our report. We have no evidence that the Argentine Government became aware of the deployment.'

This may have been due to the fact that Dr David Owen, Foreign Secretary at the time, when questioned by the Committee maintained that the fleet deployment had been covert. Dr Owen's comment on Mr Callaghan's claim is: 'It may be that they [the Argentines] were told that we were on manoeuvres in the Southern Atlantic in November 1977, but I do not think they were specifically warned about the submarine that was sent down to the Falklands themselves, although they could well have been given a general feeling that we were not without a naval capability.'[10]

On the other hand there were very many assertions concerning events in the Falklands for which the Franks Committee claimed they had 'no evidence'. At worst this was a white-washing report for the diplomats and one comprising too many negative findings; at best it merely recommended some changes in the Joint Intelligence Committee and called for 'a clearer understanding of the relative roles of the assessments staff, the Foreign and Commonwealth Office, the Ministry of Defence, and for closer liaison between them.' The events of the Argentine invasion and those leading up to it had long since made this so obvious that it hardly called for the waste in either time or money necessary for the Franks Committee to arrive at this conclusion. It should also be noted that the one man vital to this question of deterrence through a deliberate leakage of information, Sir Maurice, had died before the Committee sat, so he could not be interrogated.

The military take-over by a junta in 1976 greatly changed the situation in Argentina *vis à vis* the Falklands. The coup placed power in the hands of a few and greatly increased the influence of the Argentine Navy, which had always been the most vociferous of all the services in demanding the acquisition of the Falklands. Intelligence assessments of the possibility of an Argentine threat to the islands were made by the JIC from 1965 onwards. There seems to have been undue complacency in many of their assessments and, in fact, about the number of occasions when reappraisals needed to be made. Usually such assessments were carried out only once a year and they nearly always amounted to the view that official military action against the Falkland Islands and their dependencies was unlikely.

Oldfield had always been remarkably well informed on Latin America as a whole and had his own excellent personal contacts in the area. Over the years he had always maintained that from a Secret Service viewpoint Argentina should not be treated as a grade two post, but given a higher rating. He based his contention on commercial interests in Argentina, on the Falklands issue and the British South Antarctic outposts as a whole. He regarded the whole vast area very much in terms of global intelligence. It was a case of not just keeping a watch on what the Argentines were up to, but taking note of the Peruvians, Brazilians, of Uruguay and Paraguay and, of the utmost importance, just what schemes the Russians had in mind in the Antarctic. He knew full well that they were as anxious to extend their influence there as they already had in the Arctic region.

Strictly speaking, in the past, Antarctic intelligence would have been very much the prerogative of the Naval Intelligence Division of the Admiralty, which had always worked closely with MI 6 in some areas. There had been a time when the NID was almost the equal of the Secret Service and, in its influence, probably superior to it. But the once powerful NID had been allowed to wither in the hastily conceived integration of the Services' intelligence bodies when the late Lord Mountbatten was Chief of the Defence Staff from 1959-65. Oldfield, who felt that MI 6 had never been sufficiently consulted on these changes, commented that to make full use of naval intelligence gathering in this area 'might have cost a lot of money, but we could more than have got it back by the commercial and scientific intelligence we should have gained.' He was particularly interested in Dr Kingsley Dunham's report in 1967 of an American forecast that eventually the world would get more oil from under the sea than from the land. Oil prospects in the Antarctic had barely been explored.

In the period 1975-77 Oldfield was particularly fortunate in that the Governor and Commander-in-Chief of the Falkland Islands was a colleague for whom he had a high regard – Neville Arthur Irwin French, who in the previous three years had been Counsellor in Havana. Mr French was an old Latin American hand, having been First Secretary and Head of Chancery in Rio de Janeiro in 1966 after having been named as 'an agent of the British Secret Service' by Salisbury Radio on 25 March 1966, when he was stationed in what was then Rhodesia at the time of UDI. Mr French was a first-class assessor of intelligence.

Though the SIS were 'thin on the ground in Latin America at this time', according to one former officer, 'we were getting a first-class intelligence service on a shoestring. We knew all the junta's moves, what they were thinking, what they were planning, almost instantaneously. That might be a slight exaggeration, but it's not far from the truth.'

There was an MI 6 officer in Buenos Aires, and apart from this detailed information was provided from intercepted signals and cooperation with the Americans in reconnaissance satellites. Nor is this merely the view of an SIS man. The Americans themselves have confirmed that 'the relationship between NSA (National Security Agency) and GCHQ (the British Government Communications Headquarters) is stronger than any between the NSA and any other American intelligence agency.'[11]

But perhaps the most significant testimony of all to the excellence of British intelligence in this period came from Mr Edward Rowlands, Labour MP for Merthyr Tydfil, who was a Minister of State at the Foreign Office from 1976-79 and who had talks with the Argentines about the future of the Falklands. At the time of the invasion of the Falklands in 1982, in an emergency debate in the House of Commons, Mr Rowlands stated that he did not understand how British intelligence had failed on that occasion. 'Our intelligence on Argentina was extremely good. That is why we took action in 1977. We found out that certain attitudes and approaches were being formed. I cannot believe the quality of our intelligence has changed. Last night the Secretary of State for Defence asked "How can we read the mind of the enemy?" I shall make a disclosure. As well as trying to read the mind of the enemy, we have been reading its telegrams for many years.'

As to whether this remark at the time of the invasion was indiscreet or outrageous is not now the point. But what is very much to the point is that vital intelligence was reaching the politicians concerned – all of them – very much better and quicker and being interpreted more accurately in 1977 than in 1982. Clearly, too, this actually prevented a war. On 11 October 1977 intelligence was received that an Argentine naval party was due to land on Southern Thule in the South Sandwich Islands by 'the middle of the month'. After this it was decided to send a British force to the area to bolster the government's negotiating position. The Franks Committee stated that 'Cabinet papers show clearly that it was agreed that the force should remain covert ... The Argentine threat receded and it was agreed after the talks that the naval force could be withdrawn.'

In November 1977, two frigates and a nuclear-powered submarine were deployed in the area. It would be very surprising if the Argentine threat receded unless Argentina had learned that a British force had been so deployed. The government of the day was greatly aided by excellent liaison with the chief of the SIS and by the fact that the vital intelligence was processed and analysed so speedily. It will be recalled how both his old headmaster and various friends of Oldfield have testified to the speed with which he could absorb reading matter. One of the things he insisted upon was a speeding up in the assessment of intelligence, stressing at the same time that, from a security point of view, it was essential officials did not retain highly classified reports for leisurely reading, but perused and returned them immediately.

The crucial question is whether Oldfield used surreptitious methods for letting the Argentines know that Britain was sending a task force. The *Sunday Times* Insight team hint that this was done through 'a businessman with extensive contacts among Latin American regimes'.[12] POE, a former CIA officer, is more positive: 'Our information from Buenos Aires in November 1977 was that the Argentines had been told every detail of the British fleet movements with a certain amount of fictitious information about another force standing by to move in. It was not done directly by the British, but passed through two other sources upon which the Argentines relied. It was very cleverly planted by an agent of MI 6. Certainly these sources had nothing whatsoever to do with the politicians. The Argentines would have suspected and probably disbelieved anything coming overtly from a British political source, even through a third party. One of the sources I cannot reveal, but the other was a South African who was suspected of feeding information to the Soviet Union. It was partly through this that MI 6 and the NIS (National Intelligence Service of South Africa) got on to the trail of Commodore Dieter Gerhardt who was eventually arrested for espionage. So did we Americans. I am making a wild guess, but not, I think, an unintelligent one when I suggest that maybe two birds were killed with a single shot on that occasion.'[13]

It has been suggested that on his death-bed Sir Maurice made an admission that the late Colonel Charles Howard (Dick) Ellis, a former member of MI 6, had confessed to 'spying for the Germans, claiming shortage of money while serving abroad for MI 6'.[14]

In fairness both to Sir Maurice and to Colonel Ellis this record should be put straight. Mr Chapman Pincher states: 'At the request of Sir Maurice, who was a friend of mine, I visited him in hospital shortly before his death ... Sir Maurice, who was a very devout Christian, had forgiven him [Ellis] as, I believe, he had forgiven Philby. For doing this he had been castigated, some time previously, by one of his close colleagues on the grounds that treachery to one's country, especially in the interests of a savage regime with which war was then inevitable, is the one crime to which forgiveness should not extend.'[15]

Now in the weeks in hospital immediately preceding his death Sir Maurice was in no condition to indulge in much more than small talk and exchange jokes. Any lengthy discussion would soon exhaust him. To make an admission that Ellis was guilty either then or on another occasion would not only have been totally out of character, but a breach of the Official Secrets Act. For the investigation of Ellis had been a secret inquiry and, as a result of this, no charges had been brought against him. The matter was closed.

'Dick' Ellis, as he was known to his colleagues, was born in Australia in 1895, and joined the British Army in World War One, after which he served with missions on the borders of Russia. He married into a White Russian emigré family and worked as a free lance journalist in Geneva, Berlin and Vienna until in 1938 he became an officer in the SIS. Later he became a key figure in British Intelligence in the USA under Sir William Stephenson. Following inquiries into various matters after Philby's defection to Russia in 1963, suggestions were made in some quarters that Ellis had been a double-agent spying for the Germans. It was later hinted – and it should be stressed that it was no more than hinted on no factual evidence – that Ellis had also spied for the Russians. This last suggestion can be dismissed totally, as it was in his investigation.

As to the allegations of Ellis having acted as a German agent, he did not deny that in the course of his work for the British he had to play the role of a double-agent on occasions, thereby building up contacts inside the German ranks. This proved of enormous value when he was operating in the United States in World War Two. Ellis knew all about Dusko Popov, the double-agent code-named TRICYCLE, who was sincerely working for the British while still in the service of the Germans, yet he never betrayed Popov to the Nazis.

After the war Ellis became an SIS officer in the Far East for a while, during which time Oldfield came to know him. It was in 1965-66 that Ellis was investigated on the allegations made against him, some of them coming from dubious sources which could suggest a degree of Soviet disinformation. Nothing was proved against him, and it is worth recording that the Prime Minister, Mrs Thatcher, had written to Ellis's daughter, Mrs Ann Solwey, of New York, deploring the attacks on her father.

Mr Anthony Cavendish, one of Sir Maurice's closest friends as well as a colleague, says: 'Any connections Dick Ellis had with the *Abwehr* were simply part of his duties in working for British Intelligence. Since I knew Dick Ellis I had naturally discussed the matter with Sir Maurice Oldfield and this was his view.'[16] He added that when Sir Maurice was in hospital at the end of his life, Mr Pincher asked if Sir Maurice would see him. 'Always the gentleman, Sir Maurice agreed to a visit. However, he did not take this as an opportunity to confirm Dick Ellis's treachery, *in which he did not believe*.'

In 1975, while he was chief of MI 6, ten years after the investigation of 'Dick' Ellis, Sir Maurice wrote his old colleague two extremely friendly letters. One dated 10 February 1975 reads: 'My dear Dick, A very happy eightieth birthday from all of us – and from me in particular. You are quite right that there is too much book-making. I read the Vassall one over the weekend and have the Moraver for the week. I haven't read *Tricycle*, but will do so in due course, and I'll certainly get the Szamuely book [Tibor Szamuely was educated in Russia and Hungary before escaping to Britain and ending up as a don at the LSE]. I think I met him on one occasion with Hugh Seton-Watson. By all means pursue the Interdoc invitation.[17] There is no objection on our part, if you want to take it up. Let me have your new address when you move to Eastbourne, please, and again, many best wishes for the birthday, and it is, as it happens, the Chinese New Year – "*Kong EE Fah choi.*" Yours ever, Maurice.'[18]

An earlier letter – 10 January 1975 – refers to a comment by Ellis that 'of the making of books there is no end'.

Oldfield shrewdly comments on this: 'I don't think they matter half so much as the way in which some of our friends seem to be determined to tear themselves apart. I should like to know how much of the profits from their works the respective authors are prepared to give to the Services' charities of the organizations for which they had worked.'[19]

12

Happy Retirement

As the time for Oldfield's retirement drew near controversy about who his successor should be was fuelled by considerable argument as to whether there should be an overhaul of the whole of the Intelligence Services.

With neither of these controversies had Oldfield much patience. In his own mind there was one and only one obvious successor to himself: Arthur Temple Franks, who, like himself, was a real professional. But some advisers who had the ear of the Prime Minister, James Callaghan, believed there were arguments in favour of a more positively Foreign Office figure. One or two other unofficial advisers had talked about the need for 'tidying up' the Intelligence Services and setting up a Directorate of Central Intelligence rather on the American model, with a supremo who reported directly to the Prime Minister.

In the end Oldfield was able to smile quietly and feel reasonably satisfied. His own choice was ultimately selected as Director-General of the SIS and the Service was untouched by any gimmicky changes in its unwritten constitution. What puzzled many was why Downing Street appeared to go out of its way to alert the national newspapers that new heads of MI 5 and MI 6 were about to be appointed. Various suggestions were ventilated in the press. One was that the Prime Minister had lost patience with the system by which the SIS was under nominal Foreign Office control, while the Security Service, MI 5, reported to the Home Secretary, yet had its personnel 'attached' to the Defence Ministry. It was hinted that the Prime Minister had picked a key civil servant to master-mind a new centralized intelligence group and that this man would become chairman of the Joint Intelligence Committee and take over duties normally carried out by the Co-Ordinator of Intelligence to the Cabinet.

In fact, nothing of the kind transpired. But in April 1978, Downing Street had to acknowledge a gaffe. This took the form of an admission that 'a letter sent on behalf of Mr Callaghan, concerning changes at the head of MI 5 and MI 6, went in error to Mr Anthony Cater, editor of the *Morning Star*, the Communist mouthpiece.'[1] This paper was not supposed to receive such information, not being on the list of newspapers entitled to receive D-notices, the device by which editors and media chiefs were advised that publication of certain information could prejudice national security.

Oldfield's retirement was marked by an advancement in the Order of St Michael and St George, the Queen awarding him the Grand Cross of that Order in addition to his KCMG; the highest award ever accorded to a head of the SIS. 'Well, Maurice,' commented one of his more irreverent friends, 'you no longer have any need to repeat saying "Keep calling me God", as your KCMG indicates. With your GCMG you can truly say "God calls me God"!' It was a joke over which Maurice chuckled delightedly.

Retirement from a post such as 'C' is quite different from any other withdrawal from public life. There is always a lot of unfinished business to cope with, papers to be put in order, many queries to be answered, possibly over several months, and, in many respects most important of all, farewells to opposite numbers overseas – at least to some opposite numbers.

However, while unhurriedly 'clearing my desk', as he would put it, Sir Maurice was seriously considering how he would spend his retirement. His instincts were to return to academic life in some form or other, while never being too far distant from his beloved Derbyshire. Lord Dacre, the Master of Peterhouse College, Cambridge, who had for many years been Regius Professor of Modern History at Oxford, says that 'Oldfield asked me if I would be a referee for a place for him at All Souls, Oxford. I agreed, but I didn't think much of his choice of subject for research.'[2]

There is no doubt whatsoever that the first choice of subject which he submitted concerned the medieval clergy. However, there do seem to be some minor differences of opinion as to exactly what this subject was. Professor Michael Howard, the present Regius Professor of Modern History at Oxford, says: 'I think the initiative in arranging Oldfield's leave at All Souls came from the Foreign Office, who had fairly regularly sent us members of the Office for a sabbatical year. Their idea, as I recall it, was that Oldfield should simply have a year to settle and reorient himself immediately after his retirement, so that he could decide whether or not he wished to re-enter academic life. The college realized that he was a very exceptional case and felt that his presence would be interesting and valuable to us. His actual research project was thus not scrutinized with the kind of rigour that would be normal in such cases.

'In fact he put up two proposals. The first was that he should resume the research that he had been doing at the University of Manchester before the war on medieval bishops. We persuaded him that medieval scholarship had progressed so far during the past forty years that he could not simply take up the threads where he had let them fall and he accepted that this was therefore not possible.'[3]

Professor C.R. Cheyney, who had known Oldfield at Manchester University before he himself went to Cambridge, recalls having a letter from Oldfield 'a few years ago and we had tea at the Athenaeum. He was then thinking of retiring to Oxford, if a college would shelter him, and he was toying with the idea of returning to continue his research on the clergy in the fifteenth century parliament. I wasn't clear how seriously he was taking this, but we had a brief talk about picking up the threads after so long an interval.'[4]

Mr Peter S. Lewis, who was Dean of Visiting Fellows at All Souls at the time Oldfield went there in 1978, says that 'Sir Maurice proposed to work here on either his medieval material or a more modern topic: in the end he chose the latter. I think it's a bit unfair to say that he was "persuaded" to do so. More tidy and concise about the particular topic upon which he embarked I can't be.'[5]

One cannot help thinking that all the time Sir Maurice had in mind not one, but three or four modern topics when he was made a Visiting Fellow of All Souls. One wonders whether the suggestion of a medieval topic was made solely to detract attention from what he really wanted to do. There is always the danger when studying the character and personality of Sir Maurice of forgetting that, as one of his closest friends put it, 'he was not an intellectual'. A scholar, yes, an intellectual – especially with the implications which that word has in the English language – no. The truth is that he never lost the common touch and loved to escape from mere intellectualism.

Professor Michael Howard comments that 'his alternative proposal, and that which we accepted, was that he should undertake a study of Captain Mansfield Cumming [the first 'C'] in the expectation that he would find enough to go on in his private papers. In fact, he did not, but how seriously he ever took this I do not know. My own impression was that he spent most of his time at All Souls tying up various threads in his private life and settling outstanding business from his previous occupation. Certainly he never discussed his research with me, or, as far as I know, anyone else.'[6]

When Oldfield paid a visit to the Military Intelligence Corps Museum and Archives at Templer Barracks, Ashford, during his retirement, he told Colonel F.G. Robson, the Curator, that he was fascinated by what little he had learned of the life of Mansfield Cumming. 'He said he had looked up the files and found Cumming's first diary which contained some splendid stuff. But he couldn't find the second or any other diaries.'[7]

One SIS colleague remembers: 'Maurice was disappointed

211

at the lack of material on Cumming. "Alas," he told me, "nobody is now alive who knew Cumming, so that makes the task that much more difficult. But the fact that someone has either nicked, or lost, or destroyed some of the Cumming diaries is deplorable." '

Sir William Deakin was rather more forthcoming. 'The prospect of undertaking research and writing was a timely challenge to his intellect. Maurice's natural modesty and moral sense of security precluded him from engaging on any personal memoirs as we discussed many times and always in agreement. We often talked together about subjects on which he might appropriately direct his interest. They were, as ideas of inquiry, reduced to three: The relevance of Secret Intelligence in the decisions of government since 1912 and into the early 1920s – if overt material were available. And then, Appeasement in the 1930s as seen from certain sources. An intriguing relic of his youthful reactions to the international scene of 1939 as a hardy liberal.'[8]

Dr Rohan Butler, of All Souls, states that 'Sir Maurice did occasionally mention to me casually some interests in regard to research. I can only say that I cannot recall any specific mention of appeasement between the wars, but I think he did indicate some interest in the world of Lord Vansittart ... he never gave me any hint as to any future aims in academic life.'[9]

Sir Maurice was not merely revelling in a return to academic life, but in the freedom to turn his mind to a wide range of intriguing topics. It seems highly probable that he kept an absolutely open mind as to which subject or subjects he would take up in due course. He was undoubtedly very keen on researching the life and career of Mansfield Cumming and his preliminary research had shown him some interesting sidelines in connection with the period of Cumming's directorship of the SIS. 'Did you know,' he asked one former colleague, 'that MI 6 suffered badly from a dearth of carrier-pigeons on the Western Front in World War One? Did you also know that the pigeon was the chief means of communication at that time between the agent operating in between our own and the enemy lines and his controller?'

He was always willing, where he could legitimately do so, to use his research knowledge to help others. A young Israeli student, who had studied behavioural patterns in pigeons at Tel Aviv University, wished to research the history of pigeons used for communications in two world wars. 'I had obtained some case histories from the PDSA,' Mr Elie Weinstein told me, 'but Sir Maurice was able to put things in perspective for me. He pointed out for example that pigeons had helped to save London from V 1 and V 2 attacks when Resistance workers used them to send back messages about rocket-launching sites so that the RAF could bomb them. He also told me of a pigeon, sent on a special mission to Crete, which returned to her loft at Alexandria after having flown some five hundred miles mostly over sea, thus enabling some vital intelligence to be delivered.'[10]

During the early days of his retirement Oldfield thoroughly enjoyed visiting Intelligence colleagues in other countries to say farewell to them. His years in Syria and the Lebanon had always been an influence on his later career and he was one of the very few people who managed to be on equally friendly terms with French, Lebanese and Syrians. One particularly happy farewell party was in Paris with some of his French opposite numbers. They showed Oldfield their file on him and gave him back his pass for the interrogation centre at Beirut which he had returned to the French authorities early in 1945 when he was posted to Cairo.

Yet most of his researches during his time at All Souls remain something of a mystery. Sir Isaiah Berlin says: 'He never talked about his academic ambitions. He lived at Beechwood House, where All Souls Visiting Fellows are lodged, and I never knew what he was working on. I was always glad to see him and talk to him about current political issues, developments in Northern Ireland and the like.'[11]

While he may have had some problems in finding the material he wanted to research, it is equally probable that the authorities put some embargo on what he could set down on paper. It is also evident that he was revelling in delving into all manner of subjects, even if some of these were to be found in the less frequented archives of intelligence. From casual remarks he made one got the impression that he was bitterly disappointed, if not somewhat angry, that so many worthwhile papers had been destroyed. 'I have learned in my quest for documents that there is more to be found about the man who might have become "C" than the first "C" himself,' he said to one colleague.

'Who on earth was that?'' he was asked.

'A man nobody seems to remember nowadays, yet he is worth a little monograph all to himself. He was Captain Sir William Maxwell, who covered the Boer War for the London *Evening Standard*. Of course he was very much an agent in the field, used to operating behind enemy lines. He must have been one of the very few of our agents to be taken prisoner by a British cavalry patrol in World War One. That was outside Mons. He was head of a section of the SIS after being attached to the Headquarters in the Dardanelles expedition.'

'He told me that he was looking forward to working again in the PRO search rooms,' said Mr Jeffery Ede, who, apart from a distinguished career at the Public Record Office, had like Oldfield served in the Field Security Wing in the Middle East. 'He seemed rather uncertain of what he would be doing at Oxford, but I got the impression that he would probably – at any rate, initially – be working on contemporary papers, possibly of one or other of the agencies with whose operations he was familiar. I introduced him to one or two PRO colleagues who were greatly charmed by him and looked forward to seeing more of him.'[12]

'I knew Maurice quite well when he was at All Souls, in so far as it was possible to get to know him,' says Professor Michael Howard. 'Although a very affable and agreeable man, he had developed habits of discretion which made it difficult to get anything of great substance out of him. Like so many people in his profession, he had the capacity to appear to talk freely while in fact saying nothing at all.

'Oldfield did turn up to various seminars and lectures dealing with questions of defence and foreign policy, but he never made any very great contribution. If directly appealed

214

to, he would occasionally give factual information but never of particularly illuminating character. My own recollection of him is simply of an extraordinarily nice and companionable man who was always very welcome in Common Room, who could take part easily in any discussion that was going on, but who never gave anything away.'[13]

There seems to be a general consensus that Oldfield was a likeable figure at All Souls. 'Even though he played little part in the academic life of the College, he was a most popular member of our community,' says Mr J.S.G. Simmons, the Deputy Archivist at All Souls. 'He was one of the most popular Visiting Fellows that we have ever had here,' writes Dr Rohan Butler. 'I came to like him very much. He had an unpretentious gift for making friends with all kinds of people, academic and otherwise. I think the secret of this was that he was a good person.' 'Personally I regard him with great affection, and not only out of respect for his past. I remember, particularly, his valediction, "God bless", which he really meant,' is the tribute of Mr Peter Lewis, the Librarian at All Souls.[14]

One's impression is that at this time Oldfield was actually missing the atmosphere of Century House and suffering from some withdrawal symptoms. However much he may have longed for a return to academic life, when it came to the moment of decision he was not so sure. His work had been positive and constructive and it was something he regarded as being worthwhile in the broadest sense. Possibly, the more he saw of the academic world on his return to it, the less he felt able to fit in. It was not a case of his not being accepted, but much more whether there were not more important things he should be doing. One thing is certain: he used much of his retirement renewing acquaintance with old friends and making new friends. The outside world called him most: he was, if one likes to put it this way, a gregarious monk.

One of the old friends with whom he always kept in touch was Mr Aldo Fiorentini, a former colleague in the Middle East, now manager of Ninety Park Lane. He refers to the days when 'Sir Maurice was a regular visitor to the Savoy

Grill, which I used to manage, having his usual corner table, often shared with Mr Julian Amery and many other interesting people. He was a very charming person, and a gourmet in his own right. We would often reminisce about our times together in Cairo in a mixture of Arabic, French and Italian.'[15]

Apart from the Athenaeum, Sir Maurice was also a member of the Royal Commonwealth Society and the Royal Over-Seas League, at which clubs he often met with friends and visitors from distant lands. That heavy, stolid visage could be misleading, for behind those thick-rimmed spectacles which he often polished with his tie was a man who rarely forgot a face or a name. What was more he would remember all manner of trivialities he might be told in casual conversation with drivers and messengers. Indeed, he sometimes surprised the latter by recalling a birthday, or asking how a child was getting on at school. Yet what all this really represented was his astonishing sense of continuity in life, of following a friendship through not merely for one person, but for that person's children and sometimes even their grandchildren. He would be best man at somebody's wedding, godfather at the christening of the offspring and then present at the wedding of the offspring. Sir Bryan Hopkin illustrates this point: 'Maurice was godfather to my younger son Richard (who was christened at the advanced age of fourteen). When Richard got married Maurice came to the wedding and made a vastly amusing speech. Our last meeting was in fact at the christening in London of Richard's daughter Emma, around Easter, 1979.'[16]

At this period Oldfield became intensely interested in how journalists and other writers conducted their researches into the minefields of the world of intelligence. He was not easily accessible to them, but, realizing that intelligence was not the taboo word it had been for so long, he allowed himself to talk cautiously to a few chosen investigative journalists. Phillip Knightley of the *Sunday Times* was one who managed to arrange a meeting with Oldfield, despite the latter stating beforehand that 'I would like to help you; this is, however, unlikely to be possible for reasons some known, and some unknown to you. I suspect the OSA [Official Secrets Act] would apply.'[17]

They met at the Athenaeum Club and, though Oldfield was, as always, discreet and posing more questions than he answered, he had some interesting comments to make. Knightley asked what Oldfield thought Philby was doing during his Russian exile. 'One thing he does,' replied Maurice, 'is to keep up a voluminous correspondence with people in the West. He writes regularly to Graham Greene, for instance, and to people in this country.' At this point, remarked Knightley, 'Oldfield fixed me with his interrogator's stare, and he added, "And he tries to sow mischief in these letters. He drops hints that he has been out of the Soviet Union. One of his recent letters talked about how he had enjoyed 'sunny climes and rum in a long glass.' Philby knows that his letters are opened – at both ends, I suspect – and his scheme is to get us running around trying to find out where he had been and why. 'Sunny climes and rum in a long glass'! Has Philby been in Cuba? What the hell is he doing there? That sort of thing." '[18]

Privately, Oldfield was not merely critical, but somewhat irritated by some of the recent so-called official histories of British Intelligence in World War Two. He felt that much of these histories was 'by the Establishment for the Establishment and about the Establishment, but nothing to do with how the war was won.' His main criticism was that nearly all of the writers concerned had failed to pay tribute to the 'agent in the field', and for Oldfield the lone agent was a true hero and patriot. His comment on this was: 'You get the impression that the Intelligence war was won by committees in Whitehall, rather than by people … I'm thinking about doing a review of the book [British Intelligence in the Second World War, by F.H. Hinsley, E.E. Thomas, C.F.G. Ransom and R.C. Knight] and the first sentence will be, "This is a book written by a committee, about committees, for committees." '[19]

I have since talked with Phillip Knightley about Oldfield's feelings on this subject and he confirmed that Oldfield had said that this type of history got things out of all proportion.

'He felt very strongly indeed about it,' said Knightley, 'and he felt for history's sake that the record should be set straight.'

The more one hears of some of Oldfield's off-the-record talks with people at this time the more it becomes clear that the historian in him wanted to put quite a few records straight. Not just on the modern history of the world of espionage and intelligence, but of its earlier history, too. He told Goronwy Rees that 'in many respects Charles Babbage was the father of our modern intelligence system inasmuch as it applies to communications.' Babbage, who was born in 1792, and educated at Trinity College, Cambridge, was so far in advance of his tutors that in 1812 he founded the Analytical Society 'for promoting the Principles of pure D-ism in opposition to the Dot-age of the university'. Babbage was in effect the founder of the computer when he invented his machine for calculations. But Oldfield had delved further into his career and discovered that Babbage's theory of signalling by occulting solar lights had been brought into practice at the siege of Sebastopol and that his first model for a mechanical computer had been discussed in Italy in 1840.

'What Maurice was most fascinated by in his discovery of the material Babbage had left behind was in the Babbage Papers in the British Library,' said Goronwy Rees. 'Here one found Babbage the cryptographer who made a hobby of deciphering love messages in *The Times* in the early eighteenth century. As Maurice said, Babbage was in some ways totally equipped for being a Secret Service chief. His range of interests was so diverse that it embraced submarines, lighthouses, archaeology, lock-picking and deciphering. When a barrister was faced with the problem of coded messages in a divorce case, Babbage was asked to solve the cipher key used.'[20]

The Babbage Papers reveal that Charles Babbage spent a great deal of time working out coded love messages and plotting the probable alphabetical and numerical cipher selected. The material he deciphered makes fascinating reading for anyone romantically-minded, and one cannot help feeling that Oldfield might well have made Babbage's researches the subject of a worthwhile book. Perhaps just one brief sample of deciphering from the Babbage Papers will suffice:'... Beloved, you are the most lovely lily of the valley I know and I tell you agen [again]. I could not part with you or exchange you for anybody else ... I love you so *molto* and always did. If all the world was to make love to me, I do not think they would make me love you less. You are my dearest Seraph ... My regards 45-150 ... I understand very sweet but very wicked, and my darling what is your wish I do agree fully ... what you wish *molto* I cannot refuse ... I do not like all these things.'[21]

More often than not in this period Maurice was helping his friends in all manner of minor chores. Someone had passed on two silver chalices to St Matthew's, Westminster, but nobody seemed to know their origin. This challenged the historian in Oldfield and he immediately applied to his wartime friend, Irvine Gray, for help. It was finally discovered that the chalices dated back to the time of the Civil War and that they had been passed on from a church in Stanmore, Middlesex, to St Matthew's. Mr Irvine Gray cites an amusing letter he received from Oldfield, dated 2 November 1978, in which he said that Mr Gray's discovery warranted 'at least two masses', but added that 'if you want reward on earth where only the Inland Revenue can corrupt, please let me know.' In another letter, thanking Mr Gray for some genealogical research and referring to the latter's mentioning that 'getting on the right track had been mostly luck', Oldfield commented: 'Personally, I believe in training coupled with intuition and not in luck. Security work is a bit like genealogy.'[22]

From time to time Oldfield and Graham Greene met, and, some say, argued on theological topics. Graham Greene had himself served briefly in the SIS in wartime, watching the Vichy French in Freetown. It is said that Oldfield was angry after reading Greene's book, *The Human Factor*, when it was published in the latter part of the 1970s. He felt that it depicted the SIS in a highly unfavourable and unfair light, hinting that the Service would not hesitate to murder one of their own men if it seemed in their interests to do so. One of the SIS types in the novel tells a subordinate: 'That's your square from now on. You don't need to wory about the blue and the red. All you have to do is to pinpoint our man and then tell me. You've no responsibility for what happens in the blue or red squares. In fact not even in the yellow. You just report.' This was not at all Oldfield's way of thinking. But probably the chief objection he had to *The Human Factor* was that in it Graham Greene had actually used the cover name of one of Oldfield's most favoured agents.

Despite this, Oldfield and Greene remained friends.

13

Anguish In Ulster

Perhaps the biggest blow which Margaret Thatcher suffered on the eve of her general election victory in the early summer of 1979 was the assassination of her close friend, political adviser and campaign officer, Airey Sheffield Neave. The murder of Neave by members of the Irish National Liberation Army (possibly in collusion with other agencies) as he was driving away from the House of Commons car park meant that many of her plans had to be totally revised.

Up to the time of his death Airey Neave had concentrated on the job of shadow minister for Northern Ireland. Had he lived, it is almost certain that he would have been given the post of chief minister in Ulster in the first Thatcher government. There was a possibility, actively considered in some circles, that he might eventually have been offered the task of liaising with the intelligence services, a job similar to that given to George Wigg in 1964. Whichever post he held, it would to some extent be relevant to the situation in Northern Ireland.

Roy Mason, the Labour Minister for Northern Ireland, had proved to be hard-working, courageous and not one to offer any encouragement or inducement to those who talked glibly about seeking a political initiative for the future of the province. This seemingly negative virtue was to prove one of his soundest assets. On the other hand he was not to be compared to Merlyn Rees, who, in the eyes of the intelligence community, was the best of all the Northern Ireland Secretaries of State. The new Conservative Minister for that territory was Humphrey Atkins, who had not been groomed for the post and could hardly have been appointed at a more inauspicious moment. Not only had relations between the army and the police in Ulster deteriorated, but terrorism had suddenly been stepped up. Then came the killing of Lord Mountbatten of Burma while he was on a fishing holiday off the west coast of Donegal and the ambushing and slaughter of eighteen British soldiers by the PIRA or INLA (Irish National Liberation Army) near the Armagh village of Warrenpoint on the same day.

A significant incident in connection with the Mountbatten killing was that Oldfield, though then retired and long before he was posted to Northern Ireland, actually warned Mountbatten against going to Ireland that summer of 1979. What Oldfield might have heard, or whether he was passing on a message from others, must remain a matter for conjecture. But one point can be made categorically: Oldfield was not so much concerned for Mountbatten's personal safety as to prevent the involvement of a member of the Royal Family in an IRA killing.

After these events the Prime Minister decided that something positive needed to be done and she set about finding the right man to tackle the situation. It is, however, still far from clear whether there was any real plan as to what this man should do. To some extent it was a move made solely to placate criticism. The first names submitted to 10 Downing Street were all those of diplomats. According to one Parliamentary lobby source all of these except one declined the post of what was somewhat vaguely called 'co-ordinator'. Presumably the Prime Minister decided against the one who said 'yes'. At one time Sir Robert Mark, who had made his name as an ardent reformer with the Metropolitan Police, was tipped for the job. Increasingly, it became obvious to the Prime Minister that whoever took on the post must have rather special qualifications if he was to assert his authority, and that such talents should preferably be in the field of intelligence.

As has been seen, Mrs Thatcher had already established a rapport with Maurice Oldfield. She had sought his advice on Irish problems more than once. She also knew that Airey Neave had had a high regard for Oldfield, and this may have helped to make up her mind.

At the end of September 1979 Oldfield was staying in Over Haddon when the Prime Minister's Private Secretary telephoned to inquire if he could travel up to 10 Downing Street. The call came at the very moment that Maurice was going to Bakewell Market with his brother, and he had no hesitation in saying so. But he agreed to travel to London the next day.

'I wanted time to anticipate what this mysterious summons was all about,' he said afterwards. 'I had a hunch that it might be to do with Rhodesia, one of the subjects I was always being questioned about. Or it could even have been something to do with some security matter. The affair of Anthony Blunt was just beginning to surface then.'

He went to Bakewell Market, had a few drinks at the Wheatsheaf and then packed hastily for his return to London. Later he told his old schoolmaster, Dr Harvey: 'I didn't have any hesitation about going to Downing Street immediately. In domestic politics I thought well of the Prime Minister because one knew exactly where one stood with her. She left one in no doubt what she was trying to do and she deserved success.'

He travelled to London the following day and was told what assignment he was being offered. It was to be Co-ordinator of Security and Intelligence in Northern Ireland. He asked for thirty-six hours to make up his mind. His request was granted.

Having become used to the idea of permanent retirement from official life, it was no easy decision to take. During those hours of trial he remained alone in his London flat, while an armed detective stood outside the door. 'They were,' said Oldfield, 'the worst thirty-six hours of my life. I alone could make the decision. Nobody else could help me to do so. But I was worried, not just for myself, but for the danger I put my mother in and my whole family.'[1]

This consideration alone made him hesitate for those thirty-six hours. Deep down he felt it was his duty to accept the assignment offered to him. Yet at the same time he had to face the possibility that a bomb attack similar to that which threatened his own life in Westminster a few years earlier could be launched against members of his own family.

The next day, before going to the Northern Ireland Office, and without giving any hint of the post offered to him, he lunched with Mr Julian Amery and an old SIS colleague. 'All my life I had been dealing with the country's overseas enemies,' he said. 'Now it is something quite different. If at any time I have regretted being unmarried, it is now. The pressure is tremendous, and, having someone to talk to would have made all the difference. I can't say what this job is, but it is one I know in my heart I cannot refuse.'

Next day he accepted the Prime Minister's offer and on 2 October 1979 it was announced by Mr Humphrey Atkins that 'Sir Maurice Oldfield will assist the Secretary of State in improving the co-ordination and effectiveness of the fight against terrorism in Northern Ireland. He will be based in Northern Ireland and be supported by a joint staff drawn from the Royal Ulster Constabulary, the Army and the Civil Service, which will be operational twenty-four hours a day. The Government intends to maintain and increase the pressure by the security forces on the terrorists so as to bring them to justice.'

This announcement came within hours of the rejection by the PIRA of the Pope's call for an end to violence. The PIRA had replied to this plea by saying that 'force is by far the only means of removing the evil of British presence in Ireland.' This response was made despite the fact that the Belfast morning paper, the *Irish News*, with a mainly Catholic readership, had declared that it would be 'less than honest' not to tell the PIRA that they should heed the Pope's passionate plea and also the offer from the illegal Protestant Ulster Defence Force to match a cease-fire by the Provos.

Oldfield's appointment was cautiously welcomed by some Unionists in Ulster, but there were also some doubters in their ranks as to the real nature of this newly created post. 'There was an atmosphere of mystery surrounding it,' says Mr Enoch Powell, 'and a feeling that we Unionists were not being told all that we were entitled to know.'[2]

Mr Gerry Fitt (now Lord Fitt), the Social Democrat and Labour MP for Belfast West, without commenting on the appointment itself, said that there had undoubtedly developed a situation in which the police and army chiefs were 'not seeing eye to eye'. From time to time the Army had conducted its own intelligence-gathering operations by employing personnel wearing plain clothes in undercover work. For the most part these operations were amateurish and not very successful and had been condemned by MI 6. When Captain Robert Nairac, GC, was murdered by the IRA in 1977, one of his colleagues summed up as follows: 'It was a bloody shambles. Nobody knew what anyone else was doing. The army didn't trust the police; the police thought, rightly, that the army bungled operations.'[3]

Such an allegation was a convincing reason for bringing Oldfield to Belfast. For one of his chief functions upon arriving in Ulster was to make sure that the operations of the army and the RUC Special Branch did not overlap. His arrival in Northern Ireland had been partly precipitated by a personality clash between the Commissioner of Police, Sir Kenneth Newman, and the GOC, General Sir Timothy Creasey. The political objective at this time was that the army should be keeping a low profile and moving into the background, dealing with security problems, but playing second fiddle to the Royal Ulster Constabulary. But, paradoxically, General Creasey was a bustling 'up and at 'em' type with a positive personality to match his positive approach. On the other hand Sir Kenneth Newman had a relatively low profile and was a somewhat withdrawn and inscrutable figure. As one junior minister aptly summed it up: 'All the personal assertion was on the side of those who were meant to be withdrawn, and all the personal withdrawnness was on the side of the people who were meant to assert themselves.'

Some indications of the hazards which Oldfield faced in this new job can be gauged from the experiences of Mr Roy Mason, who was perhaps the toughest and most pragmatic of all Secretaries of State for Northern Ireland since direct rule began in 1972. Even though he was out of office in the autumn of 1979, he still lived in fear of assassination and had the life of a recluse. 'Home, if that is what you can call it, has become a mini-fortress. The gardens are patrolled, floodlights are on all night, security men live in a hut outside the door, checking all visitors, even postmen and milkmen, in a twenty-four hour vigil. The house is under total surveillance and my protection team never leave me alone,' he stated at that time. 'My wife, walking or shopping, is protected all the time, and within the house we have a multiplicity of devices which help assure our safety.'[4]

On 8 October Oldfield arrived at his office in Belfast beneath the granite towers of Stormont Castle to take on the loneliest job in his whole life. As soon as his plane touched down he was driven under armed guard straight into the appartments assigned to him, already dubbed by the PIRA as the 'Stormont KGB'. There was an instant blackout on the newcomer's movements and all a Government spokesman would say was: 'Sir Maurice has arrived and that is all we are going to tell you about him.' It was made clear that the press and other media operatives would not be allowed to meet him, not even for off-the-record briefings, and that photographers would be particularly unwelcome.

At the same time that Oldfield took up his post other key appointments in Northern Ireland were also announced. They included a new RUC chief in Mr John (later Sir John) Hermon and a new GOC in Major-General Richard Lawson, both to take effect before the end of the year. Oldfield was left to choose his own personal staff of about forty from lists supplied by the army, the police and the Northern Ireland Office, though in the case of the last-named the Foreign and Commonwealth Office also had a voice. In the meantime Sir Kenneth Newman and General Sir Timothy Creasey continued in their respective posts in the RUC and Army commands.

One reason for the new look at security arrangements in Northern Ireland was that links between the PIRA and some European, North African and Middle East terrorist organizations such as the PLO and Colonel Gaddafi's own death-dealing units had long since been established. It made sense therefore to have someone with SIS experience to cope with this problem. But probably a much more vital reason was the need to seek closer cooperation with the Irish Government on matters of security.

Shortly after the Mountbatten murder there was much unofficial talk about the need for closer links with the Irish Republic on the subject of security and for the two governments to seek a political agreement. The circumstances of the Mountbatten killing and the events shortly before and immediately afterwards were all somewhat mysterious and many Unionists, including Mr Enoch Powell, believed that the motive for the murder was a political one. That the assassination was used by some Irish Republican politicians as an excuse for bringing pressure on the British Government to achieve a political solution for Northern Ireland (which, in plain speech, meant finding a way of uniting the north with the south) was demonstrated when the Irish Prime Minister was questioned on the subject. Would the Mountbatten murder make the quest for agreement more difficult, he was asked? 'On the contrary,' he replied. 'It will make it easier.'

One section of opinion inside the British Foreign Office had for a long time taken the view that covert influences should be used to pave the way for some form of reunification of Northern Ireland with the Irish Republic. There was at the same time an unofficial exchange of views with some Americans for an undercover joint Anglo-American operation to reach some sort of reunification agreement while at the same time manipulating Ireland into the Western Alliance, as a member of NATO. At no time were any of these ideas put forward as policy, but a great deal was done to propagate them discreetly among those likely to be won over to what some saw as a neat solution of several problems in one package. Naturally, not much progress was made with the hard-line and neutralist Fianna Fail Party, but Lieutenant-General Sean MacEoin, former Irish Chief of Staff, had publicly asserted in November 1978 that 'Ireland would have little option but to become a participant in a European defence union ... Soldiers are soldiers and I would find it difficult to believe that our military people would not gladly relish participation in a cause in which they believe and which they consider must be honoured.'5

The Irish Republic had also had their undercover agents in the north and the CIA had established some links with MI 6 both in the north and the south. 'We kept a very low profile as a general rule,' says one CIA officer. 'On the whole we relied on our links with MI 6.' This officer declined to enlarge on his statement.

So it will be seen that there were some fears among Unionists as to what Oldfield's job really was. Some of them were too suspicious to believe he was solely there to co-ordinate; they were convinced that there was some hidden purpose in his appointment, that maybe he had something to do with an Anglo-American scheme for reunification on certain terms.

An advantage in the Oldfield posting was that the Security Co-ordinator would soon be dealing with a Chief Constable and a GOC who were newcomers like himself. Army and police relations in Ulster had varied from being reasonably cordial in some areas to open hostility in others. Until the beginning of 1976 the army had virtually had the final word on all security measures. This situation had changed, however, when there was an official acceptance of the conclusions of an internal Northern Ireland Office committee. This report stated that 'in the way ahead ... the police should have overall control.' Following this, the local security committee was chaired by the police instead of an army officer as hitherto. Significantly, the new Chief of Police, John Hermon, was an Ulsterman who had risen from the ranks to become Deputy Chief Constable. Sir Kenneth Newman had served in the RAF in World War Two before joining the Palestine Police and then the Metropolitan Police, having latterly been HM Inspector of Constabulary.

The problems with which Oldfield had to cope were manifold and not simply a question of improving relations between the army and the police, though this was initially a prime target. The gathering of intelligence with the aim of defeating terrorism was complicated because while some sections of the IRA supported terrorism, others did not, accepting the view that the undermining of the social structure by infiltrating political parties was more successful than terrorist tactics in the long run. So, with the two respective wings of the IRA posing different problems for the security forces, there was no simple answer to either. Admittedly, too, intelligence-gathering in Northern Ireland in recent years had been singularly unproductive.

Oldfield almost immediately looked beyond Belfast to Dublin and posed the question: 'How do the Garda [the Irish Republic's police and security force] feel about the situation between the police and the British Army in Ulster?' He got his answer from the Garda quickly enough. In strictly informal language it was this: 'We find it hard to believe any police force can get along so badly with its own army. We are baffled by the lack of co-ordination between them. How can you hope for help from us in this kind of situation?' This resulted in some unofficial communications with Mr Michael O'Kennedy, then Foreign Minister of the Republic of Ireland.

The new Security Co-ordinator was in no doubt that Belfast needed the help of Dublin and the Garda just as much as Dublin, even if less frequently, needed aid from Belfast. He discovered to his horror and amazement that up to March 1979, when a check was made, of the four hundred motor-road crossings from the north to the Republic only twenty had control points. This he described as 'a nonsense'.

But, apart from the daily threat of personal danger (he was now top of the PIRA hit list), Oldfield was shrewd enough to realize that he was very much on trial and viewed critically and suspiciously from many quarters. Surprisingly, too, he had suddenly acquired a few new enemies, chiefly from those who had got caught up in the power struggle and were looking for a scapegoat. 'The appointment of Sir Maurice Oldfield,' stated the Dublin *Irish Times*, 'has really put the cat among the pigeons. Hardly anyone, even at the very highest security levels, knows what to make of the appointment, and almost everyone suspects that something is going on. Oldfield will be greeted with politeness, but he will he watched like a hawk ... We'll have to wait and see if Sir Maurice's job is to tinker with the police, tailor the Intelligence Services, soldier with the Army, or spy on the lot of them' – an oblique reference to the title of one of Le Carré's novels about Smiley.[6]

Some in the army were initially angry because Creasey had not been made security supremo. Others back in London were angry that an SIS man had been chosen for the post rather than one with MI 5 experience. Suddenly those old enmities between MI 5 and MI 6 flared up again, the former claiming that a bias against their service existed inside Whitehall. One man – anonymously, of course – who claimed to be one of Oldfield's 'men in the field', went so far as to tell *Now!* magazine that 'he is a desk man, a paper-pusher who will find it very different when he is trying to deal with fast-breaking terrorist operations rather than sitting back and cogitating over the global strategy of defeating the KGB,' adding that 'he is too much to the Left for my taste.'[7]

Some of this hostility extended to personnel in Northern Ireland, people who had merely listened to rumour and gossip and not even met Oldfield. Yet all who knew him well would testify that he was sincerely non-political and one of the most open-minded and pragmatic men in the world. As to the ridiculous allegation that he was 'too much to the Left', perhaps this can best be answered by what Professor A.J.P. Taylor, his old tutor, told me: 'We never discussed his profession in the slightest. He once said to me, "I am a Cold War Warrior." I replied "And I am not." Nothing more ever. I had no idea of his work. We met very often at the Athenaeum Club for many years, but he told me nothing except that he was in the Foreign Office.'[8]

However, whatever some of those disappointed men

among his critics might say, Oldfield soon impressed his authority in a quiet way on those around him at Stormont Castle. In his first week he discovered widespread breaches of security, and demanded a drastic shake-up of the whole organization. He found that there were no telephone lines available to the security forces which were not liable to be bugged, and that the PIRA had equipment which could unscramble secret messages. At the time he took over virtually every radio message was liable to be intercepted by undercover Provo units lying low in high-risk areas.

Sir Philip Goodhart, MP, who held a ministerial position in Northern Ireland in 1979-80, says: 'I saw quite a lot of him. At that time he would talk very quickly, in a very low voice, so if one was a little deaf, it was very difficult actually to hear what he was saying, which added considerably to the mystique of wise inscrutability with which he was generally surrounded. Maurice's arrival resolved difficulties just because he was who he was. All Maurice had to do when the temperature rose was to say "The flowers that bloom in the spring will wither in the autumn", and everyone would nod wisely and the temperature would be reduced. Maurice, of course, said a great deal more than this, but you will get the point. It was his actual presence that mattered, because of the general respect in which he was held.'[9]

To co-ordinate the activities of some 13,500 British soldiers and 6,500 policemen in the RUC called for great tact, patience and above all quick decision-making. With Oldfield's talent for absorbing reports at a glance and devouring pages of paper in an astonishingly short while, this task was made easier. He also had to combat the fact that the RUC was a highly unpopular force in many districts. That he managed to some extent, albeit limited, to change this image was testified by the Irish political commentator, W.D. Flackes, who wrote: 'After Oldfield it was claimed that the RUC has become more acceptable in Catholic circles ... hence the steady flow of information through the confidential telephone and otherwise.'[10]

That is an Irish viewpoint, but it is amply substantiated by what little can be gleaned of Oldfield's cautious but deliberatively investigative work in Ulster. Clearly, he knew that there were many priests who equivocably supported the IRA, and that some of these included highly placed prelates. Possibly for this reason, though equally for logical reasons in connection with his work alone, he was able for the first time in his career to apply his Christian talents in the cause of his profession, though this is, of course, not to suggest that he did not always demand a fairly exacting moral code in carrying out his duties. But in Northern Ireland the medieval scholar and the student of theology was able quietly to display himself to often surprised Catholic priests of all ranks all over the territory. He had one great advantage: more than once in his life, possibly dating back to his Middle East days, he had been tempted to become a Roman Catholic, something which, with his preference for High Church Anglicanism, was almost logical. Not only had he a certain nostalgia for the Catholic Church, but on various occasions – to take a break from the pressures of work – he had actually gone on retreats to Catholic monasteries.

He fully realized that in going to see some of these priests he was putting them, even some of their flock, at risk. Thus when visiting he maintained the tightest of security, covering all parts of the province, and arriving by helicopter. He was always as anxious to protect the priests as to protect himself. Some of the Catholic clergy were astonished to find that the Co-ordinator of Security and Intelligence could possibly be the same person who half a century previously had acquired a distinction in divinity. 'He would actually discuss theology with us quite as naturally as though he had been in a monastery for most of his life,' declared one priest, 'and he explained a lot else, too of course. In many matters concerning the Church he was, to my amazement, better educated than I had been myself. Certainly he greatly aided the British cause with the Catholic community. Perhaps that is claiming that he achieved miracles. Well, not quite that, but he removed a lot of misunderstandings.'

What this priest meant was that Oldfield proved to be a highly effective ambassador. This invaluable work conducted without any ostentation also helped considerably in intelligence-gathering. Gradually, Catholics were won over as informers. Intelligence, as a general rule, came from three sources: informers, who were usually paid; the interrogation of suspects; and surveillance. The Provos' cell system had cut down the effectiveness of informers and the controversy over interrogation techniques in Castlereagh and Gough barracks had cut down the flow of information from this source. Although Oldfield's powers were limited, he nevertheless was able to exert his influence in such a way that, as chairman, he could persuade the army and the police to fulfil their respective roles more effectively. He was largely responsible for using 'deep cover' informers to identify gunmen with greater success than had been achieved previously. Oldfield was eventually able to convince his own intelligence officers that they knew next to nothing about who ran the Provos in Dublin and how the IRA was financed.

Apart from sorting out problems between the RUC and the army and tightening up security generally, the upsurge of PIRA violence in August 1979 had led to a demand for better intelligence and, if the army was to adopt a lower profile, to increased personnel in the RUC. By April 1979, the RUC strength had reached 8,684, comprised of 7,936 men and 748 women. About a thousand part-timers were on duty each evening and double that number at weekends. Most RUC officers were young and many of them had been far too occupied in carrying out their routine jobs from the very start to have sufficient time for training. Oldfield soon realized that often the RUC needed the closest cooperation of the army even when doing their own work. For example, on one occasion in the PIRA stronghold of South Armagh, while RUC officers were conducting a check on drunken drivers with on-the-spot breathalyser tests, army patrols had to protect them at a country cross-roads.

Oldfield's method of smoothing the way to the right level of cooperation and preventing any overlapping of duties was to make the security committees more effective by allowing army and police each to put their own cases while he was the neutral figure in the chair. This proved far more useful than the old method of the army and the police providing the chairman in turn.

The new Security Supremo had no doubts whatsoever that security and intelligence were indivisible and that the most important of his tasks was to improve, tighten up and achieve a more reliable intelligence system. At the same time he was well aware that, because of his previous post as head of MI 6, there was the risk that the PIRA would make international propaganda out of revelations of previous allegations of 'dirty tricks' by exponents of British espionage in Northern Ireland. He also suspected that, partly because of the attention that needed to be paid to Northern Ireland, MI 5 was finding it difficult to keep a sufficiently close watch on Soviet espionage inside the United Kingdom. Oldfield was quite sure that the KGB were fully aware of this and naturally anxious to exploit it.

During his term as chief of the SIS he had been kept posted on the presence in the Soviet Embassy in Dublin of a member of Department V of the KGB, which is responsible for assassination and sabotage. Having asked for more information, he was informed that some seven other KGB operatives had been identified in the whole of Ireland. He was fairly sure that this situation had not improved since he left Century House. Early on in his career at Stormont Castle he asked for, and eventually got, two separate reports on possible links between the KGB and the PIRA.

Throughout the history of Irish terrorist and underground organizations from the middle of the last century until today, while there has been ample evidence of links between these groups and, first the pre-Revolutionary Russians, then the Germans, and finally the Soviet, Libyans and other foreigners, rarely in the long run have the foreigners benefited much from this. Far more often they have been manipulated by the Irish. This was particularly true of the Germans in World War Two. Oldfield was always quick to remind over-zealous 'Red-watchers' of this fact: 'Watch, listen and report,' he would say, 'but never lose sight of the fact that in some cases even the Irish terrorist may take the KGB for a ride. Not always, perhaps, but when he does so, he can be doing some of our work for us.'

In the mid-seventies agents of both the Palestine Liberation Organization (PLO) and the Baader-Meinhof terrorist group had arrived in Northern Ireland. This news acquired a more sinister aspect when it was learned that a consignment of M60 machine-guns and Garand rifles had reached the PIRA. The PLO were said to be suppliers of these weapons.

Once, when told of a Polish diplomat who was visiting Belfast, Oldfield quietly replied: 'I am quite happy to know that as long as he is over here, you will monitor his movements. I see no problem in that and no need for me to have a report on those movements unless anything unusual occurs. We know that all such diplomats – Russian, Polish, Czech or whoever they may be – have to give two days' notice of plans to travel more than thirty-five miles from London. I think you can take it that such journeys are no more than what they claim to be – routine fact-finding. They know full well they are watched. What, however, I am interested in is the route between London and Belfast, where these diplomats have been just before they come here and just after they return to the UK. I suggest we might get reports on both from Liverpool and Glasgow.'

This advice paid off several months later. It was discovered that one Soviet diplomat had travelled to Belfast and Liverpool within a matter of days. While in Liverpool he had been in contact with a man known to belong to a PIRA cell. Weeks afterwards it was learned that he had been given a special assignment not only to establish links with extreme leftist organizations, but also with the IRA. After Oldfield's death sufficient evidence had been collected for the diplomat in question, Viktor Lazin, a Second Secretary in the Soviet Embassy in London, to be expelled for spying. Lazin was the first KGB officer to be deported from London since the occasion in 1971 when a hundred and five Russians at the London Embassy were declared *persona non grata*.

Oldfield set about re-organizing intelligence-gathering in a number of ways. As a former Military Intelligence officer he was, of course, fully aware of the contribution the Corps were making to improve security in Northern Ireland. Successive GOCs had testified that without the work of the MI Corps in Ulster 'our operations would have come to a halt'. The new Security Co-ordinator was also helped within a week of his arrival by a tightening up of border security by the Irish Army, and a gesture from the Republic in that British Army helicopters would be allowed to chase suspects up to ten miles inside Southern Ireland while keeping in direct contact with Irish security headquarters in Dundalk, County Louth.

Oldfield also had to curb the tendency of some Army unit commanders, usually lieutenant-colonels out for promotion, to take matters into their own hands precipitately. Sometimes Special Branch officers managed to gain the confidence of someone who knew about PIRA activities, and persuaded him to pass on information. If this intelligence was then given to an ambitious, headstrong army officer, he would sometimes exploit this in an unprofessional manner by sending in his unit in an ostentatious manner, thus drawing attention to the man who had given the information and losing a prize source of intelligence. This, of course, was a typical example of the kind of thing Oldfield hoped to check by urging a low profile by the army.

Expertise in the field of intelligence had improved over the years, particularly with a rationalization programme put into effect by the RUC since 1977. But there were still gaps in intelligence-gathering as was demonstrated by a confidential British Army document that was leaked to the press in Dublin. This document admitted that 'we know little of the detailed working of the [Provisional IRA] hierarchy in Dublin. In particular we have scant knowledge of how the logistic system works, nor do we know the extent to which the older, apparently retired, Republican leaders influence the movement.'[11]

Dr David Charters, deputy director of the Centre for Conflict Studies at the University of New Brunswick, visited Northern Ireland in August 1980, and was provided with information by the security forces. He came to the conclusion that 'the security forces have benefited from

Maurice Oldfield's expertise and guidance' and that 'deep cover' informer tactics had led to many arrests.[12]

Significant, too, were the statistics for house searches for firearms, explosives and ammunition in 1979 compared with those for the previous year. In 1978 some 15,462 searches of houses had been made, resulting in a haul of 400 firearms, 2,108 explosives and 43,512 rounds of ammunition. In 1979 fewer than 5,000 houses were searched, yet the haul from these amounted to 248 firearms, 1,979 explosives and 40,510 rounds of ammunition. Though, almost inevitably, statistics can be used to prove anything, in this instance clearly fewer searches carried out after more effective and reliable intelligence had produced more impressive results.

Not surprisingly the Provos satirized Oldfield as 'Maurice the Mole' in their magazine, and one cartoon in the *Irish Times* depicted two police officers talking on the street while in a tunnel underneath a figure captioned 'Maurice the Mole', with an eavesdropping gadget at his ear, was listening to their conversation. 'Ever get the feeling you were being undermined?' was the question posed by one of the policemen. The reason for the cartoonist adopting this theme was probably because of a mistaken belief in the south of Ireland that Oldfield had come to back the army and clamp down on the police's powers.

Yet even newspapers in the Republic came to have a respect for the new Security Supremo. David McKittrick, writing his 'Northern Notebook', said that 'Oldfield is one of the very few spymasters to have served in this secret world and left it with his reputation intact ... The chief effect of his arrival has been an increase in army activity. Now the RUC is supposed to have overall control of three important functions – raids, arrests and screening. The army is meant to consult the local RUC commander before undertaking such operations ...'[13]

Oldfield himself deliberately remained as inaccessible as possible in this period, except of course to his staff and senior army and police personnel. He refused to see journalists and politicians and even declined a request for a meeting from Mr Enoch Powell, the Unionist MP. Having been given the names and addresses of various people whom his friends had been anxious for him to meet, he politely took note of all these, but refrained from making contact with them. Nobody could have been more scrupulous about not getting himself involved in other people's affairs and political viewpoints. Some Irish newspapers declared that he had never been seen in Ulster and raised the question: 'Has he ever been to Northern Ireland? Or was his posting just a propaganda ploy to deceive everybody?'

Throughout his stay in Belfast no journalist was ever able to find him and no photographer succeeded in getting a photograph of him except for the *Down Recorder*, which was said to have secured one picture. He was able to go in and out of Ulster without his movements being discovered. Sometimes on leave from Northern Ireland he would attend a service at St Matthew's Church, Westminster. He sat at the back of the church as usual, flanked by two bodyguards. Once he confessed that, though he never feared death, he was appalled at the prospect of falling into the hands of the PIRA. On the other hand he also told his vicar, Prebendary Irvine, that in some ways he 'found the Ulster Loyalists' paramilitary organizations just as sinister, if not more so, than those of the IRA.'

His family and the possibility of some harm being done to them were always uppermost in his thoughts. But equally so was the idea that he might bring tragedy upon his friends. When invited to the country one weekend to stay with friends who had a baby son, he declined on the grounds that he did not want 'to draw the lightning'. For the same reason his visits to his family became less frequent. When, occasionally, he returned to Over Haddon, it was simply for a day trip and there was generally a helicopter overhead keeping watch on the area. Once, when he was back at the farm, there was a telephone call insisting that he must leave Derbyshire right away in his own and his family's interests. The reason for this was that police had located a car, packed with explosives, on its way to Over Haddon. A hit-gang was on Oldfield's trail. This was but one of a number of alarms about assassination attempts in this period.

Despite all these worries and the intensive work incurred in Belfast, Oldfield still found time to remember old friends. Fred Bardwell, on his twenty-first birthday, was pleasantly surprised to get a personal call from Oldfield and an assurance that the latter would attend his birthday party.

One hostile reference was made to his appointment in Ulster by the Social Democratic and Labour Party, the main voice of the Roman Catholic moderates in Northern Ireland. In a lengthy paper, drawn up by the SDLP, they stated that 'The primacy of law and order has been challenged by the appointment of a former undercover supremo to head security and by the announced expansion of undercover activities which are inherently dismissive of legal conventions.'[14]

No such official announcement about undercover activities had, of course, been made. The SDLP statement was based solely on speculation in the press. It certainly did not help the situation, especially at a time when one of Oldfield's aims was to see that the army and the police won the confidence of the Catholic community. Yet it must be remembered that, as a result of the recruitment of some singularly unsuitable characters for undercover work against the IRA by MI 6 in the early seventies, the Catholic community was still highly suspicious of the machinations of the British Secret Service in Ulster. It is some measure of Oldfield's skill behind the scenes that he was able to dispel many of these suspicions at least through his contacts with the priesthood.

Oldfield was acutely aware of the need for attempting to change the atmosphere of suspicion within the Catholic community, while at the same time altering the tactics of intelligence-gathering in Northern Ireland because of the embarrassments which activities such as those of the Littlejohn brothers and Howard Marks had caused in the past. But perhaps because of this both his appointment and his actual role became the subject of misgivings among some inside the Unionist Party. Many Unionists were suspicious because of the suddenness of the appointment and the fact that nobody had spelt out Oldfield's exact role and terms of

239

reference. But behind this suspicion was the fear that Oldfield might be used as a tool of the Foreign Office, for in the eyes of many Unionists the British Foreign Office was equated with the appeasement of Irish nationalism and paving the way for the independence of all Ireland.

It was noted with some misgivings that there was a Foreign Office observer at the Ulster Unionist conference in October 1979. Possibly there was a good reason for this as, after all, the Foreign Office had its own Irish desk. But what some Unionists really feared was that a combination of the Foreign Office, the US State Department and some of NATO's advisers would ultimately bring about the absorption of Northern Ireland into the Republic. The Republic was not a member of NATO, whereas Ulster, as part of the United Kingdom, was. Thus the argument ran that if a deal could be struck so that a united Ireland, including Ulster, could be persuaded to join NATO, in terms of world politics there could be no real objection to the British withdrawing from Ulster.

What such optimistic thinking conveniently ignored, however, was that any such move as the reunification of Ireland would be seen as a triumph for the forces of terrorism and the extremists and that these people would call the tune in deciding what kind of a country the unified Ireland should be. Most of them were hard-line neutralists, opposed to joining NATO or any other defence union. The real risk of any such experiment would be that the PIRA and INLA would destabilize Ireland and exploit the resulting chaos as they armed for a centralized single-party dictatorship on Marxist lines. Fifty years ago the influence of the Catholic Church might have prevented this in Catholic Ireland. Today, as has been seen in Nicaragua and elsewhere in Latin America, many of the Catholic clergy have swung over to the side of the terrorists and left-wing dictators, or would-be dictators. That, of course, was the pessimistic side of the picture, but such were the political, religious and psychological minefields through which Oldfield had to plough his way.

His first task was to encourage a genuine rapport between

240

Sir John Hermon, the Chief Constable, and Major-General Richard Lawson, the new GOC. He also encouraged the long-term tactics of winning informers from the ranks of the IRA, or from those closely associated with one or other of the wings of that organization. Informers of this type have often proved to be more reliable than agents infiltrated into the IRA.

It would appear that MI 6 activities in the Republic produced rather better results in this period than they had done previously. Not the least of their tasks was the constant monitoring of the significantly large embassy staff of the USSR in Dublin. Another organization closely watched by MI 6 was the Irish-Arab Society. But MI 6's main success was in establishing agents inside the Garda, the Irish Army and government departments. One of the most vital informants was a senior Garda officer who (up to 1981 at least) was still in that force. He had not only provided information on the PIRA, but on the activities of the former Irish Premier, Mr Haughey, and other prominent political figures.

14

The Last Tragic Year

Oldfield had never really been happy while in Northern Ireland. In many respects this was perhaps the unhappiest period of his whole life. Not only did he feel cut off from his friends, but from life itself. For in his own way he was a very outgoing and gregarious person. What irked him more than anything else was the sense of being permanently hemmed in by a bodygurd who went everywhere with him.

By the spring of 1980 the strain was beginning to tell, and he was feeling far from well. His first instinct was to attribute this to the worry and responsibilities of the job, while telling himself that it was unlike him to worry about responsibilities. But he also complained about the food served up in the Stormont canteen, saying that this was 'nearly always fried and not at all what a good diet should be'. When he duly consulted doctors in Northern Ireland it was thought that he might be suffering from the early stages of diverticulitis.

One highly controversial and politically dangerous subject which Oldfield had to handle without becoming too involved in it was the allegation made from various quarters that the CIA had been concerned in the assassination of Earl Mountbatten of Burma. No evidence has ever been put forward to substantiate this allegation which could emanate from either PIRA, INLA or even Soviet sources. The only public reference to this was made only as recently as January 1984, when Mr Enoch Powell stated in a letter that 'the Mountbatten murder was a very high level "job" not unconnected with the nuclear strategy of the United States.'[1]

Some few months before he was murdered Lord Mountbatten made a controversial speech in Strasbourg about nuclear arms. He expressed the opinion that the nuclear arms race had no military purpose and questioned the growing opposition to the SALT agreement within the United States. Secret Service reports suggested that the Kremlin had been shocked and even agitated by the Mountbatten murder, for the Russians had long regarded him as a useful communications link in the West and one who was not unfriendly towards the Soviet regime. He had indeed opened up secret and personal communications with the Soviet Defence Ministry when he was First Sea Lord through the British naval attaché in Washington, Captain Geoffrey Bennett. Apart from this the American Intelligence Services had long regarded Mountbatten as something of a security risk for NATO. It would therefore have been in the Soviets' interests to work up propaganda suggesting that the CIA had engineered the killing. This may have been one reason why Oldfield declined to meet Mr Powell.

The Security Co-ordinator would have been the last man to take credit for himself for some of the improvements in security in the province. He was all the time only too aware of the complexity of the problems with which he had to cope. He always stressed to his staff that this was very much a team operation and that his task was simply to advise, suggest and guide. Many of the results of his work became obvious as long as three years after he left Belfast. By the autumn of 1983 army levels in the province had settled at consistently below 10,000, including headquarters staff and ancillary forces. This compared with more than 22,000 army personnel in Ulster at the height of the troubles in the early 1970s, thus allowing the RUC and the Ulster Defence Regiment to play a more dominant role. There were then

8,000 RUC together with reserves and 7,000 Ulster Defence Regiment soldiers to enforce law and order.

It is now admitted in Intelligence circles – albeit unofficially – that infiltration of the PIRA would have been far more effective and the policy of encouraging informers more productive, if the Maze Prison break-out had not occurred. Yet, despite this incident which led to stepped-up terrorism, the overall situation has improved. British intelligence has won the cooperation of informers with promises of freedom, new identities and subsidised new lives away from Northern Ireland. Within eighteen months of Oldfield's coming to Ulster some thirty informers had given evidence which led to the arrest of more than three hundred suspected terrorists. IRA bombings were reduced in number and terrorist murders were halved in two years.

'The Year of the Informer' was how some dubbed 1983 in Ulster. Serious inroads into the terrorist underworld sowed the seeds of mistrust, disillusion and demoralization. Some nine informers were given new identities and jobs abroad and, as a result of their evidence about former colleagues, at least two hundred people have been implicated in a total of six hundred crimes.

'We are getting men who are disillusioned with themselves,' declared Sir John Hermon. 'They see the futility of terrorist activity. They see no future in it for their families. They have been involved in it, some of them for several years, and they have learned of the true tactics of these terrorist organizations. We have not offered large sums of money, but we do offer to people who give us the evidence on which we can convict terrorists a safe haven because they know, and we know, that their lives will be terminated very quickly should the PIRA get close to them.'

Towards the early spring of 1980 not only was Oldfield's health deteriorating, but he was becoming increasingly worried by what seemed to be a calculated attempt by some factions to start a whispering campaign against him. The object was clear: somebody obviously wanted him removed from Belfast. About this time Mrs Elizabeth Roberts, answering a telephone call from Oldfield to her husband,

Brigadier Roberts, who was then too ill to talk, recalls that Maurice sounded very depressed. 'He said to me, "if they don't get me one way, they'll get me another", and I assumed by this some kind of a smear campaign was being mounted against him.'

Shortly after this doctors diagnosed Sir Maurice's ailment as an inflammatory condition of the bowel, subsequently confirmed following a visit to a London hospital. By the end of May 1980, he had asked the Prime Minister to relieve him of his post on the grounds of ill health: evidence of his positive conviction that something was seriously wrong. Then on 12 June it was formally announced that he was to leave Ulster within a few weeks.

Although this Northern Ireland appointment was the least enjoyable of his career, Oldfield would unquestionably have liked to accomplish a few more improvements in the security set-up over there before he left. 'The spirit was willing,' he declared to a colleague afterwards, 'but the flesh has become very, very weak. There were a few loose ends I should have liked to tie up.' He was succeeded in his post by Sir Francis Brooks Richards, who had been the intelligence co-ordinator at 10 Downing Street for the previous two years and before joining the Cabinet Office had been Ambassador to South Vietnam and Greece.

In Belfast, as in London, Singapore, Washington and elsewhere, Oldfield was always especially popular with the female staff. The female civil servants at Stormont thought highly of him. 'Sir Maurice was such a nice man, more like a father than a spy-master,' said one. 'He was a real gentleman who always had a kind word for us. All the time he was over here morale just soared. And he never needed to raise his voice.'

So, somewhat sadly, (for he hated what he called 'unfinished business') Oldfield returned to his London flat and started to pick up the threads of his old life. His vicar, the Reverend Prebendary Irvine, remembers being dismayed when he first saw Sir Maurice on the latter's return from Ireland. 'He just said he had diverticulitis and would be having some treatment. I felt at the time that his gruelling spell on duty in Northern Ireland had taken a toll of his health. I still think it had. He looked so very ill. I remember his showing me a letter from the Prime Minister, warmly thanking him for his work in Ulster.'

In a statement issued by the Northern Ireland Office at the time of his retirement the following tribute was paid to Sir Maurice: 'The Prime Minister and the Secretary of State are very grateful ... for all that he has done to make more effective the security effort against terrorism in Northern Ireland.'[2]

But retirement brought no relief, either from physical or mental pain. The nagging problems associated with Northern Ireland would not go away. Suddenly a story was planted not simply in Ireland north and south, but in Fleet Street, too. It was something so ridiculous that it could easily be dismissed by all but the ultra-credulous, or those so devoted to sensation that they would grab at any whisper regardless of its source. In short, the story was that Oldfield had been sent home from Northern Ireland because he had not been cleared by positive vetting!

This may seem so silly that a biographer might well be asked why he brought it up. To have ignored it might be equally dangerous, because there is no worse sin than that of omission. The truth is that, despite the fact that Oldfield was obviously a sick man, Fleet Street started to investigate the story. A watch was kept on Oldfield's flat in Marsham Street by reporters. All comings and goings were noted. Nothing was published in the United Kingdom, but some editors obviously thought a scandal might be in the offing. This was another unwelcome burden which Oldfield had to bear.

Who were Oldfield's enemies? Who wanted to hound him even in retirement and, if possible, to destroy him totally? These were questions which I felt it imperative to try to answer. I tried to track down the source of these various stories which became embroidered as time passed, but there was nothing positive one could go on other than word of mouth gossip. My information is that the first report came not from the IRA, but from an undisclosed Ulster Defence Regiment source. Later sources suggested the stories came from inside the British Army.

Did the PIRA manipulate the UDR and the British Army, or was this a Protestant-inspired plot? And, whoever it was, what was the motive, especially as Oldfield had retired? What is remarkable is that, even after his death, no attempts were made to revive these smears even in the most sensational section of Fleet Street.

On his return to London some of those close to him noted that in private conversation he tended to regard the Protestant extremists as being far worse and more malicious than the Catholic and PIRA opposition. But, as these views have come to the author second-hand, it is not easy to get a balanced view of them. There seems no doubt that Oldfield felt that, to sustain their own case, Protestants should behave much more correctly both in a political and a religious sense. What is abundantly clear is Oldfield's own summing up of the policy he believed in when he returned to London. He told a close friend: 'You can infiltrate rogues as agents in Northern Ireland and you can pay the price by being shown up as the employer of rogues. It is a risk with doubtful promises of success. Or you can try to win over some of the terrorists, which offers no easy solution, but a rather better chance of success, though it can still be misinterpreted by the PIRA as concocting evidence. There is absolutely no safe and sure way to defeat terrorism, but on balance I prefer to win informers.'

It was soon obvious to his closest friends that the last thing he wanted was for his family to be worried about the state of his health. He particularly wished for the news to be kept from his mother – 'whatever happens to me, she is not to be told, as far as this is possible.' His mother's memory was failing at that time, though she still enjoyed her son's occasional visits. But his wish that she should not be told was faithfully observed. When his mother died in 1982, at the age of eighty-nine, and was buried in the grave next to his in the churchyard of St Anne's, Over Haddon, she had not been told of her son's death.

Eventually it became clear that Oldfield's ill health was much more serious than just inflammation of the bowels. One of his agents in the field says: 'I begged him to see a rather special consultant, an SIS doctor, and I was much relieved when he agreed to do this. Only then was the dreaded verdict given – that he was suffering from cancer.'

He was admitted to the King Edward VII Hospital in Marylebone where he had two operations, the first of which was purely exploratory. By this time the cancer had obtained an inexorable grip on him. Yet despite the essentially drastic chemo-therapy treatment to which he was subjected, he remained cheerful and alert until very nearly the end of his life. The same colleague from overseas who had urged him to see another doctor told me: 'He was lucid to the last and still trying to advise on intelligence matters, if any ideas occurred to him. I saw a lot of him in hospital and we had some inspiring talks. He once told me in a quite forcible manner: "There's going to be more trouble in the Middle East. You must go back to ——. You will be invaluable there because —— is going to be important from the point of view of oil supplies." '

Mr George Carver, a senior CIA officer, who had long been a friend of Maurice, last saw him on 17 February 1981, just three weeks before he died. 'We sat and talked,' he said. 'I had found a relatively new book of the poems of the German poet, Johann Christian Hölderlin, in a bilingual edition, which I gave to him, and he seemed to be delighted with that. He said he would keep himself happily employed checking the accuracy of the English translations and started rifling through it immediately to start the work. He was wan and tired, but everything about him was very much in keeping with the qualities that he had displayed over the years and which had engendered such respect and affection in all of us who were privileged to know him and to count him as a friend.'[3]

Mr George K. Young, a former deputy chief of the SIS, visited Sir Maurice a few days before he died. He was able to reassure him that he had 'checked through his *Times* obituary notice and it was very good. He inquired anxiously: "Have they put in that bit about 'Nothing worth nicking there, Guv'?" When I said that was the concluding phrase in the obituary, a peaceful smile came over his face as he settled back on his pillow.'[4]

A much appreciated visitor during these last days of his life was the Prime Minister, who called to see him the Saturday before his death. Mrs Thatcher's presence at his bedside raised his spirits enormously for a short while.

All his visitors pay tribute to the fact that he put up an astonishing piece of play-acting to make out he was feeling better than he was. 'He was a natural play actor in these circumstances,' said the Reverend Gerald Buss. 'He made a great effort to put people at ease and to raise a laugh, though he sometimes exhausted himself in the process. He did his best to make light of his suffering even to the nursing staff. Towards the end he would still be play-acting, with great effort pulling himself up in bed and saying "Ah, nurse, how nice to see you again." Then he would fall back on his pillow exhausted.'

Mr Harry Chapman Pincher, who also visited him in hospital, has recalled 'hilarious intelligence experiences such as the occasion when a report to the Foreign Secretary, which should have read "according to a source with good access" was mistyped as "a source with God access".'[5]

Fred Bardwell, another visitor in this period, says: 'By this time we were close friends and we understood each other so well that it was impossible to pretend. But I shall always recall the courage and calmness with which Maurice faced death. There he was, with tubes everywhere, but his first words to me on one occasion were: "This way I die without pain." He said this to put me at my ease. He received the Last Sacrament three days before he died.'

It was one of Oldfield's great regrets that, fond as he was of animals, he could never have a pet of his own. As a bachelor who could never be sure when he would have to travel overseas at a moment's notice, this was impossible. But he did become very fond indeed of the pets of some of his friends. When he was dying he asked for a photograph of a favourite dog of his named Abdullah belonging to his friend, Anthony Cavendish, to be placed in a frame on his bedside table. It was the only photograph he had with him and it remained there till he died.

On 11 March 1981 Maurice Oldfield died at the relatively early age of sixty-five. In an instant tribute to him Mr Humphrey Atkins, the Northern Ireland Secretary, said: 'The people of Great Britain and Northern Ireland have lost a great, loyal and valued servant.'

If he had been a totally uncontroversial figure in his lifetime, the news of his death aroused a certain amount of harmless controversy in the media. This was the period in which the television films based on the character of George Smiles in John Le Carré's novels were being shown, and so there was a revival of the hotly disputed legend that Smiley was a barely disguised portrait of Maurice himself. The *New York Times* stated: 'Sir Maurice Oldfield, believed to be the inspiration for George Smiley in John Le Carré's spy novels and "M" in Ian Fleming's James Bond books, is dead ... Ian Fleming, a fellow wartime Intelligence officer, is popularly believed to have used him as the model for "M", the chief of Intelligence who sent James Bond on his missions.'[6]

But the New York paper added: 'Unlike the grave, plodding Smiley, Sir Maurice was noted for a sense of humour and cheerful demeanour.'[7]

Oldfield would have been the first to be horrified at any suggestion that he could have master-minded the somewhat ill-conceived, aggressive assignments upon which James Bond might be despatched.

Even the London *Times* and other papers in the United Kingdom mentioned that Oldfield was said to be the model for both Smiley and Fleming's 'M'. There was some excuse for this in that not only were some of Oldfield's idiosyncrasies portrayed in the character of Smiley in Le Carré's books, but Le Carré had known Oldfield personally.

In the television programme *News at Ten*, Le Carré was quoted by name as saying that Maurice was the model for George Smiley. This drew a denial from Le Carré himself when he wrote to *The Times*, insisting: 'I have never in my life made such a statement, least of all on the day of Sir Maurice's sad death ... The truth, once and for all, is this. I never heard of Sir Maurice either by name or in any other way until long after the name and character of George

Smiley were in print. I knew him, whether by reputation or personally, scarcely at all. Our social contact, such as it was, occurred after his retirement, and amounted to a couple of lunches, over which he was inclined to rebuke me, albeit amiably, for what he regarded as the unflattering portrait I had given of his former Service. At his request, I once produced Sir Alec Guinness for him, for the good reason that he had always been, in his modest way, one of Sir Alec's fans. Sir Maurice was tickled pink.'[8]

Sir Alec Guinness has this to say on the subject: 'I met Maurice Oldfield only once – at a lunch arranged by John Le Carré at La Poule au Pot in Ebury Street. I found him out-going and charming and amusing. We corresponded a couple of times and he wrote to me after the end of *Tinker, Tailor, Soldier, Spy*, saying "I *still* don't recognize myself." We arranged to meet for dinner in London, and then he was called to Northern Ireland. Then he invited me to Oxford to dine, and he was taken gravely ill and died.

'I knew of his passion for the Church of England. He told me his favourite book was St Augustine's *Confessions* and that he read it every year. I was a bit surprised that his Derbyshire accent came through, but saw no reason to use it in my Smiley stuff.'[9]

This reference to Oldfield's accent is interesting as it may reveal a subtle attempt by Sir Maurice to mask his own personality. For most of his friends seem to agree that his accent was classless and with no touch of any dialect. On the other hand he could quite easily put on a Derbyshire accent, and one very close friend says: 'Curiously, I did notice that sometimes, and with some people, *after* he became "C", he would occasionally let himself talk with a Derbyshire accent. I never asked him why.'

It is worth recording what, according to the press agency UPI, Oldfield himself had to say on the subject of Smiley: 'I'm certainly not the model for "M". I don't think I am the model for Smiley – perhaps some of the characteristics are mine, and John Le Carré did ask me to lunch with Alec Guinness.'[10]

Back in 1979 I was myself asked to write an article for a

251

national newspaper on the subject of Oldfield and Smiley, and 'The Real Face of George Smiley' was the title suggested for this piece. However, I never thought that the character of Smiley had more than a superficial and incidental resemblance to him. When an editor has a fixed idea in his head as to exactly how an article should be written and his contributor takes an opposing view, the editor usually wins. Consequently, though paid for, my article was never published. I wrote that 'the real face of George Smiley does not reside behind the figure of Sir Maurice Oldfield. True, there are some physical resemblances and both men were educated at grammar schools, were South-East Asia specialists and have a passion for medieval history. There the similarities end. Oldfield is a bachelor; Smiley suffers from his appalling problem wife, Anne. Nor can I imagine Sir Maurice breaking the news, say, of Philby's defection, to a colleague in El Vino's bar in Fleet Street as Smiley did about Haydon "one rainy midday".'

Another vital difference, of course, was that Smiley was not even the chief of MI 6. Indeed, I found many more clues to people other than Oldfield spattered among the descriptions of characters in the Le Carré novels. 'The Optimates ... an upper-class Christ Church club, mainly Old Etonian ... a private selection tank for the Great Game': substitute the Apostles for the Optimates and Trinity College, Cambridge, for Christ Church, Oxford, and the picture fits. As for Karla, I have no doubt he was based on a Soviet recruiter, active in the thirties, but today either dead, liquidated or in retirement. Le Carré, with an accuracy that makes fiction truer than much of what we read in newspapers, states that 'most of the English moles were recruited by Karla before the war and came from the higher bourgeoisie ... and became secretly fanatic, much more fanatic than their working-class English comrades.'

'Small, podgy and at best middle-aged, he was by appearance one of London's meek who do not inherit the earth. His legs are short, his gait anything but agile ... he wore no hat, believing rightly that hats made him ridiculous.' Such is the description which Le Carré has given to his best-known character. Oldfield was short, stocky and bespectacled and one of his friends said he had 'the same flat-footed way of walking as Smiley and also the same habit of frequently wriggling his thick-lensed glasses.' His talent for anonymity was also shared with Smiley who had learned 'to love the crowds who pass him in the street without a glance.' Yet Oldfield could be very nimble on his feet in a surprising way. Fred Bardwell has testified that when Maurice flew over from Stormont specially to attend his twenty-first birthday party, 'he showed that he could dance both the old-time stuff and that of today. He thoroughly enjoyed himself and was as good a dancer as any of them.'

Nevertheless the fleeting similarities between Smiley and Oldfield made the excuse for the editor of the *New Statesman*, then Bruce Page, one of the co-authors of *The Philby Conspiracy*, to put this heading on a profile of Oldfield, published in that journal: 'Sir Maurice Oldfield of the Secret Intelligence Service – original of "George Smiley" in the Le Carré spy novels – The Honourable Grammar Schoolboy.'[11]

One has the feeling that Oldfield quite enjoyed playing his own little game both with John Le Carré and Alec Guinness, subtly and amiably, of course, but a game nevertheless. Nobody could leave his listeners guessing at what he meant more skilfully than Maurice when this was a role he felt he must play. Whereas previous heads of MI 6 would have been horrified at the idea of being portrayed in fiction, Oldfield was mildly amused by the idea. By this time he had retired and he knew it couldn't possibly harm the Service. But he was seriously concerned that Le Carré's portrayal of how British Intelligence officers worked, and what they were like, might give the public a false picture.

When Oldfield decided he had a role to play, however, there must be a reason for it, and on the occasions he met Sir Alec Guinness maybe it was to show that he wasn't really like Smiley. Nobody would know better than Maurice that, with today's emphasis in spy fiction being on the 'factional', there was a need to disinform and to baffle on the subject of any resemblance he might have to Smiley, purely to try to dissociate such a fictional character from his beloved Service. For there is no doubt that in an unostentatius way he was very proud indeed of the Secret Service and of having been its chief.

Oldfield knew full well that the KGB had their own section of 'literary watchers' to try to sift fact from fiction in this field. He was well aware that they had recruited a Bulgarian novelist, Andrei Gulyashki, to invent a Soviet spy to counteract the popularity of Fleming's James Bond. Thus Gulyashki had created Avakum Zakhov, whose chief task was 'to destroy the vile imperialist agent, James Bond', serializing his book *Avakum Zakhov versus 07* in the Communist youth paper, *Komsomolskaya Pravda*. [12]

What dismayed Oldfield more than anything, and what he hoped to counteract, was the kind of image which le Carré in his fiction had given to MI 6, or 'the Circus', as the author called it. The recurrent theme of the Smiley books was the bureaucratic jungles of the Circus and the way in which the Establishment class was equated with treachery and hypocrisy.

Sir Alec Guinness found Oldfield 'garrulous, informative and unshy', yet he also declared that originally he had thought the part of Smiley 'would be easy, but the more I studied it, the less it seemed so. He is both vulnerable and anonymous.' In fact, on the silver screen the portrait of Smiley was not remotely like Oldfield except when Alec Guinness employed Maurice's quirk of playing with his spectacles on occasions. Maurice succeeded, to some extent at least, in a superb piece of disinformation.

This diversion to the subject of Oldfield in relation to Smiley may seem strangely out of place and irrelevant at the very moment his death is being recorded. Yet, paradoxical as it may seem, it is important that the 'Oldfield was Smiley' theme, which appeared in so many obituary notices, should be put in its proper perspective at this juncture. As Lady Clanmorris (Madeleine Bingham, the author) has commented: 'As long as he was alive, we were led to believe that Sir Maurice Oldfield was the model for Smiley. Only when he was dead were we informed that this wasn't the case.'

Madeleine Bingham was once inspired to write a book entitled *Smiley's Wife*, but which for various reasons (none of which seem to have been either fair or sensible) was withdrawn from publication. 'As far as the content of the book is concerned it is simply the story of one Intelligence officer and his family and the introduction was designed to defend the Intelligence Services against the ludicrous attacks of David Cornwell [John Le Carré].'[13]

One last comment on this subject. Let the final word be with The Reverend Dr Vivian Green, who was Senior Tutor at Lincoln College, Oxford, when David Cornwell was his pupil. 'When David and his wife stayed with me last October,' he said, 'they brought a present of caviar and vodka with a card reading "With love from Karla!"'For it has recently been revealed that it was not Oldfield, but Dr Green who is named as the original model for Smiley. This much had been confirmed by David Cornwell and Dr Green.[14]

A notice in the press after Oldfield's death stated that a requiem mass for parishioners would be held at the ruined church of St Matthew's, Westminster, and that there would be a family funeral at St Anne's Church, Over Haddon. The notice added: 'No flowers, but donations if wished, to St Matthew's Church, St Anne's, or Imperial Cancer Research.'

His funeral was conducted exactly as he had asked and his body was taken to St Matthew's on the evening before the requiem service. Evensong of the Dead was recited and a continuous 'Watch of Prayer' was kept in the ruined church from 4.30 pm on the Monday until the service the following day. The burnt-out church was kept open to the public all this time and, despite the fact that the scarred hulk of the building was exposed to gusts of wind and rain, a steady stream of mourners, mainly parishioners, came in and stopped to pray. 'We were sorry,' said the vicar, 'that the announcement of the service said it was for "congregation only", as many stayed away because of this. Even so, parishioners were still coming to pay their respects well into the night.'

Prior to the requiem mass being held Scotland Yard received a tip that the PIRA had planned to plant a bomb on Oldfield's coffin while it was in the church. This was one of the most sickening of all threats – to inflict such barbarity on a man who had died and whose body awaited burial. There was even a suggestion that it might be wise on this occasion to substitute an empty coffin for the real one. But there is no confirmation as to whether this was done.

At the requiem service Oldfield was described by his friend, Canon Peter Pilkington, headmaster of King's School, Canterbury, as 'a devout Christian who could have found a safer and less worrying path in life'.

One former colleague of Oldfield's (an agent in the field), who had visited him in hospital, had asked Maurice if he could provide some solace by writing to one of Oldfield's sisters. 'My dear chap,' replied Maurice, 'you shouldn't write to one any more than another. Write to them all.'

Among those who went to pay final tribute to him at St Matthew's were Mr Phillip Whitehead, who described Sir Maurice as 'being like an elder brother', and his former master at Lady Manners School, Dr R.A. Harvey. Quite a few of his former agents in the field slipped into the church late at night to show their last respects to a much beloved chief.

His burial service at Over Haddon followed immediately afterwards, when he was laid to rest beside his father. The service was a simple one, just for family and close friends, the vicar, the Reverend Edmund Urquhart, presiding. One of Maurice's favourite queries when he rang up a very close friend was : 'Is all well?' On one of the wreaths on his grave was the message: 'All's well, Maurice, all's well.'

Oldfield's will was a simple and straightforward affair, typical of the man himself. He left an estate valued at £111,940 net, and everything was bequeathed to his sister, Miss Irene Annie Oldfield, of Mona View Farm, Over Haddon.

A memorial service was held at the Chapel of St Peter and St Paul at the Royal Naval College, Greenwich, on 12 May, when the Reverend John Oliver, RN, and the Reverend

Halsey Colchester, formerly a colleague of Oldfield overseas, officiated. One of the reasons for choosing this venue was that, being inside a naval establishment, it was easier to organize protection against possible terrorist activities. But there was another good reason in that the chapel was a favourite of his and that he had played the organ there. One old friend says that this was one of his favourite organs, too, while Mr Gordon St John Clarke, who was appointed organist at the College chapel in 1975, and who played the organ at the memorial service, states: 'If Sir Maurice did play the organ here, it would probably have been only after a dinner or similar function in the relaxed company of friends.'[15]

Quite considerable security precautions were taken concerning the memorial service. Though it had been announced in the press, every pressure was applied to stifle publicity and, particularly, to keep hidden the identities of many of those who attended. There was no official list of mourners and even the local newspaper, the *Kentish Independent*, stated that it 'did not carry a report on the memorial service for Sir Maurice'.

Police and Ministry of Defence guards kept a close watch on all who approached the gates of the College, which were kept shut throughout the service. No one was allowed in without producing a special pass. One report of the memorial service in the national press by a correspondent named Peter Hardy stated that 'the Spymaster himself might have enjoyed the challenge of breaching the massive security ring that surrounded his memorial service yesterday. The combined force of the Metropolitan and Defence Ministry Police launched a unique operation in Greenwich at sunrise ... The problem police faced was the protection of the 500 guests who had accepted personal invitations to attend the service held in the Royal Naval College Chapel. So sensitive were the identities of some of the guests that photographers were warned that their films would be confiscated. Some of them [the mourners] gave their names. Sir Dick White, former head of MI 6, willingly offered his. But other more shadowy figures were reticent. "Same club," replied one astonished guest when asked in what capacity he was present. "Understood names weren't being taken," protested another.'

Other mourners were equally tight-lipped when asked who they were, or who they represented. 'Same firm,' was one typical reply, constantly repeated. M. Armand Maribout, who attended on behalf of the French counter-espionage organization, DST, was, however, sufficiently courteous to explain: 'The DST is more or less the same as your MI 5.' Which was probably not only the most courteous, but also the most constructive of all responses from the guests.

Sir William Deakin, who gave the address, opened by saying that he was speaking to the congregation as 'one personal friend, and not as a former colleague, which I have never been. Army service, for which Maurice promptly volunteered, led him into Field Security in the Middle East (where we first and briefly met) ...

'The other morning I returned at a quiet hour, to a place where Maurice and I went to lunch and dine frequently in recent years. Members of the staff gathered to talk of him. As one of them put it: "Sir Maurice knew us ordinary people as friends. His constant personal interest in our lives made us feel that he shared in our small amusements and troubles, and was one of us. On his many journeys abroad he would never fail to send postcards to our families, and he knew every name."

'This one example is symbolic of an invisible "grand company" of ordinary friends whom he knew and remembered in all corners of the world, as in the Middle East and the Far East. Maurice was himself in a special sense an ordinary man gifted with a natural simplicity ... As a compassionate and above all fascinated observer of his fellow human beings, he was unequalled, and perhaps here lay one of the central secrets of his professional achievement.

'... As an experienced scholar, Maurice was leery of absolute judgements, and aware of the imperfections of evidence. He would have approved of the warning of Sir Walter Raleigh in the preface to his *History of the World*:

"The historian of antiquity pursueth truth too far off, and loseth her sight, and loseth himself. But whosoever, in writing a modern history, shall follow the truth too near the heels, it may happily strike out his teeth." '

Perhaps this last comment was in the nature of a depth-charge to be deliberately dropped in the vicinity of any who might seek to write a life of Sir Maurice. If so, the warning is duly regarded, for what is unclear today may be much clearer tomorrow. On the other hand if things do become clearer tomorrow, they may well lack the authenticity of first-person evidence if many of those who knew Sir Maurice had by then passed on. Some of those leaving the memorial service expressed the view that even this tribute omitted something of the rather special qualities of Maurice Oldfield. 'He was very elusive in some ways,' said one, 'not in the sense of being devious or ambivalent, but in being like a conjuror who held all manner of virtuous tricks up his sleeve. He would pull these out when one least expected it. But he did this in an impish way, not that of some omnipotent do-gooder. Yes, that was Maurice Oldfield – he managed to do good without making one feel guilty about his doing it. Or should I say feel guilty about not being as good as he was?'

There were some who served with him who took a much more critical view of Oldfield as head of MI 6. To give a balanced picture it is only fair that some of these criticisms should be noted. One former MI 6 officer says: 'He was a very complex character, very politically-minded, not in a party sense, admittedly, but in always paying heed to political opinions and bending over to listen to the party in power. He was an absolutely first-class officer. That is to say, give him a complex case to analyse and he would tackle it superbly. But I do not think he was the right man for chief. On the other hand you could say that MI 6 is a splendid service which has nearly always had chiefs who were not really good enough for the job. Maurice could also be highly indiscreet on occasions and he did mix with some very odd types.'

This view, with modifications, has been expressed to the

author by one other member of the Service. Yet, if it is right to include criticism as much as praise, it is also right to provide a biographical answer to the criticisms where this seems called for. First, the suggestion that Oldfield was too 'politically-minded', that he paid too much attention to the political effects of some action or project. The quick answer is that all intelligence chiefs are servants of the government of the day. That is the constitutional and democratic way of doing things. However, some SIS personnel would say – not without a degree of justification – that situations could arise (and have arisen in the past) where an incompetent, or ambivalent government could put the nation at risk and that it was a patriotic duty of the Secret Service to take what actions it saw fit in defence of the realm. From all one learns about Maurice Oldfield it seems clear that this was something he well understood. On the charge that sometimes he could be indiscreet, one can only point to the abundant evidence that he was the soul of discretion. However, it should be stressed that Oldfield had a fear of becoming a prisoner of a system, that he felt it was necessary to move around in a wide range of social and political circles and even to draw someone out by the occasional deliberately indiscreet remark. He was well aware of his critics and he had them in mind when he widened his circle of acquaintances which latterly he did more and more. As to the suggestion that he was not the right man for 'C', if one looks at the history of heads of all Western intelligence chiefs, one can see that they have all come under intense fire. Even some of the ablest, as James Angleton would probably ruefully agree, have been lambasted and sacked.

Mr Norman Mott, who spent the war years in the SOE and later was a close colleague of Sir Maurice, speaks of 'his very high, almost phenomenal professional competence and his deep humanity. He was generous almost to a fault and the number of lame ducks he befriended must be legion – as, too, must be his god-children! As a boss he was totally accessible to the whole range of his staff and was quite without pomposity. I expect others will speak of his appreciation of the occasional joke at his own expense, but you may care to have one example he told me himself with great glee. He was having a drink in his "local" at Bakewell during a visit home before going overseas. "Hullo, Maurice, what are you doing here?" said one of the locals. "I'm on my way to Singapore," said Maurice, thinking to make a bit of an impression. "Oh, I didn't know Bakewell were on way to Far East," was the reply.'[16]

Could this be said to be one of his indiscretions?

For my own part I feel that the end of this attempt to capture something of the life and character of Maurice Oldfield should dwell on a constructive note – the kind of note, or advice, which he would have liked to pass on to future generations. Beneath that character there was a sturdy, if unobtrusive patriotism and also a message for the future. One of his favourite books of modern times touching on the subject of intelligence was *Secrets, Spies & Scholars: Blueprint of the Essential CIA*, by Ray Cline, former Deputy Director of the CIA. In the foreword to this book the author expressed an opinion with which Oldfield was not only in full agreement, but which very nearly represented his own philosophy. Because of this, and also because it contains a worthwhile message for the future of all Western intelligence services, it makes a fitting end to this book.

Cline explained that his book was 'a contribution to political science – an analysis of how the main elements in American intelligence operations can contribute information and ideas to decision-making and national policy.' He went on to say: 'Scholars and spies can give to our national strategy and to our foreign policy the enormous benefit of objectivity if, but only if, our national leaders are disposed to protect our open society by maintaining and using, not abusing, a sophisticated secret intelligence service. A free nation with accurate knowledge of the world around it, particularly of hostile and secretive closed societies, is more likely to survive and prosper than one that relies on wishful thinking. Spies and scholars can give significant clues to future opportunities and dangers, if kept at work on a systematic, stable well-co-ordinated programme calculated to find facts that interpret them objectively.'[17]

Chapter Notes

FOREWORD

[1] *The Times*, 12 March 1981. This obituary was compiled by Professor R.V. Jones.

[2] *The New York Times*, 9 February 1973.

[3] Capt. Sir Mansfield Cumming in collaboration with Admiral Sir Reginald Hall ordered the murder of one of their own spies, Alexander Szek, a 20-year-old student of wireless telegraphy who had been born to an English mother and Austro-Hungarian father and acquired dual nationality. Employed by the Germans in Brussels in World War One, he was recruited by the NID and MI 6 and asked to obtain the German cipher book. The order to kill was given by the British to prevent the Germans discovering that their ciphers had been handed over. See also *Admiral of the Fleet Lord Beatty*, by Capt. Stephen Roskill, Collins, London, 1980.

[4] *Daily Telegraph*, November 1983.

[5] 'Z' network had its headquarters in The Hague where it was quite separate from the MI 6 network, but still controlled from London. Its Hague office was run by Capt. Best Payne, who was later kidnapped by the Germans. The fatal mistake was made by Sinclair, head of MI 6, in sending a memorandum to Dansey, head of 'Z' network, at the outbreak of war, telling him that 'Z' section must combine with MI 6's network.

[6] *A Record of Events before the War, 1939*, compiled by Lord Halifax, Foreign Office 800/317.

CHAPTER 1

[1] Author's conversation with Dr R.A. Harvey, 1 November 1983. See also *The Story of the School of Grace, Lady Manners, Bakewell*, by R.A. Harvey, J.W. Northend, Sheffield, 1982.

[2] *Ibid*.

[3] Letter to the author from Mrs Greta Nimse, 22 February 1984.

[4] *The Peacock* (Lady Manners School magazine), December 1934.

CHAPTER 2

1 *A Personal History*, by A.J.P. Taylor, Hamish Hamilton, London, 1983.
2 Letter to the author from Sir Bryan Hopkin, 24 November 1983.
3 Letter to the author from Mr David Wiseman, 1 August 1983.
4 Letter to the author from Professor Norman Dees, 2 November 1983.
5 Manchester University Records.
6 Letter from Oldfield to Mr David Wiseman, 16 November 1939.
7 Letter from Professor C.R. Cheney to the author, 29 February 1984.
8 This is a reference to the James Klugmann who achieved some notoriety later through his pro-communist machinations while working in the SOE Balkans office in Cairo in World War Two. He became an executive member of the CPGB and was official historian of the British Communist Party.
9 Address to the Queen by the Colonel Commandant of the Military Intelligence Corps at Ashford, 25 March 1981.

CHAPTER 3

1 An article entitled 'The Private Life of a Man Called "C"', by David Potts, *Observer*, London, 15 March 1981.
2 Letter to the author from Mr H.M. Trethowan, 3 January 1984.
3 Conversation between the author and Mr Irvine Gray, 9 February 1984.
4 Letter to the author from Mr H.M. Trethowan, 3 January 1984.
5 Letter to the author from Mrs Jeanne Smith, 11 March 1984.
6 Conversation between the author and Mr H.M. Trethowan, 29 January 1984.
7 Conversation between the author and Mr Alan Cutbill, formerly of the Military Intelligence Corps, 4 January 1984.
8 *Ibid*.
9 From the original smoking concert ditty, reproduced with kind permission of Mr Irvine Gray. Regarding the authorship of this ditty sung to the tune of 'Oh, dear, what can the matter be?', Mrs Jeanne Smith recalls it being sung 'at one Christmas staff party' and she suspects it was 'composed by Oldfield with the assistance of Irvine Gray'.
10 *The Times*, 12 March 1981.

CHAPTER 4

1 See also *Master of Deception: Tangled Webs in London & the Middle East*, by David Mure, William Kimber, London, 1980; and *Chief of Intelligence*, by Ian Colvin, Gollancz, London, 1951.

263

[2] Statement to the author by Mr David Mure.

[3] Letter to the author from Mrs Jeanne Smith, 11 March 1984.

[4] *Master of Deception*, David Mure.

[5] Letter to the author from J.W. Eppler, 18 March 1983.

[6] *Handbook for Spies*, Alexander Foote, Museum Press, London, 1949.

[7] *The Invisible Writing*, Arthur Koestler, 2nd vol. of *Arrow in the Blue: An Autobiography*, Collins with Hamish Hamilton, London, 1954.

[8] *The Great Game*, Leopold Trepper, Michael Joseph, London, 1978.

[9] Statement to the author by former NID agent, code-named CALPE.

[10] Papers of the British War Office, PRO, Kew: WO 169/19510; 3 Field Security Section Middle East Forces, 'War Diary'.

[11] *Ibid.*

[12] Extracts from War Diaries & British Embassy papers – Egypt 1946/49, PRO, Kew.

[13] Conversation between the author and Mr Alastair Horne, 21 March 1984.

[14] War Office Diary for February 1946, GSI Branch, GHQ, Middle East Forces, CSDIC, PRO, Kew.

[15] *Ibid.*

[16] Letter from Mr Teddy Kollek, Mayor of Jerusalem, to the author, 1 February 1984.

[17] Papers of the British Colonial Office, PRO, Kew: CO 537/2269.

[18] Report by Sir Charles Wickham on the Palestine Police & Papers of the Colonial Office: CO 537/2269.

CHAPTER 5

[1] Letter from Professor Norman Dees to the author, 1 November 1983.

[2] Sir Charles Wickham's report on the Palestine Police, Colonial Office Papers CO 537/2269, PRO, Kew.

[3] Article entitled 'The Honourable Grammar Schoolboy', *New Statesman*, 7 July 1978.

[4] Letter to the author from Sir Bryan Hopkin, 24 November 1983.

[5] *My Silent War*, by Kim Philby, Grove Press, New York, 1968.

[6] *Ibid.*

[7] *Ibid.*

[8] From a statement made by Alexander Foote and not previously published. Much later Foote was most anxious that this statement should go to the Home Secretary direct, as he did not trust personnel in the Home Office or members of MI 5 to whom it might first be shown.

[9] Article entitled 'Dinner with the Spymaster', by Phillip Knightley, *Sunday Times*, 15 March 1981.

[10] *My Silent War*, Kim Philby.

CHAPTER 6

[1] Letter to the author from Mr Peter Ellis, of Ottawa, 29 September 1983.

[2] Conversation between the author and Mr John Carrington, 4 January 1984.

[3] The 'K' in 14-K was added to signify 'karat' of gold, after the members of a rival tong, who proclaimed the superior virtues of softer non-karat local gold, were hacked to death in a street confrontation with knives and swords.

[4] Anthony Short writes in *The Communist Insurrection in Malaya: 1948-60*, Frederick Muller, London, 1975, that 'many of the *Wah Kee* groups had committed themselves to the government side, but at the same time they had taken and were taking advantage of their position for material profit.'

[5] Conversation between the author and Sir James Easton, 30 November 1983.

[6] Letter to the author from Professor Purseglove, 21 November 1983.

[7] Letter to the author from Mr Ray S. Cline, 30 January 1984.

[8] *Ibid.*

[9] Conversation between the author and Mr L.A. Choong.

[10] *Ibid.*

CHAPTER 7

[1] Letter from Dr. R.A. Harvey to the author, 26 November 1983.

[2] Letter from Mrs Jeanne Smith to the author, 11 March 1984.

[3] Sixth Report from the Select Committee on Estimates, 1957-58, Question 1507.

[4] Conversation with Mrs Elizabeth Roberts, 6 March 1984.

[5] A US Department of State letter of 9 January 1956 urged Britain 'to take the lead in developing a policy of independence for the colonial peoples' (ref. 0024880).

[6] Dept. of State ref. 002561, letter from the Secretary of State.

[7] Joint Chiefs of Staff memo. CM-222-25, 26 October 1955 (Dept. of Defense, USA).

[8] Letter from Mr Ray S. Cline to the author, 30 January 1984.

[9] Letter from Sir Robert Thompson to the author, 23 November 1983.

[10] Interview with former US Intelligence officer, code-named POE.

[11] News item entitled 'Russia Can Beat Lie Test – Pentagon' by staff correspondent in Washington, *Sunday Telegraph*, London, 24 July 1983.

[12] CIA Declassified Papers, MKULTRA Projects, released August 1977.

[13] Interview with Mr Fred Bardwell, 7 December 1983.

CHAPTER 8

[1] See London *Times* obituary of Oldfield, 12 March 1981.

[2] See *Secrets, Spies & Scholars: Blueprint of the Essential CIA*, by Ray S. Cline, Acropolis Books, Washington, DC, 1977.

[3] Letter from Mr Ray S. Cline to the author, 30 January 1984.

[4] Conversation with Mr Alistair Horne, 21 March 1984.

[5] *Twice Through the Lines: The Autobiography of Otto John*, translated from the German by Richard Barry, Macmillan, London, 1972.

[6] *Ibid.*

[7] Conversation with Mr Phillip Whitehead, 7 December 1983.

[8] Letter from Dr Otto John to the author, 22 October 1983.

CHAPTER 9

[1] US State Department Papers: informative memo. from Richard H. David, Bureau of European Affairs, to the Secretary of State, 9 July 1965.

[2] State Department Papers: memo. of conversation (J. Wayne Fredericks, and Sir Algernon Rumbold, 24 March 1965.

[3] Conversation between Lord Wigg and the author, 21 November 1977.

[4] *George Wigg*, by Lord Wigg, Michael Joseph, London, 1972.

[5] Conversation between Lord Wigg and the author, 21 November 1977.

[6] *Ibid.*

[7] Letter from the Right Reverend Kenneth Skelton to the author, 21 May 1984.

[8] *Guardian*, 27 January 1978: 'Death of the Department that Never Was'. *Observer*, 29 January 1978: 'How the FO Waged Secret Propaganda War'.

[9] *The Times*, 2 October 1981.

[10] Conversation between Prebendary Irvine and the author, 3 October 1983.

[11] The Reverend Conrad Noel, nicknamed the 'Red Vicar' of Thaxted in Essex, was, with his peculiar brand of Anglican communism, an early influence on the young Tom Driberg.

[12] The actual document also confirms the name and address of the British agent concerned, stating that he 'is the only person able to dispose of the goods described above – i.e. to give us instructions for the trans-shipment of these goods to a seagoing vessel, to be designated by him, for further transport to the place of destination.'

[13] Letter from Mr Jeffery Ede to the author, 20 February 1984.

[14] Article entitled 'British Spies in Ireland', *Irish Times*, 22 April 1980.

CHAPTER 10

[1] Article entitled 'The Pincher Profile', *The News Magazine*, London *Evening News*, 7 December 1979.

[2] *A History of the Chinese Secret Service*, Richard Deacon, Frederick Muller, London, 1974.

[3] 'MP seeks end to ban on press naming spy chief', *The Times*, London, 7 August 1973.

[4] See reports of the trial of Dennis Howard Marks in the *Daily Telegraph*, November 1981. Also an article entitled 'Secret Life of an Amateur Spy', by John Coates and Colin Simpson, *Sunday Times*, 22 November 1981.

[5] *The Times*, 16 October 1973.

[6] *The Times*, 2 November 1973.

[7] *Daily Mail*, London, 24 July 1974.

[8] Letter from Mr Julian Amery to the author, 29 February 1984.

CHAPTER 11

[1] Letter from Mrs Susan Crosland to the author, 8 December 1983.

[2] *New York Herald Tribune*, 23 December 975.

[3] Conversation between Prebendary Irvine and the author, 3 October 1983.

[4] Conversation between Dr David Owen and the author, 16 January 1984.

[5] *Ibid.*

[6] BBC Radio 4: *The Profession of Intelligence* programme, HNT 351 Y406N, 30 August 1981.

[7] *Daily Express*, 11 July 1977.

[8] BBC Radio 4: *The Profession of Intelligence*, 30/8/81.

[9] 'MI 6 "tipped off Argentina" ' *Observer*, London, 30 January 1983. Also see *The Battle for the Falklands*, by Max Hastings and Simon Jenkins, Michael Joseph, London, 1983.

[10] Letter from Dr David Owen to the author, 12 December 1983.

[11] *Sunday Times*, London, 14 March 1982.

[12] *The Falklands War: The Full Story*, the *Sunday Times* Insight Team, André Deutsch, London, 1982.

[13] Letter to the author from POE, 11 March 1983.

[14] Letter to the *Daily Telegraph*, 17 May 1984, from Mr Chapman Pincher.

[15] *Ibid.*

[16] Statement to the author from Mr Anthony Cavendish, 17 May 1984.

[17] Interdoc is an international documentation and information centre, based at the Hague, which studied East-West relations as they affect the Atlantic Community.

[18] Letters reproduced by kind permission of Mrs Anne Solwey, daughter of Col. Charles Ellis.
[19] *Ibid.*

CHAPTER 12

[1] *Daily Telegraph*, 25 April 1978.
[2] Lord Dacre in a personal conversation with the author, 27 January 1984.
[3] Letter from Professor Michael Howard to the author, 13 October 1983.
[4] Letter from Professor Cheyney to the author, 29 February 1984.
[5] Letter from Mr Peter Lewis to the author, 11 March 1984.
[6] Letter from Professor Michael Howard to the author, 13 October 1983.
[7] Conversation with Col. F.G. Robson, 21 September 1983.
[8] Memorial service address for Sir Maurice, given by Sir William Deakin, 12 May 1981.
[9] Letter from Professor Rohan Butler to the author, 7 March 1984.
[10] Conversation between Mr Elie Weinstock and the author, 7 March 1984.
[11] Letter from Sir Isaiah Berlin to the author, 13 April 1984.
[12] Letter from Mr Jeffery Ede to the author, 21 February 1984.
[13] Letter from Professor Howard to the author, 13 October 1983.
[14] Letters from Mr J.S.G. Simmons, Dr Rohan Butler and Mr Peter Lewis to the author.
[15] Letter from Mr Aldo Fiorentini to the author, 28 March 1984.
[16] Letter from Sir Bryan Hopkin to the author, 24 November 1983.
[17] Article entitled 'Dinner with the Spymaster', by Phillip Knightley, *Sunday Times*, London, 15 March 1981.
[18] *Ibid.*
[19] *Ibid.*
[20] Conversation with Dr Goronwy Rees: also letter from Dr Rees to the author, 6 November 1978.
[21] Babbage Papers, British Museum, Add MS 37205 ff, 65-227, Charles Babbage Papers, Dept. of Manuscripts.
[22] Letter from Mr Irvine Gray to the author, 12 February 1984.

CHAPTER 13

[1] A comment made by Oldfield to Dr R.A. Harvey. See also *The Story of the School of Grace, Lady Manners*, by R.A. Harvey.
[2] Conversation between the author and Mr Enoch Powell.
[3] *Sunday Times*, November 1977.
[4] Cited in an article entitled 'The Endless Ordeal of Ulster's No. 1', *Now!* magazine, 12 October 1979.

⁵ Quoted in *The British Intelligence Services in Action*, Kenneth Lindsay, Dunrod Press, Dundalk.

⁶ The *Irish Times*, 17 November 1979.

⁷ 'Can the Spymaster Outwit the IRA?' by Ronald Payne and Christopher Dobson, *Now!* magazine, 12 October 1979.

⁸ Letter from Professor A.J.P. Taylor to the author, 22 November 1983.

⁹ Letter from Sir Philip Goodhart, MP, to the author, 18 November 1983.

¹⁰ *Northern Ireland: A Political Directory, 1968-79*, by W.D. Flackes, Gill & Macmillan, Dublin, 1980.

¹¹ Quoted in the *Irish Times*, 17 November 1979.

¹² See *Trends in Low-Intensity Conflict ORAE Extra-Mural Paper No. 16*, by Dr David Charters, Dominick Graham & Maurice Tugwell, Ottawa, 1981. Also report in the *Globe & Mail*, Toronto, 2 December 1981.

¹³ The *Irish Times*, 17 November 1979.

¹⁴ *The Times*, London, 1 February 1980.

CHAPTER 14

¹ *The Guardian*, London, 9 January 1984, article entitled 'Powell Says CIA Had Hand in Earl's Murder'.

² *The Times*, 13 June 1980.

³ BBC Radio 4: *The Profession of Intelligence* programme, HNT 351 Y406N, 30 August 1981.

⁴ Letter from Mr George K. Young to the author, 6 May 1984.

⁵ 'The Man who led a Secret Life', by Chapman Pincher, *Daily Mail*, 12 March 1981.

⁶ The *New York Times*, 10 March 1981.

⁷ *Ibid*.

⁸ Letter from John Le Carré (Mr David Cornwell) to *The Times*, London, 17 March 1981.

⁹ Letter from Sir Alec Guinness to the author, 17 September 1983.

¹⁰ UPI message from London, 17 March 1981.

¹¹ *New Statesman*, 7 July 1978.

¹² See *Who's Who in Spy Fiction*, by Donald MacCormick, Elm Tree Press, London, 1977, entry under Fleming, Ian.

¹³ Letters from Lady Glanmorris to the author, 1 September, 1980, and 6 October 1983.

¹⁴ Article entitled 'Who Was Who', by Alan Bold, *Telegraph Sunday Magazine*, 15 April 1984.

¹⁵ Letter from Mr G. St John Clarke to the author, 30 March 1984.

¹⁶ Letter from Mr Norman Mott to the author, 10 April 1984.

¹⁷ *Secrets, Spies & Scholars: Blueprint of the Essential CIA*, by Ray S. Cline.

Index

Smellie, Craig, 174
Smith, Sir Howard, 16
Smith, Mrs Jeanne, 46, 59, 110, 263-5
Smith, Joseph, 90
Snepp, Frank, 198
Socotra, report on Soviet intentions, 173-4
SOE, (Special Operations Executive), 15, 54, 63, 88, 263
Solwey, Mrs Ann, 206, 268
South Staffordshire Regiment, 39-40
Spears, Maj.-Gen. Sir Edward, 43, 47
Spratley Isles, oil prospects, 180
St John Clarke, Gordon, 257, 269
St Matthew's Church, Westminster, 126, 152-3, 219, 238, 255
Stalin, Josef, 81, 147
Stephenson, Sir William, 205
Stewart, Michael, 149-50, 152
Stirling, Col. David, 155-6
Strong, Sir Kenneth, 121, 135
Sun Yat-sen, 93
Sûreté Generale aux Armées, 43
Szamuely, Tibor, 206
Szek, Alexander, 262

Tawney, Professor R.H., 36
Taylor, Professor A.J.P., 29-30, 230, 263, 269
Temple, William, Archbishop of Canterbury, 36
Templer, Maj., (later Fld.-Mshl. Sir Gerald), 39, 92, 97-8
Thatcher, Mrs Margaret, 16, 187, 193, 195, 221-3, 249
Thomas, E.E., 217
Thompson, Sir Robert, 122, 265

Thurloe, John, 3
Tongs, the, (see also Triads), 93
Trend, Sir Burke, (later Lord Trend), 121, 135
Trepper, Leopold, 63, 264
Trethowan, H.M., 41-2, 45-6, 48, 59, 263
Triads, the, 93-5, 98
TRICYCLE, (agent: see also Popov, Dusko), 205-6

UDI in Rhodesia, 148-9, 202
Ulster Defence Force (UDF), 224, 243-4, 246-7
ULTRA, 47
US Defense Dept., 101, 125, 129
Uttley, Alison, 28

Vermehren, Dr Erich, 63-4
Vivian, Col. Valentine, 8
Volkov, Constantin, 78, 148

Wadsworth, Janet, 117
Wah-kee, secret society, 95, 265
Wang Ching-wei organization, 95
Warsaw Treaty Political Consultative Committee, 100
Way, Keith, 89
Weidenfeld, Lord, 184
Weinstein, Elie, 213, 268
West German Federal Internal Security Service, 141
West German Secret Service, 141
'Whisper Box' in Malaya, 97
White, Sir Dick Goldsmith, 5, 9, 13-15, 117, 121, 130, 137, 141, 150-1, 178, 257